THE MEANING OF TREASON

REBECCA WEST

The Meaning of Treason

THE VIKING PRESS

NEW YORK · MCMXLVII

Grateful acknowledgment is made to *The New Yorker,* in which the first two chapters in Part One and the first two in Part Two originally appeared, and to *Harper's Magazine,* in which the Epilogue was published.

SET IN BASKERVILLE AND BULMER TYPES
AND PRINTED IN U.S.A. BY THE HADDON CRAFTSMEN, INC.

TO

HAROLD ROSS

NOTE

Parts of this book, relating to William Joyce and John Amery, appeared in *The New Yorker,* and I reprint them here with a strong sense of gratitude to that periodical. The material I collected for the most part by attending various civil trials and courts martial; and I have supplemented this in certain cases by information supplied by friends and relatives of certain persons accused of treachery. In cases where convicted persons seem likely to return to the outer world after a short period, and have not received much mention in the press, I have alluded to them by other names than their own.

For he was numbered with us, and had obtained part of this minis-
try. Now this man purchased a field with the reward of iniquity; and
falling headlong, he burst asunder in the midst, and all his bowels
gushed out. And it was known unto all the dwellers at Jerusalem;
insomuch as that field is called in their proper tongue, Aceldama,
that is to say, The field of blood. For it is written in the book of
Psalms, Let his habitation be desolate, and let no man dwell therein:
and his bishoprick let another take.

THE ACTS OF THE APOSTLES, I:17-20

TABLE OF CONTENTS

I

THE REVOLUTIONARY

I

EVERYBODY in London wanted to see William Joyce when he was brought to trial as a radio traitor, for he was something new in the history of the world. Never before have people known the voice of one they had never seen as well as if he had been a husband or a brother or a close friend; and if they had foreseen such a miracle they would not have imagined that the familiar unknown would speak to them only to prophesy their death and ruin. All of us in England had experienced that hideous novelty. It was difficult not to chance on Joyce's wave length when one was tuning in to the English stations, and there was an arresting quality about his voice which made it a sacrifice not to go on listening. It was a rasping yet rich voice, like Father Coughlin's, and it was convincing in its confidence. It seemed as if one had better hearken and take warning when he suggested that the destiny of the people he had left in England was death, and the destiny of his new masters in Germany life and conquest, and that, therefore, his listeners had better change sides and submit. This was often terrible to hear, for the news in the papers confirmed it. He was not only alarming, he was ugly; he opened a vista into a mean life; he always spoke as if he were better fed and better clothed than we were, and so, we now know, he was. He went further than that smug mockery of our plight. He sinned that sin which is the dark travesty of legitimate hatred because it is felt for kindred, just as incest is the dark travesty of legitimate love. When the U-boats were sinking so many of our ships that to open the newspapers was to draw into the nostrils a smell of drowned sailor, he rolled the figures of our lost tonnage on his tongue. When we were facing the hazard of D-day he rejoiced in the thought of the English dead that would soon lie under the Westwall.

So those who were at once robust and curious went off to the Central Criminal Court on September 17, 1945, when he came up for trial. It is an odd place to visit these days, for it stands in a district once congested with unlovely commercial buildings, which the blitz has converted into a beautiful desert. Churches stand blackened but apparently intact; birds, however, fly through the empty sockets of the windows and long grass grows around their altars. A red-brick Georgian mansion, hidden for a century by sordid warehouses, now looks at the great Renaissance dome of St. Paul's across acres where willow herb, its last purple flowers passing into silver clouds of seed dust, grows with the yellow ragwort from the ground plan of a lost city drawn in rubble. The courts themselves startle the eye that knew them as they were, housed in a solid building built of grey stone in the neo-classical style. Its solidarity has been sliced as if it were a cake, and the walls of the slice are raw new red brick. At the time of Joyce's trial, because of the sealing off of the bombed parts, and the heavy blackout, which could not yet be removed owing to the lack of labour, all the halls and passages and stairs were in perpetual dusk. The courtroom—the Court No. 1 where all the most famous criminal trials of modern times have taken place—was lit by electric light. Daylight used to stream in through a glass dome cold as justice itself, but that had long been shattered. Bare boards filled it in, giving an odd-come-short look to what used to be an austerely fine room.

The strong electrical light was merciless to William Joyce, whose appearance was a surprise to all of us who had not seen him before. His voice had suggested a large and flashy handsomeness. But he was a tiny little creature and, though not very ugly, was exhaustively so. His hair was mouse-coloured and grew thinly, particularly above his ears. His nose was joined to his face at an odd angle, and its bridge and its point and its nostrils were all separately misshapen. Above his small dark-blue eyes, which were hard and shiny, like pebbles, his eyebrows were thick and pale and irregular. His neck was long and his shoulders were narrow and sloping. His arms were very short and very thick, so that his sleeves were like little bolsters. His body looked flimsy yet coarse. There was nothing individual about him except a deep scar running across his right cheek from his ear to the corner of his mouth. But this did not create the savage and marred distinction that it might suggest, for it gave a mincing immobility to his mouth, which was extremely small. His smile was pinched and governessy. He was dressed with an intent and ambitious spruceness which did not succeed in giving any impression of well-being, but rather recalled some Eastern European peasant, newly driven off the land by poverty into a factory town and wearing his first suit of Western clothes. He moved with a jerky formality which would have been thought strange in any society. When he bowed to the Judge, his bow seemed sincerely respectful but entirely inappropriate to the occasion, and it was difficult to think of any occasion to which it would have been appropriate.

At right angles to the dock, against the wall of the court, sat the jury, none of its members greatly blessed by nature, though there was one woman, slender and high-nosed, of the colonel's-daughter kind, who had an irresistible charm. Day by day the journalists who watched the case became more and more convinced, for no reason at all, that she was a very good sort. But the members of the jury were all middle-aged, since the armies had not come home, and though they were drawn from different ranks of life, there is no rank in which English people are other than puffy or haggard. But at that they were all more pleasant to look at and more obviously trustworthy than the homely and eccentric little man in the dock; and, compared with the judicial bench which he faced, he was of course at an immense disadvantage, as we all should be, for its dignity is authentic. Against oak panels columns run up to a pediment framing the carved royal standard and the sword of justice, which is affixed to the wall in its jewelled scabbard. At the foot of the wall, in a high-backed chair, sat the Judge, dressed in his scarlet robe, with its neckband of fine white linen and its deep cuffs and sash of purplish-black taffeta. Beside him, their chairs set farther back as a sign of their inferiority to him, sat the Lord Mayor of London and two aldermen, wearing their antique robes of black silk with flowing white cravats and gold chains hung with chased badges of office worked in precious metals and enamel. These two sorts of pompous trapping are always given some real meaning by the faces of the men who support them. Judges are chosen for a combination of intellect and character; city honours are usually earned by competence and character and the patience to carry out a routine of tedious public duty over decades. These qualities have to be possessed in both classes to a degree which is bound to leave an imprint on the features.

Looking from the bench to the dock, it could be seen that not in any sane state would William Joyce have had the ghost of a chance of holding such offices as these. But when he was asked to plead he said, "Not guilty," and those two words were the most impressive uttered during the trial. The famous voice was let loose. For a fraction of a second we heard its familiar quality. It was as we had heard it for six years, it reverberated with the desire for power. Never was there a more perfect voice for a demagogue, for its reverberations were so strong that they were certain to awaken echoes in every heart that was tumid with the same appetite. What could the little man do—since he so passionately desired to exercise authority, and neither this nor any other state would give it to him—but use his trick of gathering together other luckless fellows, that they might over-turn the sane state and substitute a mad one? That was the most profound cause which had brought him to the dock; but there was another which quickly became apparent.

This trial, like the great treason trial of the last war, when Sir Roger Casement was sent to the gallows, was an Irish drama. From the first, rumours had been current that Joyce was Irish, but they had never been officially confirmed, and his accent was dif-ficult to identify. But there was little doubt about it when one saw him in the dock. He had the real Donnybrook air. He was a not very fortunate example of the small, nippy, jig-dancing type of Irish peasant, and the appearance of his brother, who attended the court every day in a state of great suffering, was proof of the family's origin. Quentin Joyce, who was then twenty-eight, was eleven years William's junior. He was much better-looking, with a sturdy body, a fresh colour, thick and lustrous brown hair, and the soft eyes of a cow. Nobody in his senses could mistake him for anything but an Irishman from the provinces. There were also strong traces of Irish origin in the followers of Joyce who watched the trial. These included some singular figures. There were some women who especially attracted attention by an almost unearthly physical repulsiveness, notably an ageing and floozy blonde in a tight Air Force uniform, who sucked sweets and wept, as she swung an ankle creased with fat from crossed knees that pressed up against her drooping bosom. But she and her like, it seemed probable, had been merely on the fringe of the British Fascist movement and were sympathizers with Joyce rather than his associates.

These could be seen every day gathered round Joyce's brother, and his solicitor (as the English call the lawyer who prepares the case for the lawyer who actually conducts it in court) and his clerk, who were the oddest pair of figures I have ever seen in the law courts. The solicitor was a hunchback dwarf with blond hair and a pale sensitive face. He was a well-known solicitor who was acting for Joyce not because he wished to have him as a client or had any sympathy with British fascism, but because Joyce, being without means on his return from Germany to England, had had to apply for the services of a lawyer under the Poor Prisoners' Defence Act when he first came up before the minor judge we call a magistrate for the preliminary stages of his trial. This meant that the magistrate had had to select at random the names of certain lawyers from a rota, and call on them to perform the duty of defending Joyce, a summons which they were not in practice able to refuse. The task must have been extremely repugnant to this lawyer, who was a practitioner of high standing and had no need for notoriety. But he could not have behaved with more exquisite loyalty to his client, nor soothed more kindly the grief of the many persons associated with the case which he must heartily have wished he never had seen. Each day he bore himself amiably towards them, aided by his clerk, who was a strange figure, not from eccentricity but from modesty. She obviously thought of herself as invisible. She was a girl in her twenties, with long and elaborately curled hair, bareheaded and dressed as if for the beach walk of a summer resort, with flowered frock, fleecy coat, and light shoes, and there could not have been a figure more discordant with the peculiar dry decorum of the English courts. But she too was conscientiously gracious to Joyce's friends, the chief of whom was a thin man with fierce black eyes blazing behind thick glasses, a tiny fuzz of black hair fancifully arranged on his prematurely bald head, and wrists and ankles as straight as lead piping in their emaciation.

He was a Scotsman named Angus MacNab, the editor of a Fascist paper and Joyce's best friend. He was plainly a foredoomed eccentric, and a variation in circumstances might have found him just as happily a spiritualist medium or a believer in the lost ten tribes of Israel. As for the rest of the followers, men of violent and unhappy appearance, with a look of animal shyness and ferocity, and, in some cases, a measure of animal beauty, they were for the most part darker in complexion than one would expect in sub-scribers to the Aryan theory. One, especially, looked like a true gipsy. Most of them had an Irish cast of feature and some bore Irish names. It must be remembered that these men were not followers of Sir Oswald Mosley, who picked a more varied and more cheerfully brutal type. Joyce had seceded from Mosley's movement some years before the war and started his own. This was his private army, part of his individual hell.

The story developed during the first day and the morning of the second, and it was certainly an Irish story. At first our attention wandered from Joyce's personality because the lawyer for the Crown was Sir Hartley Shawcross, the Attorney-General appointed by the new Labour Government. He is young for the post, charming in manner and voice, and he set out a beautifully lucid argument, and we were pleased, and pleased to be pleased. For the English were pathetically eager to approve of whatever the new government did; we were tired out by such excitements as had produced this trial, and what we wanted was to hear the machine ticking over. But the interest of the trial presently shifted from personalities to a fantastic and ironical story of a family who, for obscure reasons springing from one convulsion of history, engaged in disingenuous conduct which, long after, brought their dearest member a peculiarly nonsensical doom in another con-vulsion of history.

That the proceedings were to be odd was indicated by the three indictments which were brought against him. He was charged with three offences against the Treason Act of 1351, by adhering to the King's enemies elsewhere than in the King's realm, to wit, in the German realm. On the first count he was charged with having on divers days between the eighteenth day of September, 1939, and the twenty-ninth day of May, 1945, whilst "an open and public war was being prosecuted and carried on by the German realm and its subjects against our lord the King and his subjects, then, and on the said several days, traitorously contriving and intending to aid and assist the said enemies of our lord the King against our lord the King and his subjects, did traitorously adhere and aid and give comfort to the said enemies in parts beyond the seas without the realm of England, to wit in the realm of Germany, by broadcasting to the subjects of our lord the King propaganda on behalf of the said enemies of our lord the King." On the second count he was charged with having purported "to become naturalized as a subject of the realm of Germany" on the twenty-sixth day of September, 1940. On the third count he was charged with broadcasting between certain dates during the period named in the first count, beginning when it did and ending on the second of July, 1940. In each indictment it was stated that these were offences, if William Joyce had committed them, because he was "a person owing allegiance to our lord the King." Later the first two indictments were amended, and he was described in them, but not in the third, as a "British subject."

It seemed, in the early stages of the trial, as if William Joyce must be convicted on these two first indictments. He himself had again and again described himself as a British subject, and his father had done the same. The first evidence to this effect came from a lady in early and spruce middle age with marcelled grey hair and a spirited red straw hat, the kind of lady who is photographed in women's magazines as having taken a prize for preserves at a country fair, who, oddly enough, turned out to be the assistant secretary of the Committee for Military Education in the University of London. When one thought of the blond and boar-like young man or the Brunhilde-like young woman who would have held such a post in a German university, it became a better joke than ever that we had won the war. She was present because someone with a prodigious memory had recalled that in August 1922 William Joyce, then a boy of sixteen, had sent a letter of application for entrance to the London University Officers' Training Corps, in which he had described himself as a British subject, a description which was supported by his father, Michael Joyce.

The boy's letter threw a light on the inner ferment that had brought him to the dock. In this letter he had said that he wanted to study with a view of being nominated by the University for a commission in the Regular Army; but it was obvious that he would find difficulty in following that road. His letter was a little too highfalutin, even for a boy of sixteen. Doubt would have crossed the mind of anybody who read it. And the letter from his father, the loving letter of a father eager to do his best for his son, was too illiterate. But they made themselves plain enough on the subject matter of the correspondence.

"I must now," wrote the young Joyce, "mention a point which I hope will not give rise to difficulties. I was born in America, but of British parents. I left America when two years of age, have not returned since, and do not propose to return. I was informed, at the brigade headquarters of the district in which I was stationed in Ireland, that I possessed the same rights and privileges as I would if of natural British birth. I can obtain testimonials as to my loyalty to the Crown. I am in no way connected with the United States of America, against which, as against all other nations, I am prepared to draw the sword in British interests. As a young man of pure British descent, some of whose forefathers have held high position in the British army, I have always been desirous of devoting what little capability and energy I may possess to the country which I love so dearly. I ask that you may inform me if the accident of my birth, to which I refer above, will affect my position. I shall be in London for the September Matriculation Examination and I hope to commence studies at the London University at the beginning of the next academic year. I trust that you will reply as soon as possible, and that your reply will be favourable to my aspirations." At an interview with an official of the O.T.C. he conveyed that he was "in doubt as to whether he was a 'British subject of pure European descent,'" a doubt which must have been honest if he expressed it at all in view of the ardent hope expressed in his letter; but he asserted that his father had never been naturalized. This the father confirmed when the official wrote to him for further particulars. "Dear Sir, your letter of 23rd October received. Would have replied sooner, but have been away from home. With regard to my son William. He was born in America, I was born in Ireland.

His mother was born in England. We are all British and not American citizens."

But why, when William Joyce was making later declarations that he was a British subject, had he sometimes said that he was a British subject, had he sometimes said that he was born in Ireland and sometimes that he was born in America, when he had a birth certificate which gave his birthplace as Brooklyn? The answer is that he was probably never sure of the real facts regarding his own and his father's status till he learned them from his own defence lawyers just before the trial. In the statement he made to the Intelligence officers on his arrest he expressed himself uncertainly. "I understand, though I have no documents to prove any statement, that my father was American by naturalization at the time of my birth, and I believe he lost his American citizenship later through failing to renew it, because we left America in 1909 when I was three years old. We were generally treated as British subjects during our stay in Ireland and England. I was in Ireland from 1909 till 1921 when I came to England. We were always treated as British during the period of my stay in England whether we were or not." But the truth was disclosed when Mr. Gerald Slade, K.C., counsel for the defence, got going with the case for Joyce and told—with a curious dry and ascetic fervour which recalls that in his spare time he is a temperance advocate—a story which would have charmed a snake if read to it at dictation speed. For it turned out that William Joyce's father, Michael Joyce, had been a naturalized American long before William Joyce had been born at 1377 Herkimer Street, Brooklyn. Therefore William Joyce was by birth an American citizen and owed the King of England no allegiance arising out of British nationality. All his life he had described himself as a British subject, and his father had done the like; and they had been lying. There was no doubt about it. The documents of naturalization were present in good order, dated in 1894, and a torn certificate, printed in that early nineteenth-century type which we used to regard as hideous and now nostalgically think charming, proved that Michael Francis Joyce and Gertrude Emily Brooke had been married in All Saints Church, at 129th Street and Madison Avenue, New York, by Roman Catholic rites, on the 2nd of May, 1902.

Then, to confirm all this, came Mr. Frank Holland, who was a difficult witness. An old gentleman, white-haired and shrivelled and deaf and palsied and quavering, he stoutly gave evidence that he had been born in 1883; and there was apparently no mistake about it. Added to this, he was Irish beyond the normal provisions of nature, with the emphasis of art; he might have been one of the Dublin players taking part in a Sean O'Casey play. He also suffered from an eerie form of deafness, the inverse of a banshee's wail; one saw even the baritone of Sir Hartley Shawcross, which is as audible as an actor's voice, come to his ear and be attenuated and disappear into nothingness. Added to that, he had a mind which, in one sense fragile, was in another vigorous. He did not fly off at a tangent—flying things can be brought down—but he crept off at tangents, and not the entire forces of the Central Criminal Court could bring him home. The defending counsel had announced that he was calling Mr. Holland to certify that when Michael Joyce was leaving America for England, his passport had arrived after he had left his home in Brooklyn to go down to the steamer, and that Mr. Holland had waited to take it from the postman and had carried it down to his friend at a Hoboken pier, and that Mr. Holland had then seen it was an American passport. But when the relevant questions were put to the old man, he bridled. They appeared to him to cast aspersions on his gentlemanliness. Yes, he had helped his friend by fetching him his passport, but how was he to know what kind of passport? His attitude sharply indicated that other people might know no better than to be inquisitive, but he had his manners. As the examination went on, old age could be seen shifting itself from the shoulders of Mr. Holland to those of the examining counsel; yet Mr. Holland contributed some effective evidence.

Long ago he had known a girl named Gertrude Emily Brooke. She was called Queenie, he told us, with a sudden affectionate chuckle. She had married a man named Michael Joyce, who worked in America. It was on Michael Joyce's advice that Mr. Holland himself had gone to America and followed his calling of civil engineer under the employment of the Pennsylvania Railroad Company. He and his wife had seen much of the Joyces in America; with a burst of cynical candour the old gentleman announced that he and his wife had visited the Joyces so often for the simple reason that they were the only people they knew in

New York. And indeed they were lucky to have friends with such a pleasant home. For the Joyces' house, which has since been reconstructed and is now a realtor's office, stood on a corner lot in a broad street planted with trees, which is now occupied at one end by Negroes and at the other by Italians, but was then a centre of the Irish community. The German quarter was not far away. He went on to describe how Michael Joyce had told him that he had become an American citizen and advised him to do the same. He took the advice, but came home to England after the outbreak of the First World War; he was greatly inconvenienced by his American citizenship, for he had to register under the Aliens' Act which was passed in 1915 and report all his movements to the police. At this time he had visited Queenie, then settled in Lancashire, and had exchanged commiserations with her, because she was incommoded in the same way. His cracked old voice evoked two people grumbling together thirty years ago. That they had so grumbled could not be doubted.

This witness's evidence recalled the acting of Sir Henry Irving. It was impossible to hear a word of what Irving said for years before he left the stage, and as his memory had gone that was just as well; but the melodic line of his murmurs and the gesture of his gauntness never failed to evoke the truth concerning Shylock, because his intellect possessed that truth and charged such means of expression as still remained to him with instructions to transmit it. Mr. Holland was as unsatisfactory a witness as could be imagined. The name of Gertrude Emily Brooke's birthplace, the town of Shaw in Lancashire, inspired him to dazzling feats. He swore he had been born there, that he had never been there, that he had seen the Joyces there, and that he had not seen them there, and that he had visited the Joyces in 1919 at a house in which they had in fact settled in 1923. But he had known the Joyces for fifty years; he did recognize the prisoner in the dock as the William Joyce who had been a baby in Herkimer Street, Brooklyn; he had heard Michael Joyce say he was an American and Gertrude Emily Joyce grumble about the necessity to register as an alien; and he was telling the truth. It showed in the irritable twitch of his eyebrows when he was asked to put the truth he knew into a form more likely to convince the jury, the impatient wail of his voice as he made what seemed to him the superfluous repetition.

The case against William Joyce, so far as it depended on his British nationality, lay dead on the courtroom floor when Mr. Holland left the witness-box.

There came to confirm that evidence a police official named Woodmansey who proved that in the last war Mr. and Mrs. Michael Joyce, oscillating between Galway and Lancashire with their children, had been registered as Americans. They had broken the rules by failing to report their movements and this had produced an illuminating correspondence between the police in Lancashire and the Royal Irish Constabulary in Galway. This revealed that both Michael Joyce and his wife had oddly met the situation with the nonsensical tale which we had heard before, that they were not really aliens, because Michael had failed to re-register as an American citizen within two years after leaving the United States. What was odder still was that the Galway constabulary—which must have known that it was nonsense, for there was nothing that an Irish policeman knew better than the American laws that affected Irish emigrants—recommended this preposterous story sympathetically to the Lancashire police, urging that Michael Joyce was "one of the most respectable, law-abiding, and loyal men in the locality, and one who has been consistently an advocate of the 'pro-Allied' cause since the beginning of the war," and expressing doubt "whether these people are aliens at all." The Lancashire police crisply resisted the suggestion, but dealt with the case by a caution. The Galway constable who had administered the admonition came to give evidence—a thin and aged giant, so disabled by blindness and partial paralysis that he had to be led to the witness-box and propped up in it, a tall, blanched obelisk. It was odd to find that to this incident Mrs. Joyce, who was by all accounts a person of scrupulous character, had contributed her own lie. She told the police that though her husband had been in the United States he was "only three or four years there altogether." It seems unlikely that she should not have known that he had lived there for eighteen years preceding their marriage.

The oddity of the situation was emphasized by the evidence of Quentin Joyce. There passed between him and the man in the dock a nod and a smile of pure love. One realized that life in this strange family must sometimes have been great fun. But it evidently had not been fun lately. Quentin told the court that his father had died in 1941, shortly after the house in which he had lived for eighteen years had been destroyed by a bomb, and his mother had died in 1944. Out of the wreckage of the house there had been recovered a few boxes full of papers, but none had any bearing on the question of the family's nationality, and there was a reason for that. Michael Joyce had told young Quentin, when he was ten years old, that he and all the family were American citizens but had bade him never speak of it, and had in later years often reiterated this warning. Finally, in 1934, the boy, who was then sixteen, had seen him burn a number of papers, including what appeared to be an American passport. He had given a reason for what he was doing, but the witness was not required to repeat it. The date suggested what that reason must have been. By that time the police knew William Joyce as a troublesome instigator of street-fighting, and attacks on Communists and Jews, and in November 1934 Joyce was prosecuted, together with Sir Oswald Mosley and two other Fascists, on a charge of riotous assembly at Worthing; and though this prosecution failed, it indicated a serious attempt by the authorities to rid themselves of the nuisance of Fascist-planned disorder. Michael Joyce had every reason to fear that, if the police ever got an inkling of his secret, they would deport his son and not improbably the whole family.

The courtroom was by now in a state that would have puzzled those Americans who think of the British as a comfortably homogeneous people; for some of the spectators could not make head or tail of this old story, and some of them knew perfectly well where they were, even if they did not know exactly what was going on in that peculiar field. The people who knew where they were had two characteristics in common: they had Irish antecedents and they were not young. They knew what Ireland was before it was Eire, and the dreary round by which men, often brave and good men, kept in check, by a complicated mechanism of oppression and espionage, other men, also often brave and good, who retorted by shooting them from behind stone walls and burning down their houses. Because Michael Joyce had been married in a Roman Catholic church, and because of the surname he bore, which is extremely common in certain counties, it could be known that he was one of the native Irish, the mass of whom were against the English and on the side of the people who shot the English from behind stone walls. But when an officer of the Royal Irish Constabulary described him as one of the loyalest men in Galway, it meant that he was on the side of England. There were many such native Irish who turned against their own kind and worked with the alien oppressor, and we forget now how many of them were passionately sincere. Doubtless the bribery dispensed by Dublin Castle was the prime nourishment of this queer community, but many were people who honestly loved law and order and preferred the smart uniforms and the soldierly bearing of the English garrisons and the Royal Irish Constabulary to the furtive slouching of a peasantry distracted with poverty and revolutionary fever. The error of such people was insufficient inquiry into first causes, but for simple natures who went by surface indications their choice was very natural; and it must have come very natural indeed to the Joyce family, who, as could be seen from the nervous neatness of both William and Quentin Joyce, and their bearing in court, had been reared to cultivate military smartness and to appreciate ceremonial to such a degree that their appreciation did not entirely desert them even when the ceremonial belonged to a trial at which one of them stood charged with a capital offence. These native Irish who had made that choice often felt a love of England which struck English people as excessive and theatrical: such a love as William Joyce had, at sixteen, expressed in his letters to the secretary of the London University Committee for Military Education, such a love as led him in after-life habitually to make a demand—which struck many of his English acquaintances as a sign of insanity—that any quiet social evening he spent with his friends should end with the singing of the national anthem.

There was, in that letter he wrote when he was sixteen, an astonishing sentence. "I have served with the irregular forces of the Crown in an Intelligence capacity, against the Irish guerrillas," wrote the boy. "In command of a squad of sub-agents I was subordinate to the late Capt. P. W. Keating, 2nd R.U.R., who was drowned in the *Egypt* accident. I have a knowledge of the rudiments of Musketry, Bayonet Fighting, and Squad Drill." The *Egypt* was sunk off Ushant in May 1922; which means that if this story is true the boy was engaged in guerrilla fighting with the Black and Tans—as the British irregulars who were sent over to pacify Ireland after the last war were called—when he was fifteen years old. It seems likely that that story was true. Schoolboys realize that correspondence with school authorities is apt to come the way of parents, and no son would like to be caught by his father making an unfounded boast. He repeated the statement later on an official form, giving the duration of his service as four months, and the name of the regiment with which he had been associated as the Worcestershires; he must have known that this particular gave the authorities such a very easy way of checking his story, and during his trial at the Old Bailey an old man from County Galway stood in the crowd outside and gave rambling confirmation to the story. He illustrated the Irish conception of consistency by expressing to bystanders his hearty desire that William Joyce should be hanged for treason against the King of England, on the ground that when he was a boy he had worked with the Black and Tans in persecuting the Irish when they were revolting against the English. The crowd, with that tolerance which foreigners, possibly correctly, suspect of being a form of smugness, was amused and sympathetic. It is typical of the irony which determined William Joyce's life that not only did that service he thought he rendered England mean ultimately nothing, since now we see the severance of England and Ireland as a historical necessity, but even at the time it can have recommended him hardly at all to the Englishmen who read his letter. The Black and Tans were terrified men, set down in a country where it was impossible to tell friend and foe, and assassination was the only art of the people; they burned and slew with the ferocity of fear. Even those who thought that England should not have relinquished Ireland were ashamed at this reminder of the inevitable impudicity of the conqueror's sword; and to all, a child who had partaken, even with gallantry, in such deeds, would have seemed to have had his childhood outraged.

To the end of his life this love of an obsolete England persisted in William Joyce, to be rebuffed by contemporary England. Its climax was related at the trial by an officer with the superb name of Alexander Adrian Lickorish, who described how it came about that William Joyce fell into the hands of justice at the end of the war. He might never have been arrested had it not been for his desire to do a service to two English officers whom he did not know, whose only value to him can have been that they were English officers. In November 1944 he had been given a fake passport, apparently for the purpose of enabling him to escape recognition if he fell into the hands of the British. This is the only recorded instance when the Germans showed any concern for the safety of any of the traitors who had been working for them; but it was a very convincing document. It was made out to Wilhelm Hansen, but the holder was stated to have been born in Galway, Ireland, a detail which would have been likely to arouse the interest of any Intelligence officer. After William Joyce had made his last broadcast on April 30, 1945, a broadcast in which, not without dignity, he acknowledged the coming of the night, he took this false passport and with his wife went into hiding. On May 28th, when evening was falling, Captain Lickorish and a Lieutenant Perry were walking in a wood near Flensburg, on the Danish frontier, looking for some branches to make a fire, when they came on a man who was wandering aimlessly among the trees. He watched them for a time, and then called to them in French, "Here are a few more pieces." Presently he said in English, "There are a few more pieces here." At once the voice betrayed him. The two officers conferred together, and then Lieutenant Perry said to him, "You wouldn't happen to be William Joyce, would you?" The man put his hand in his pocket, and Lieutenant Perry, thinking he was about to draw a revolver, shot him in the leg. He fell to the ground, saying, "My name is Fritz Hansen." Fritz is not an abbreviation of Wilhelm; but the slip did not matter, for when they searched him they found not only the civil passport (*Reisepass*) made out to Hansen but a military passport (*Wehrpass*) made out in the name of William Joyce.

It was this love, slanting across time, which made him a Fascist. He had been brought up to believe in an England who held Ireland by force, and felt betrayed when Home Rule was given. This meant an actual, material betrayal. The family had to leave Ireland, like many other loyalist Irishmen. Thus William Joyce found himself exiled from his real motherland, Ireland, which his blood must have loved, and confined in England, for love of which he had betrayed Ireland, and which showed no gratitude for that sacrifice. Though the loyalists often received financial aid, Michael Joyce plainly suffered heavy loss through his exile. He was a builder and contractor who had come back from America with handsome means and owned, at the time of the First World War, considerable house property in County Mayo and County Galway, as well as managing the horse-tramway system in Galway town. He came to England for three very good reasons of diverse sorts. The horse-tramways in Galway were abolished. He was universally suspected of being an informer, and without British protection it might have gone ill with him. And, perhaps the most cogent reason of all, he was confused in many people's minds with another informer, also named Michael Joyce, who had denounced to the Black and Tans a priest whom they murdered. With exile he entered on a declining scale of prosperity and on his death in 1941 left nothing but effects valued at six hundred and fifty pounds. William Joyce himself could not restore the family fortunes—in spite of his intellectual equipment, which was sufficient to give him a degree at the University of London, with first-class honours in English language and literature—because of his personal limitations, the clownish extravagance which left him, even after he had played a uniquely sinister part in history, with the comic nickname of Lord Haw-Haw, the odd vulgarity which made it almost impossible to believe, looking at him or listening to him, that he was a University graduate or the child of people with a position in a community. After finishing his studies he at once gained a position, and not an unremunerative one, in a tutorial college, but it would have been inconceivable that he could have arrived at any position of distinction in the academic world. He had in early youth joined the Conservative Party and spoken for it, but it would have been unlikely that any local committee could have nominated him as Parliamentary candidate. If he had remained innocent as snow he would still have looked dubious, and at that comically dubious.

Therefore the Fascist movement was a godsend to him. Its leader was himself on the grotesque side; and he was determined not to modify but to obliterate all those standards by which Joyce would have been excluded. In 1931 Sir Oswald Mosley stood for Ashton-under-Lyne as Parliamentary candidate representing his New Party, which was to be a socialist party more drastic and

dashing than the Labour Party, and was defeated. When the
results were announced at the town hall on election night he
looked down at a sea of jeering faces who were exulting at his
defeat for the stupidest and meanest of reasons, who were guffaw-
ing because a rich baronet should profess socialism and because a
man who was brilliant and handsome had suffered disappointment
and humiliation, and he said to a friend, "These are the people
who have got in the way of everybody who has tried to do anything since the last war." It was a sensible enough observation;
but, making it, Mosley fell into the sin of Lucifer. In his pride he
violated the just pride of others. He decided not to wrestle with
the vulgarity of the vulgar by argument and by example, but to
exploit it, and he deliberately planned propaganda which would
deceive them into crediting himself with a like vulgarity, so that
he could seize power through their support. Joyce was therefore
valuable to Mosley for those very qualities which would have
prevented his becoming an army officer or a don. So the Fascist
movement gave him a place in a hierarchy, with which there went
acclamation, a certain amount of money, travel abroad, and company which was of a certain distinction. It also gave him an opportunity to use that superb courage which his people have wrung
out of their terrible history, and to gratify that itch for plotting
and intrigue which is another product of Irish history. It also
gave him the hope that under fascism England might become
what Ireland had been to him and his family before there was
Home Rule, a police state where spruce tyrants held down the
unworthy and rewarded those who submitted to them. It also
gave him cause to use that voice, that really extraordinary voice,
in which his discontents were fused into a powerful demon able
to call to all like demons in other men's hearts and stir them into
comradeship.

It must have also nourished a strain in William Joyce that was
implanted in him by his family life. Michael Joyce was a mysterious person. It is difficult to see why, loving England as he did,
he went to America and stayed there for many years. In the nineteenth century it was still economically advantageous to emigrate
to England, and emigration to America was more commonly the
resort of the anti-English Irish. There were, of course, some pro-
English Irish who went to America to act as informers on the anti-

English Irish, who at that time were very actively supporting the Fenian movement. It is still more difficult to see why, when Michael Joyce returned to England and found his American citizenship such a burden that he warned his children to keep it a deadly secret, he never took the simple steps which would have readmitted him to British nationality. It would have cost him only a few pounds; and he was in those years well-to-do. It cannot have been the legal technicalities which baffled him; his wife's brother was a solicitor. The official resistance to the process was not great; his friend Mr. Holland described his readmission to British nationality without any of the complaint for which he had a natural turn. Can Michael Joyce have feared to remind either the British or the American government of his existence? Had he once, in fulfilling some mission, failed and got a black mark against his name? Was he working his passage home when he gained the good opinion of the Royal Irish Constabulary? There is probably nobody alive now who knows. All that we can be sure of is that the story was probably incredibly complicated. Nothing was simple in that world of espionage and counter-espionage, treachery and counter-treachery, vengeance and vendetta; and complication is to the soul what condiments are to the palate and alcohol is to the nervous system. During the last century Europe has been debauched with an increasing debauchery by this particular form of complication. Sweet it is to be not what the next man thinks one, but far more powerful; to know what he wrote in the letter he was so careful to seal before he sent it for quite a different person's reading; to charm the confidences from the unsuspecting stranger; to put up one's finger whimsically through the darkness and touch the fabric of the state, and feel the unstable structure rock, and know it one's own doing and not a soul suspecting it; and to do all this for nobility's sake. It is the misfortune of our age, with its high degree of political fluidity, that the life of the political conspirator offers the man of restricted capacity but imaginative energy excitements and satisfactions which he can never derive from overt activities.

In the complexities of that life, the shifts and disguises and evasions, the little man nearly found shelter from justice. For he owed the Crown no allegiance at all of the sort which springs from British birth. The immunity he had for the moment established by proof of his American birthright can be realized better if his position in regard to the second indictment is considered first. He had, it now appeared, committed no offence whatsoever in becoming a naturalized German subject on the 26th of September, 1940. That would have been high treason had he been a British subject, for a British subject is forbidden by law to become the naturalized subject of an enemy country in wartime. But when he took out his naturalization papers in Germany he was an American citizen, and even the American government could not have questioned his action, being then at peace with Germany, which did not declare war on the United States until the 11th of December, 1941. It followed then that his broadcasting was, if only his nationality had to be considered, an offence against nobody. Up till the 26th of September, 1940, he had been an American working for a friendly state; and after that he had been a good German working for the fatherland. He would have walked out of the court scot free if society had been conducted on lines as arbitrary as is imagined by those who are Fascist, who desire, that is to say, government by a minority on a non-contractual basis. Allegiance is not exacted by the Crown from a subject simply because the Crown is the Crown. The idea of the divine right of kings is a comparatively modern vulgarity. According to tradition and logic, the state gives protection to all men within its confines, and in return exacts their obedience to its laws; and the process is reciprocal. When men within the confines of the state are obedient to its laws they have a right to claim its protection. It is a maxim of the law, quoted by Coke in the sixteenth century, that "protection draws allegiance, and allegiance draws protection." *(Protectio trahit subjectionem, et subjectio protectionem.)* It was laid down in 1608, by reference to the case of Sherley, a Frenchman who had come to England and joined in a conspiracy against the King and Queen, that such a man "owed to the King obedience, that is, so long as he was within the King's protection." That is fair enough; and indeed very fair, if the limitations which were applied to this proposition were considered. For in Hale's *History of the Pleas of the Crown*, in the seventeenth century, it was written: "Because as the subject hath his protection from the King and his laws, so on the other side the subject is bound by his allegiance to be true and faithful to the King. And hence it is, that if an alien enemy come into this kingdom hostilely to invade it, if he be taken, he shall be dealt with as an enemy, but not as a traitor, because he violates no trust nor allegiance. But if an alien, the subject of a foreign prince in amity with the King, live here, and enjoy the benefit of the King's protection, and commit a treason, he shall be judged and executed, as a traitor, for he owes a local allegiance."

There could be no doubt whatsoever that William Joyce owed that kind of allegiance. He had certainly enjoyed the protection of the English law for some thirty years preceding his departure to Germany. The lawyers for the defence, in proving that he did not owe the natural kind of allegiance which springs from British birth, had found themselves under the necessity of proving beyond all doubt that he owed this other acquired kind; and there were the two damning sentences in his statement: "We were generally counted as British subjects during our stay in Ireland and England. . . . We were always treated as British during the period of my stay in England whether we were or not." Thus, though an alien, William Joyce owed the Crown allegiance and was capable of committing treason against it. But a further question arose. In the reference to Sherley it was defined that such an alien "owed to the King local obedience, that is, so long as he was within the King's protection." Obviously this opened the door wider and wider, as communications improved, to conduct which no nation could tolerate, and in 1707 an assembly of judges laid it down that "if such alien seeking the Protection of the Crown having a Family and Effects here should during a War with his Native Country go thither and there Adhere to the King's Enemies for purposes of Hostility, He might be dealt with as a Traitor. For he came and settled here under the Protection of the Crown. And though his Person was removed for a time, his Effects and Family continued still under the same Protection."

Now, the letter of this judgment did not apply to William Joyce. He had taken his wife with him to Germany, and by his marriage with her he was childless. (He had two children by a former marriage, but they were in the care of their mother, and are irrelevant to this case.) If he possessed any effects when he quitted England they were sure to be of such a trifling nature that it would have been fairer to regard them as abandoned rather than left under the protection of the Crown; had he retained any substantial property in the country he would not have had to avail himself of the provisions of the Poor Prisoners' Defence Act. But he was within the sphere of the spirit of the judgment. Joyce disappeared from England at some time between August 29, 1939, when he issued an order dissolving the National Socialist League, the Fascist organization of which he was the head, and September 18, when he entered the service of the German radio. He was the holder of a British passport, it was part of his lifelong masquerade as a British subject. He had declared on the application papers that he had been born in Galway, and had not "lost the status of British subject thus acquired." He obtained this passport on the 6th of July, 1933, and there is perhaps some significance in that date. He had become a member of the British Fascists in 1923, when he was seventeen, but had left this organization after two years, to become later an active member of the Conservative Party. In January 1933 Hitler seized power, and later in the year Mosley formed the British Union of Fascists, which William Joyce joined. This passport was, like all British passports, valid for five years. When July 1938 came round he let it lapse, but applied on September 24, 1938, for a renewal for the customary period of one year; and there is, perhaps, some significance in that date also, for the Munich Agreement was signed on the 29th of September. The next year he was careful not to let it lapse. He made an application for renewal over a month before its expiry on the 24th of August, 1939, and there was certainly some significance in that date, for war broke out on the 3rd of September. Each of these renewals was dated as if the application had been made when the passport expired. So when William Joyce went to Germany he was the holder of a British passport which was valid until the beginning of July 1940. That was why the third count of an indictment charged him with committing high treason by broadcasting between "the eighteenth day of September, 1939, and on divers other days thereafter, and between that day and the second day of July, 1940, being then, to wit, on the said several days, a person owing allegiance to our lord the King." It was, in fact, the case for the prosecution that a person obtaining a passport placed himself thereby under the protection of the Crown and owed it allegiance until the passport expired.

No ruling on the point existed, because no case of treason involving temporary allegiance had been tried during the comparatively recent period when passports, in their modern sense, have been in use, so the Judge had to make a new ruling; and for one sultry afternoon and a sultrier morning the prosecuting and defending counsel bobbed up and down in front of the bench, putting the arguments for and against the broadening of the law by inclusion of this modern circumstance. People with legal minds were entranced, and others slept. Joyce enjoyed this part of the trial very much, and frequently passed down to his counsel notes that were characteristically odd. Like all prisoners in the dock, he had been given octavo sheets to write on, and could certainly have had as many as he wanted. But when he wrote a note he tore off irregularly shaped pieces and covered them with grotesquely large handwriting, so large that it could be read by people sitting in the gallery. One ended with the words, "but it is not important." His enjoyment of the argument was not unnatural in one who loved complications, for no stage of it was simple. Much depended on the nature of a passport, and this had never been defined by the law, for a passport has been different things at different times and has never been merely one thing at a time. It was originally a licence given by the Crown to a subject who wished to leave the realm, an act as a rule prohibited because it deprived the King of a man's military services; but it was also a licence given to an alien to travel through the realm; and it was a pass given to soldiers going home on leave, or paupers discharged from a hospital. Through the ages it changed its character to a demand by the issuing state that the person and property of one of its subjects shall be respected by other states when he travels in their realms; a voucher of his respectability, demanded by the states he intends to visit, as a precaution against crime and political conspiracy; and a source of revenue to the states, which charged heavily for such permits. But of its protective nature in our day there can be little doubt, since the preamble on every passport announces that "we," the Foreign Secretary of the day, "request and require in the Name of His Majesty all those whom it may concern to allow the bearer to pass freely without let or hindrance, and to afford him or her every assistance and protection of which he or she may stand in need." In 1905 the Lord Chief

Justice of that day, Lord Alverstone, defined a passport as "a document, issued in the name of a Sovereign, on the responsibility of a Minister of the Crown, to a named individual, intended to be presented to the governments of foreign nations and to be used for that individual's protection as a British subject in foreign countries."

The arguments that Joyce's counsel brought against the obvious inference were peculiarly masculine: they were tainted with that decadence which befalls all human activities, art, literature, science, medicine, and law, when the game becomes less important than the rules. This was not due to the imperfection of Mr. Slade's mind, which is an admirable machine. It happened because the case against Joyce rested on principles evolved in the classic phases of the law, when rules were laid down in order that the game should be played the better. The argument that William Joyce, an alien by birth who had acquired a temporary and local allegiance, extended its sphere by taking a passport with him when he went to the Continent could not be met on its own plane of forthrightness. It had to be met by the incomplete plea that a British court has no right to try an alien for a crime committed abroad, which was obviously true, but not applicable, since William Joyce was not simply an alien, he was an alien who had acquired a temporary allegiance to Great Britain. This involved maintaining that a temporary allegiance could in no circumstances be carried over by an alien to the Continent, that he must divest himself of it by the mere act of passing beyond the three-mile territorial limit; which committed Mr. Slade to the view that an alien who had been a resident of England and was the holder of a British passport could pop across the Channel, conspire with an enemy of England at Calais, and pop back again, not only once but hundreds of times, and never be tried for treason, because at three miles' distance from Dover he lost his duty of allegiance.

There was another fantastic argument which was appropriate to the case, because it went back to the Ireland of Michael Joyce and the transatlantic journeys made alike by his kind and their enemies. Just after the last war an Irishman named Johnson who was a naturalized American returned to Ireland and took part in the treasonable activities of the Sinn Fein. He was discovered, and some property of his was confiscated by the government as

"an act of State," which is a process not applicable to British subjects but only to aliens. He then sued for the return of his property
on the ground that an act of State could not be directed against a
friendly alien resident in Great Britain; to which the government replied that, whatever rights a friendly alien might enjoy
through residence in Great Britain, he had forfeited them by
reason of his treasonable activities. The point was in fact never
decided by the judges who tried it, obviously because they regarded
the proceedings of the rebel Johnson and the civil servant who had
confiscated his property as equally anarchic. But on the basis of
the civil servant's defence Mr. Slade argued that whatever protection had been afforded to Joyce by his British passport he must
have lost the moment he began to commit treason by aiding the
Germans. However, he also argued that Joyce's passport could
give him no protection, because he had acquired it by a false
statement; yet it was hard to see how it could fail to protect him
until the fraud was discovered and the passport was withdrawn.
Supposing that William Joyce had fallen out with the Germans
during 1940 and had become a civil internee, he could have called
on the assistance of the Swiss Embassy in Berlin, as Switzerland
was "the protecting power" appointed to safeguard the interests of
Britons in hostile territory during wartime.

All this filigree work delighted the little man in the dock, who
watched his lawyers with a cynical brightness, as if he were
interested in seeing whether they could get away with all this
nonsense but had no warmer concern with the proceedings. He
showed no special excitement, only a continuance of amused
curiosity, when, on the third day of the trial, at the end of the
morning, the Judge announced that he would give his ruling on
these legal submissions after the luncheon interval; and at two
o'clock returned to the dock still with his usual eccentric excess of
military smartness and his sustained tight-lipped derisiveness.
The Judge announced that "beyond a shadow of doubt" William
Joyce had owed allegiance to the Crown of this country when he
applied for his passport, and that nothing had happened to put an
end to that allegiance during the period when the passport was
valid. In other words, he ruled that a person holding a British
passport owed allegiance to the Crown even when he was outside
the realm. This ruling made it quite certain that William Joyce

was going to be sentenced to death; and if the sentence were carried out he would die the most completely unnecessary death that any criminal has ever died on the gallows. He was the victim of his own and his father's lifelong determination to lie about their nationality. For if he had not renewed his English passport and had left England for Germany on the American passport which was rightfully his, no power on earth could have touched him. As he became a German citizen by naturalization before America came into the war, he could never have been the subject of prosecution under the American laws of treason.

Now it was certain that the little man was to be sentenced to death; and nobody in court felt any emotion whatsoever. That was what made this case more terrible than any other case that any of us could remember in which a death sentence was passed: it was not terrible at all. People wanted Joyce to pay the proper legal penalty for his treason, but not because they felt any personal hatred against him. They wanted to be sure that in any other war this peculiarly odious form of treachery, which climbed into the ears of frightened people, would be discouraged before it began, and that was about the limit of their interest in the matter. At no other such trial have the spectators, as soon as the jury went out to consider their verdict and the Judge retired from the bench and the prisoner was taken down to the cells, got up from their seats and strolled about and chattered as if they were at a theatre between the acts. At no other such trial has the jury come back from considering their verdict looking as if they had been out for a cup of tea. At no other such trial has the Judge assumed the black cap—which is not a cap at all but a piece of black cloth that an attendant lays across his wig—as if it were in fact just a piece of black cloth laid across his wig. He spoke the words of the sentence of death reverently, and they were awful, as they always must be: "William Joyce, the sentence of the Court upon you is, that you be taken from this place to a lawful prison, and thence to a place of execution, and that you be there hanged by the neck until you be dead; and that your body be afterwards buried within the precincts of the prison in which you shall have been confined before your execution. And may the Lord have mercy on your soul."

But the effect of these words was, on this uniquely shallow occasion, soon dispersed. It was indeed pitiful when Joyce was asked if he wanted to make a statement before sentence was passed on him, and he shook his head, the hungry and inordinate voice in him at last defeated. He had been even more pitiful earlier in the trial, when the Judge had warned the jury to consider very carefully their verdict because a person found guilty must be sentenced to death, for he had put up his hand and touched his neck with a look of wonder. But that he deserved pity was noted by the intellect; pity was not felt. Nor was anybody in the court very much moved by the extreme courage with which he bore himself, though that was remarkable. He listened to the sentence with his head high, gave one of his absurd stiff bows, and ran down to the cells, smiling and waving to his brother and his friends, acting gaiety without a flaw. Such a performance would once have moved us, but not now. All has changed; and even a trial for a capital offence is quite different from what it was before the war. Then the spectators were living in a state of security, and the prisoner was an exceptionally unfortunate person who had strayed into a district not generally visited, perhaps for lack of boldness. But every man and woman who attended Joyce's trial had at some time during the past six years been in danger of undeserved death or pain, and had shown, or witnessed in others enduring such peril, great courage. These attributes in William Joyce made no claim on them, themselves pitiful and brave; and he could not arouse their interest by his exceptional destiny, since he was in the dock by reason of failure to acquit himself in their common destiny. So they turned away from him and left the court as if it had been a cinema or concert.

But in the dark corridor a woman said: "I am glad his mother's dead. She lived near us in Dulwich. She was a sweet little lady, a tiny little woman. I often used to stand with her in the fish queue. In fact, that's how I met her. One day after the blitz had been very bad, I said something about that blasted Lord Haw-Haw, and someone said, 'Hush, that's his mother right beside you,' and I felt dreadful. But she only said—but she was ever so Irish, and I can't speak like she did—'Never mind, my dear, I'm sure you didn't mean it unkindly.'" This story recalled the lilt of affection in the aged Mr. Holland's voice when he had spoken of Queenie. The dark corridor passed to a twilit landing. Down a shadowed staircase the band of Fascists were descending, tears shining on their astonished faces. Joyce's brother walked slowly, his eyes that were soft and brown like a cow's now narrowed and wet, and the hunchback solicitor just behind him. There was a block, and for a minute the crowd all stood still. The hunchback plucked at Quentin Joyce's jacket and said kindly, "This is just what he expected, you know." "Yes," said the brother, "I know it's just what he expected." The crowd moved on, but after it had gone down a few steps the hunchback plucked at the young man's jacket again and said, "It's the appeal that matters, you know," and Quentin said, "Yes, I know. The appeal's everything."

At the counter where the spectators had to collect their umbrellas and coats, the charming jurywoman was saying good-bye to one of her colleagues. They were shaking hands warmly and expressing hopes that they would meet again. They might have been people parting after a cruise. Jostling them were the Fascists, waiting for their raincoats, garments which they affected in all weathers, in imitation of Hitler. The young man who looked like a gipsy held his head down. Heavy tears were hanging on his long black lashes. He and his friends still looked amazed. They had wanted people to die by violence, but they had not expected the lot to fall on any of their own number. Another dark and passionate young man was accosted by a reporter, and he cried out in rage that he had been four years in Brixton Jail under our Security Regulation 18B, all for patriotism, and he had come out to see the persecution of the finest patriot of all. His black eyes rolled and blazed about him. They fell on another bystander, who was not the best person to receive his complaint, for her name had been on the Gestapo list, recently discovered in Berlin, of persons who were to be arrested immediately when the Germans invaded England, and it was doubtful, had this happened, if it would have led to anything so comfortable as four years in Brixton Jail. But the bystander did not blaze back at him. Not possibly could she have achieved this force. There was this new universality of horrible experience, these vast common martyrdoms, that made these unhappy egotists, insisting on their own particular revolts and heroisms, seem so pathetically obsolete. Not with any degree of picturesque intensity could the bystander have struck an attitude on the ground that she was on that Gestapo list, because about twenty-three hundred other people had also been on it.

The little band of Fascists gathered together in a knot by the door, and after they had wiped their faces and composed themselves, they went out into the street. In the open space in front of the building was a line of parked cars, and behind them stood a crowd of silent people. The Fascists walked away from this crowd, down a street that narrowed and lost itself in a network of alleys. Nobody followed them, but they began to hurry. By the time they got into the shelter of the alleys, they were almost running.

2

THE fight between the Crown and William Joyce over the continuance of the breath that shook his flimsy little body was waged throughout four months and all across London. It began in the golden warmth of September in the Old Bailey, which stands, prosaic but wholesome as boiled mutton, in the melancholy-mad landscape, stranger than the surface of the moon, of the ruins round St. Paul's. There the sentence of death was passed upon him. He appealed, and his case was reviewed during some bright November days by the Court of Appeal, in another damaged building, the Royal Courts of Justice, usually called the Law Courts. They stand something under a mile to the southwest, just where the Strand and Fleet Street meet, where the church of St. Clement Danes stands in the middle of the road, always an obsolete and beautiful inconvenience, now a poor lovely charred skeleton. The Court of Appeal confirmed the sentence of death. Then Joyce took his last chance and appealed to the House of Lords, and there for a week stood his trial, in the precincts of Westminster Palace, which, hugger-mugger within from bomb damage, looked across the river through the light December mists at one of the most moving memorials of the blitz, St. Thomas's Hospital, still operating but hideous in dilapidation.

The forms of the Law, changing with each stage of the case,

symbolized the increasing intensity of Joyce's ordeal. In the first trial, he faced one judge as he stood in the dock, with a wide court behind him, where numbers of his supporters formed groups expressing apostolic grief and loyalty. In the Court of Appeal, which is a simple, small, square library lined with law books, three judges faced him, and the number of his supporters who attended was no longer large enough, or distant enough, to be seen as a group of wild and unhappy young men in Hitler rain-coats with a look of Irishry about them, but appeared as indi-viduals. One could note the weak eye glaring in imitation of the two dictators, forgetful that they had both died in disgrace, and other features bespeaking the soul who, being nothing, passion-ately wanted to be something. Last of all, in the House of Lords, there were five judges to try the prisoner, and the most restricted and remote accommodations for spectators. Only his brother and his two best friends were present in court, and they were hidden from him. Nor would it have profited him if he could have seen them, for they were by this time neither a group nor indi-viduals but personifications of anxiety. While the forms of the Law changed round Joyce in the courts, the hatred against him in the world outside remained constant and severe. It was related to the ruin that had touched and surrounded every building in which he was tried. The people remembered that while they had fought fires and lost their kin and homes, a man who had lived all his life amongst them had mocked at their misery and rejoiced at the thought of their deliverance to their enemies. Those of us who attended the trials heard, if we mentioned to casual acquaint-ances, hairdressers and porters and shop-assistants, what we were doing, a monotonous, unimpassioned, but definite hope that he would not escape the gallows.

Joyce experienced a considerable change of architectural en-vironment in the course of the trials. The Old Bailey is the standard official building that people liked putting up in the first twenty-five years of this century, whether in London or Paris or Berlin or Washington—unimaginative but well adapted to its purposes. What an advance that represented could be seen when the case went to our preposterous Law Courts. Erected in the full frenzy of the Victorian passion for the Gothic, the building is a swollen replica of a mediæval monastery. The lofty but obscure hall, which is used for no purpose whatsoever except to exhibit a few small notices, is, as it were, an abbey church; and many of the officials have to work underneath it in a crypt. The Press Association is to be found down there, functioning in a monastic cell. Upstairs, curved and vaulted staircases lead to side chapels, which are the courts, and to other apartments that are all strictly loyal to the prevailing fantasy. Even the ladies' room preserves an ecclesiastical appearance, and is presided over by a woman with a dedicated air, whose costume blends the concepts of a wardress and a nun. She lingers in the memory because of her exceptional amiability. Many of the other officials and attendants have been infected by the oddity of their surroundings, and resemble the more unpleasant characters in Dickens. They were insolent to the press, insolent to Ministries which rang them up for seats for distinguished foreign journalists, insolent to the general public who exercised their right to hear the case. Into this corner there had silted a last vestige of the most odious side of the Victorian Age: its snobbishness, its ill manners towards strangers, its stupidity. These people did not know enough about their own preoccupation, the law, to understand why the world should be interested in the trial of William Joyce.

Down at the House of Lords it was very different. Corporeally the Houses of Parliament are a muddle of exquisite mediæval architecture and capable but mediocre Victorian Gothic. They have been constructed according to the needs of the passing centuries, with occasional cancellations owing to fire and accident. Of the three places where Joyce was tried, it was the only one which was fully alive, alive like an old English or American house where sensible and pleasant people have lived for centuries, adapting it according to the knowledge of their generations. It was impossible to frequent the House of Lords without growing fond of it and being compelled to laugh aloud at it. Being alive, it presented the unpredictable quality of life. Yes, even at its threshold; for in the queue which waited every day at the entrance for admission to the public gallery were many African Negroes and Hindus, including some young women, very pretty and shapely in saris. Nothing seemed more unhappily clear than that these must be discontented members of the British Empire's subject races, sympathetically attending the trial of a fellow-rebel. But eavesdropping showed that they belonged to that large class of person, to be found in all races, which delights in the technicalities of Western Law for their own sake, and would exchange a native dance or the Taj Mahal any day for a good tort. They were interested in Joyce only as a golfer might be in a ball that has taken up an unusual position in the rough.

Each day of the third trial the spectators went up a stone staircase to a lobby full of gossiping lawyers, outside the chamber where the Lords were meeting temporarily, because their real home had been damaged by a bomb. They were then taken in hand by the attendants of the House of Lords, a body of spare and anonymous-looking men in ordinary white-tie evening dress, with the gold badge of the Royal Standard worn at the waistline. These men are a race apart, resembling the djinns in the *Arabian Nights*, though the magic never breaks down into malice. Their drill is perfect, their courtesy never cracks, and, since they belong to a supernatural order, they see no difference between the children of men and are no respecters of persons. Nothing could have been more determined yet detached than their ejection of the wife of a judge, and a very important judge too, who had usurped the seat allotted to a not at all important young journalist. They owe their strongly individual character to the circumstance that they are employed by the Lord Chamberlain, one of the three great officers of the Royal Household. This is much more than it sounds. His office is a department of state, like the War Office or the Admiralty, and it administers all the royal palaces and the establishments, such as the Houses of Parliament, which pertain to the Crown not only in the person of the King but in its impersonal existence as the supreme authority of the state. This department is conducted with remarkable efficiency, owing to the very long shadow cast by the shortest of our English sovereigns. As Queen Victoria grew up she realized that the Royal Household was in a state of squalid and spendthrift confusion and addressed herself very seriously to the task of putting it on decorous and economical lines that at once would do credit to the state and avoid extravagance. Her son Edward VII, her grandson George V, and her great-grandson George VI have all been compelled by the grim magnet of her will into perpetuation of that effort.

The attendants, who were under the supervision of a most elegant retired general, whose appearance and manners would have delighted Ouida, shepherded all the pressmen and the prisoner's friends into the Royal Gallery, a hall conceived and executed in the British monarchical equivalent of the brown-stone-house style. There is the same feeling that everything rich, and not just plum cake, should be dark. On the walls, strips of mulberry-and-gold brocade divide vast blackish frescoes in which a welter of arms and legs set at every angle around a few war horses suggests military effort; about the doors are dingy gilded figures of kings and queens; and in an alcove two toga-clad figures, quite black, though obviously they represent persons belonging to the white race, make expansive political gestures of a meliorist type. It is very like the downstairs dining room in the old Hotel Majestic that used to stand in New York at Seventy-second Street and Central Park West. In one corner there is a glass-covered show table, in which there lies a book inscribed with the names of all the peers and their sons who were killed in the 1914-1918 war. Each day a fresh page is turned. It has the heart-rending quality, more unhappy than normal grief, which pertains to all memorials of the last war.

Every morning, while we waited, a bishop in black robes and huge white lawn sleeves hovered at the door of the chamber in which the Lords sit, ready to go in and say the prayers which open the day's session, until an attendant cried, "Make way for the Mace!" and we were all ordered off the strip of oatmeal matting which runs across the ugly tiled floor. Then a procession came in, never quite at ease, it was so small and had never had enough start to get up the processional spirit. The Sergeant-at-Arms came first, carrying the Mace, which is a great golden pepper-pot on a stalk, the stylization of the ancient weapon with which the Sergeants-at-Arms of the Lords and Commons used to be sent to "demand obedience" from those who had disobeyed the instructions of Parliament. Another attendant followed, carrying, in a pouch embroidered with the Royal Standard, the Privy Seal, which has to be affixed to all important state documents before the King affixes the Great Seal. Then came the Lord Chancellor, Lord Jowitt, one of the handsomest men in London, superb in his white full-bottomed wig, its curls lying in

rows on his shoulders, and wearing a long black silk gown with
a train carried by an attendant. He supported between the fore-
finger and thumb of each hand the black velvet bag which rep-
resents the Privy Purse, the financial resources of the Crown.
The ritual is not mere foolishness. The procession and the sym-
bols are a mnemonic guide to the constitutional functions of the
House of Lords, and are part of a complicated convention into
which most of the legislative and judicial activities of Parliament
fit conveniently enough, and which nobody would much care to
rewrite, in view of the trickiness of procedure. It is fairly safe to
say that this is not one of the features of English life which will
be altered by the Labour Government.

We had to stand a long time after that, for the opening prayers are lengthy. Around the room ran a shiny quilted red-
leather bench, broken by ugly drab radiators, but nobody ever
sat on it except Joyce's solicitor, the fair-haired hunchback. He
looked much older than he had at the first trial; and it is not
easy to estimate what it must have cost him to have conducted
for four months, with an efficiency which was remarked on by
all the lawyers who followed the case, the difficult defence of one
who must have been repulsive to him as a traitor, whom he had
never chosen to defend. He did not seem quite so friendly as he
had been with William Joyce's brother Quentin, who also looked
much older. At the Old Bailey he had been a fresh-faced boy,
seeming younger than his twenty-eight years. Now he might
have been forty. Deep furrows had appeared in his forehead,
and his eyes were small and sunken, and, in the morning, red
with weeping. His face was bloated with grief and he had put
on weight. With him were two friends; tall, gaunt Angus Mac-
Nab, ex-internee, who was plainly superior in education and
social standing to his companions—the cranky gentleman so
often, as Henry Adams complained, produced by the British
people; and a young man named MacNeill Sloan, whose cold
grey-blue eyes showed that he had escaped from the world into
his dreams, which were not wider and kinder than the existence
around us, as the dreams of most people are, but narrower and
harsher. All three were lifted to the heights of dignity by their
grief for William Joyce, whom assuredly they were mourning

as the early Christians might have mourned a brother about to go into the arena.

Some rumour of this cult had been spreading abroad since the trial began. The City of London greatly respected a certain aged stockbroker, belonging to a solid Scottish family, who conducted a large business with the strictest probity and was known to his friends as a collector of silver and glass and a connoisseur of wine. He had a beautiful house, which was kept for him by his sister, a tall and handsome maiden lady given to piety and good works, whose appearance was made remarkable by an immense knot of hair twisted on the nape of her neck in the mid-Victorian way. The old man's last years were afflicted by a depressing illness, during which he formed a panic dread of socialism, and for this reason he fell under the influence of Sir Oswald Mosley, to whom he gave a considerable amount of money and whose followers he often entertained. This is a repulsive thought when it is remembered that many of those followers were very ugly scoundrels; one was prosecuted for living on the earnings of a prostitute. The old man had a special fondness for William Joyce, who, being a lively, wise-cracking, practical-joking little creature, was able to cheer up an invalid; and after his death his sister, who carried on all his enthusiasms, treated Joyce like a son. She let him use her country house as a meeting-place for the heads of his organization, and entertained him there so often that it was one of the first places searched by the police at the outbreak of war when they found that Joyce had left his home.

This woman, then over eighty and crippled by a painful disease, rose from her bed to travel up to London, an apocalyptic figure, tall and bowed, the immense knot of hair behind her head shining snow-white, and went to see William Joyce in prison. She returned weeping but uplifted by his courage and humility and his forgiveness of his enemies and his faith in the righteousness of his cause. To all those whom she especially loved she sat down and wrote letters describing her visit to this holy and persecuted man which truly might have wrung the heart, and she followed them with copies of the letters that he wrote to her from prison, in which he said that he knew well that the issue of his trial might be against him but was not dismayed,

since he could think of no better death than dying for his faith.
These pretensions on behalf of a man who worked to enable
Hitler and Goering to set up Naziism in England were obviously
sickening, and there was only a minute and crazed fraction of
the population which would accept them. Yet there was, as
could be seen from day to day during these trials, some reference
to reality in these pretensions, though the difficulty of seeing
that, or anything else relating to the trial, in the House of Lords
was very considerable.

Because the House of Commons had not then been repaired,
having been very heavily blitzed, the Commons were sitting in
the House of Lords, while the Lords sat in the Robing Room
used by the King and Queen at the Coronation and the opening
of Parliament. This had been hastily converted into an ersatz
House of Lords, though it is no bigger than the auditorium of
a women's club in a small American town and has no gallery
for the press or the public. Improvisation had not been very
successful. The spectators climbed a staircase steep as a ship's
companion-way and found a small shelf with two tiers of seats
for the press and a third for the press or the public, from which
nothing whatever could be seen of the Joyce trial. Instead, they
could see very clearly, were indeed forced into intimacy with,
some of the most horrible Edwardian frescoes imaginable. All
that could be said for them was that they were appropriate to a
chamber that was to be used as the House of Lords, in view of
the notorious obsessional devotion of the British aristocracy to
the horse. That had been traceable outside in the Royal Gallery,
for in the blackish frescoes the horses had been the only living
creatures which in a scene of catastrophe had remained the
right way up. Within, the tribute was even more ardent. The
fresco beside the gallery had the word "Hospitality" written underneath it, and showed a lot of people in old Metropolitan
Opera Wagnerian costumes on the set which the old Metropolitan always used when an abbey was needed, all of them welcom-
ing a man who, oddly enough, was riding in on a horse. But that
was not really hospitality. They were plainly glad to see him
because he was riding a horse. Behind the gallery the word "Generosity" was written under a fresco showing a horseman refrain-
ing from killing a man lying on the ground, on the advice of his

horse, who was turning an elder-statesman muzzle toward him. There was a horse in every fresco except one, in which there was a divine person instead.

As well as the frescoes, the spectators could see the two royal thrones at the end of the Chamber—the Queen's carefully built a little lower than the King's—raised on a dais with two steps. In front of the thrones, on the floor of the house, was the Wool-sack, a red, stuffed *pouffe* on which the Mace was lying; during normal sessions of the House the Lord Chancellor sits on it. On the floor of the House there is also a table covered with very new and bright red leather, at which a clerk in wig and gown sat throughout the trial, cutting up paper with scissors as if he were preparing to amuse an infinite number of children. Running lengthwise on each side of the floor were the two rows of benches on which the peers sit, and there some were sitting. But they were no part of Joyce's trial, they were spectators like the rest of us. For though a prisoner appeals to the whole House of Lords for judgment on his case, the House refers the matter to a small committee of judges, drawn from a panel of law lords. In Joyce's case these judges numbered four, with the Lord Chancellor as a fifth. The counsel address this committee not on the floor of the House but from the bar of the House, and the committee sits at a table pressed as close to the bar as possible. The improvised gallery was over the bar of the House. To follow the case the spectators had to listen to a thin thread of sound by invisible speakers under their feet. Quentin Joyce had to partake in this general inconvenience. Surely Hell could provide no greater torture than to follow thus a brother's destiny.

Yet there was something to be seen before one went up to one's seat. Pausing at the foot of the steep staircase and looking across the twilit space under the gallery, one saw the barristers, in wig and gown, sitting in silhouette, their faces turned towards that one of their number who stood speaking into the brightness of the lit chamber beyond, where there sat at the table, fantastic companions to the Lord Chancellor in his robes, the four old Judges, dressed in lounge suits and swathed in steamer rugs against the bitter cold. And in the furthest corner of the darkness under the gallery, with four warders to guard him, was William Joyce, his face altered by new wisdom and as yellow

with prison pallor as if it were stamped on a gold coin. Time
had acted on him during the trials as strongly as on his brother,
but differently. Some of the change had been wrought by the
eye of the beholder. At the Old Bailey he had seemed meanly
and repulsively ugly. At the Law Courts, where he appeared
before the Court of Appeal, he was not so. He was certainly puny
and colourless, but his face had an amusing, pleasant, even pret-
tyish, character. It was not good-looking, but it could be imagined that people who knew him well would find it easy to believe him far better-looking than he was, although he would
probably make no such reciprocal generosity, for his own vice
was plainly the icy coldness of the charmer. The alteration in
effect was in part due to a considerable improvement in his
health. He had arrived in England shabby and tousled and
sickly, pulled down by the hardships of his months of homeless-
ness between his last broadcast and his arrest and by the wound
in his leg; but during his imprisonment he had eaten well and
slept soundly, and was said to be the only prisoner who had
ever consistently put on weight while under sentence of death.
But the alteration in effect was also due in part to the circumstance that, while he had sat at the Old Bailey with the right
side of his face towards most of the spectators, at the Law Courts
he had turned the left side towards the court, and the left side
was unscarred. The cut that had run from the lobe of his right
ear to the right corner of his mouth had not only left a scar, it
had destroyed the moulding and meaning of that side of his
face.

He had received this wound during the years of adolescence,
when pride and self-doubt fuse into anxious vanity. For he was
full of pride in the sense of impatience with anything less than
glory. That was written in his early letter to the secretary of the
Committee for Military Education, and it was shown in the
course of his education. His first bent was scientific, but when
he sat for his Intermediate Science at the age of seventeen he failed
in two subjects, and though this was natural enough, as his
schooling had been interrupted by the family's hegira from Ireland to Lancashire and London, he turned his back on science
and studied for a degree in arts. To cause him self-doubt, there
was his tiny stature and his love of women. The scar, when it

was new and red, must have been a terrifying disfigurement. It was another handicap which he had to overcome, for which he had to compensate. More fuel was given to his huge ambition, and he was committed to a certain career. It is not certain just how he received this wound. A man who worked in the Fascist movement beside Joyce for many years never heard him account for it, and his followers told so many different stories, most of them improbable, of how he received it, that he was tempted to believe it the result of a commonplace accident. But at the time William Joyce suffered the injury he was a student at Battersea Polytechnic, and it was then believed by his fellow-students and at least one of the staff that he had either been slashed with a razor-blade concealed in a potato or mauled with the leg of a chair by a Communist in a street-fight arising from a British Fascist meeting.

Whoever followed William Joyce from the Old Bailey to the Law Courts found themselves thinking of him no longer as base and shabby, but as damaged and deformed. For, of course, it had not mattered how much he hungered for glory, how he cancelled the disadvantages of pygmyhood by courage and learning and the use of his prodigious voice. There was something there which would have been a bar between him and advancement, whatever he had made of himself. Passionately he longed to enjoy certain things which are the fruits of a highly developed civilization, such as the pleasure of administering complex systems for the benefit of the community; but though it is the essence of those things that they exist to be shared, few who enjoy those fruits would not have felt panic at the idea of sharing them with William Joyce. He could never have been trusted not to make a mistake, of such grossness as the mistake which led him, loving England, to plan her salvation through subjugation to the architects of Belsen and Buchenwald. There was at some point a partial blackness, as if a perforated ear-drum or a detached retina, and the consequence was barbarity. This was apparent even when the unscarred side of his face revealed his humour and acuteness, to a degree that was remarkable. Prisoners in the dock laugh more freely than is generally imagined; judicial jokes which so often annoy the newspaper reader are to them an opportunity for relaxation. But Joyce's amusement at his own appeal was more subtle than that. One of the Judges on the bench was most picturesquely comic in appearance and might have come straight out of the *commedia dell' arte*. William Joyce watched him with delight; and he followed the legal arguments with as unusual detachment, once nodding in approval when a point was decided against him.

But here at the House of Lords he had endured a further change. He had still his humour and his love of glory. Every morning he was taken into the court before the counsel came in, and he never failed to express to his warders, laughing at himself but nevertheless making an honest confession, how much he enjoyed making this ceremonial entrance to the Mother of Parliaments. He still followed the legal argument with a bright eye. But the long contemplation of death had given him a dignity and refinement that he had lacked before. It could be recognized when he turned his eyes on the spectators who paused to look at him before they went up to their seats in the gallery. At the Old Bailey he had soon come to recognize those who were sitting through the whole trial, and it had entertained him to catch their eyes and stare them out. At the Court of Appeal he had more effectively, though involuntarily, disconcerted the gaze of the critical by the evident coincidence of his field of reference with what they could have claimed for their own. His following of the argument showed that he was not just an eccentric criminal. Intellect and humour he had, and books he had evidently used; and courage, he knew all about that too. The ordinary human equipment for dealing with time had been his. At the House of Lords he had gone past comparison, looking at us from a territory governed by another time than ours, and listening to the striking of an hour that had not yet struck for us. Against the mystery of his expression a mocking spirit might recall the jest which Dr. Johnson uttered when a wag, who knew well that he had written the sermon preached in prison by Dr. Dodd the forger when he was awaiting execution, commented on the marked superiority of the sermon to any others that the criminal clergyman had ever preached. "Depend upon it, sir," he said, "when a man knows he is to be hanged in a fortnight, it concentrates his mind wonderfully." But how far that was a jest Dr. Johnson knew, who went in great fear of death.

In order that William Joyce's process of enlightenment should not continue indefinitely, the lawyers swung their argument back and forth for four days. It was difficult to follow the unseen speakers, because what could be seen was often incongruous enough to be captivating. Midmornings, a stately attendant glided across the scene of baronial pomp bearing a very common little tea tray for the comfort of the shivering Judges. Peers dropped in to listen and sat about on the red rep benches, some of their eldest sons exercised a curious right and squatted on the steps of the dais beneath the thrones. One peer lived through a most painful moment of his life during the trial. Following an intricate point, he ran his finger thoughtfully up and down behind the lapel of his coat, but suddenly stopped. A look of agony passed over his face, and he turned back the lapel. He had found a moth hole and for a long time was unable to think about William Joyce. But our attention was always drawn back by the unfolding story, which became more ironical each time it was restated in court, of a man who was being strangled by the sheer tortuousness of his family destiny. He was an American by birth who, by his father's wish, had pretended all his life to be British. Why? In the third trial, as in the first and the second, that question was never answered. It had become more perplexing as more knowledge about William Joyce had come into currency. He had stood as a candidate at municipal elections and had at that time had to swear an oath that he was a British subject; the penalty for making such a false declaration is a fine up to a hundred pounds and anything up to five years' imprisonment. Why did the father—who by all account loved his eldest son very dearly, and must have acquired a reasonable notion of the law's view of such ongoings in the course of his life as a close friend of the British police government of Ireland—keep his own and his family's status as close a secret as if their lives depended on it? But perhaps they did. Such hooded figures live in a land not ruled by likelihood. This mysterious imposture, and this alone, brought Joyce to the gallows. The arguments of his counsel could not disguise the ineluctable process.

The legal content of each of the trials was slightly different; different as, say, three performances of the same piano concerto by the same conductor and the same soloist but by three separate orchestras. But that comparison fails as regards the proportion of constants and variables. The thematic material and the harmonies were the same, but the interpretation varied; and the conditions of the second and third trials permitted, as it were, the polish that comes of prolonged rehearsal. At the Old Bailey the fantastic novelty of the case and the disturbing excitement of William Joyce's presence, the Judas of our blood, overwhelmed the Court, and the proceedings were disordered in their spontaneity. It was not surprising that the shorthand notes of Mr. Justice Tucker's address to the jury should have read:

Now as you have been very rightly told and reminded—you have been told already once—William Joyce would play a very small part in the world's history, and our demeanour, the way we comport ourselves in the proceedings in this case, is of greater importance to us than is William Joyce—observations that are very true, but I only add this, that it is not only the way we outwardly comport ourselves in the proceedings in this court, but it applies, and applies with even greater force, to the way you comport yourselves when you retire to consider your verdict, to be sure that you arrive at what you honestly believe to be a true verdict according to the facts, regardless of opinion or anything of that kind, and it applies to me in the very responsible decisions of law that I have had to come to in this case.

The contentions on which Mr. Slade asked the Court of Appeal to reverse the verdict returned at this initiatory trial were four, and of these, three were repetitions of the legalistic ingenuities which had been brought forward in Joyce's defence at the earlier trial. The Court, it was said, had wrongly assumed jurisdiction to try an alien for an offence against British law committed in a foreign country. The learned Judge was wrong in law in holding, and misdirected the jury in directing them, that the appellant owed allegiance to His Majesty the King during the period from the 18th of September, 1939, to the 2nd of July, 1940. (Because he had gone out of the country and had not left his wife and effects behind him.) There was no evidence that the renewal of the appellant's passport afforded him, or was capable of affording him, any protection, or that the appellant ever availed himself or had any intention of availing himself of such protection. This third contention was argued on grounds which seemed to the lay mind curiously frivolous. Contrary to vulgar opinion, it is rare that what is said in a court of law runs directly counter to common sense, although the manner of saying it may be gibbering with excessive precaution or stuccoed and cockleshelled with obsolescence. But this argument propounded something sillier than our human custom; we do not live our daily lives on the plane where it would be true that the protection which attracted allegiance was not protection *de facto* but protection *de jure*, not actual protection but the right to it, and that therefore a man who obtained a passport by fraud (as Joyce had done) would not owe allegiance in return for the protection he derived from it. According to this line of argument, a man who fraudulently obtained a British passport was in a better position than a man who obtained it legally, because he had to give nothing in return. The obvious way for the community to handle such a situation would be to prove that he had obtained the passport illegally and deprive him of it but make him discharge all the responsibilities he had incurred by possessing it up till the time when he forfeited it. Mr. Slade again made the submission that the moment the holder of a passport committed treason the power which granted the passport withdrew its protection, as the passport-holder had failed in his allegiance and therefore had no claim on the corresponding protection. This was obviously a catch, a Christmas-party riddle which had lost its way and could only have been made tolerable by mince pies and kissing under the mistletoe. The Judge who looked like a character in the *commedia dell' arte* thought little of this point; he puffed out his cheeks and spouted out air through his leathery old lips as if he were a dolphin. William Joyce watched him with a lively delight.

The fourth contention related to the oddly incoherent summing-up of the Judge at the Old Bailey. If there were any evidence that the renewal of William Joyce's passport had afforded him any protection, or was capable of doing so, and that he had ever availed himself of this protection, or had tried to do so, it was for the jury to decide whether this evidence was true, and the Judge had failed to direct them on this issue. There was much more substance in this contention than in any of the others, or, rather, it seemed to be so; for its plausibility arose from the impotence of the written word to convey the significance of an occasion determined by speech. At the Old Bailey, Mr. Justice Tucker had said to the jury: "My duty is to tell you what I believe to be the law on the subject, and that you have to accept from me, provided you believe the facts about the passport, going abroad, and so forth. If you do not believe that, you are entitled to reject it and say so, because you are not bound to believe everything, but if you accept the uncontradicted evidence that has been given, then, in my view, that shows that this man at the material time owed allegiance to the British Crown." None of us who had sat through the trial had the faintest doubt that he was directing the jury that they must decide whether they did believe or not that William Joyce had gone abroad with a British passport and had retained it for use. In the psychological situation built up by the arguments and personalities of the figures involved, those words had that meaning and none other. But when those words lay cold on the typewritten or printed page, they looked vague and perfunctory. Nevertheless, though the argument had that much in its favour, Mr. Slade dwelt on it only briefly, and the Judges did hardly more than mention it in a judgment that was a workmanlike essay on the two sorts of allegiance.

There in the House of Lords there was being given a performance far finer than the highest level of the proceedings in the Court of Appeal: as far superior to that, as that had been superior to the Old Bailey. When these four old Judges had a passage with counsel, it was as good as first-class tennis. They had been chosen for this work because they had supremely good minds, as well as the physiological luck that makes a man able to go on through the seventies into the eighties doing what he has done all his life better and better, even though he may not be able to address himself to new tasks or work continuously. The voice of each old man was characteristic enough to be easily identifiable, and often, in the quieter moments, recalled what was generally known about him. One amongst them had a small manor house set in a forest lying under the Wiltshire Downs. He lived there with a wife much younger than himself, who was perhaps the most celebrated professional horsewoman in England. At night he sat at his end of the table surrounded by his pupils, who had come to learn from him the subtlest mysteries of the law, and she sat at her end surrounded by her pupils, who had come to learn from her the subtlest mysteries of foxhunting and horsebreaking. The two groups were hardly able to communicate with each other, owing to the extreme specialization of each, but, as there is nothing so civilizing as scholarship and craftsmanship which have not lost touch with life, the Judge and his wife lived together in the most agreeable amity. Again, as at all trials of Fascists, there was suddenly audible the discord of natural injustice which is ordinarily silenced by the artificial harmonies of civilization. These old men's lives were pressed down and running over with earned honours and sagely contrived pleasures; the young man sitting next to me, whose sports jacket was too brightly checked in crimson and emerald green and cream, whose head was held too cockily, whose face was too coldly aggressive to permit confidence, was empty with an emptiness which would never be filled.

The third trial of William Joyce began on a Monday, and it looked as if the verdict would be given on Thursday afternoon. At one o'clock on Thursday counsel had finished their arguments, and the Lord Chancellor dismissed the court and bade it reassemble at three. Joyce's brother Quentin and his friend Mac-Neill Sloan rose miserably and went off to look for some lunch. This would be difficult to get, for in London everybody now lunches early and there is not a table free at one. Outside the Houses of Parliament everyone knew who they were and eyed them with wonder, aware of their peculiar grief, their terrifying sympathies. They crossed the street and passed into the crowds of Whitehall, and there they became two young men in raincoats among ten thousand such. Here lies the real terror in the international war of ideologies; that a city knows not whom it entertains.

When everyone had reassembled, the Lord Chancellor announced that the Judges required more time to consider their verdict, and dismissed the court again until Tuesday morning. Tears stood in Quentin Joyce's eyes, and he and his friends pressed past me to get out of the hated place as soon as might be. But the attendants held us back, and we stood together at the head of the steep stairs, looking down on William Joyce as he was marched out among the four policemen on his way back to jail. The courage he had shown in the dock at the Old Bailey had not greatly impressed a court in which most of those present had some experience of facing danger and had found themselves able to acquit themselves creditably enough; but now he was doing something more difficult, being a prisoner who had lain four months under the threat of death and had not heard the sentence he had braced himself to hear, and was a little, ill-made man surrounded by four drilled giants. He held his chin high and picked his feet up, as the sergeants-major say, and though he held his chin so very high that his face was where the top of his head ought to have been and though his feet flapped on his weak ankles, his dignity was not destroyed, but was made idiosyncratic, his very own. It appeared that there could be such a thing as undignified dignity. It also appeared that Joyce's body had the same resistance to culture as his mind. He was a graduate with honours of London University, but there was a quality about all his sayings and doings which suggested illiteracy; he was a good rider, he swam and dived to Polytechnic standard, he had tried hard as a featherweight boxer, he fenced, but his body looked as if he had been a poor child without exercise.

The postponement of the verdict was to have a graver consequence for Joyce and his friends than mere anguish. England was anxious to see Joyce suffer the just penalties of the law, but it was very anxious, too, that no penalty should be inflicted which was not just. Both in the towns and in the villages people were asking themselves whether the trial was perfectly fair and whether we were being careful to be loyal to our tradition of impartial justice and to escape the Nazi contamination of our troubled times. In legal circles it had been remembered that the most conspicuous prisoner under a capital charge whose case had ever gone through the Court of Appeal to the House of Lords had been reprieved, though he was a most repulsive scoundrel. He was a night-watchman who had enticed a little girl into his hut with the intention of assaulting her and had suffocated her because she persisted in crying for help; his case had gone to the supreme tribunal because he was in a state of drunken delirium at the time and the law had not till then defined its view of the extent to which a man insane by reason of intoxication was to be held responsible for his actions. Ugly as the crime was, it had been felt that no civilized community should keep a man hanging over the abyss of death so long and then push him over, and he was not only reprieved but, it is said, was informed in advance that if he were found guilty he would be reprieved. Lawyers, remembering this, felt there was a considerable case for reprieving William Joyce, who was a criminal not because he was an animal but because he was unable to manage those ideas which differentiate the man from the animal.

Unhappily, during the postponement Sir Oswald Mosley had a rally of his followers at a London hotel. It was necessary for his organization to deceive the owners of the hotel as to the purpose for which their assembly room was taken. The attendance was a matter of hundreds, and most of them were oddities like Captain Gordon-Canning, the ex-Guards officer who had recently paid five hundred pounds for the bust of Hitler which was sold at the auction of the German Embassy: a man in his late fifties whose sheeplike face was as unlined as if he were a young child. But the English public was disconcerted to find that even some hundreds of the anti-British and pro-Nazi people who had caused so much brawling and confusion before the war were gathering together with the plain intention of causing further brawling and confusion. It was most unfortunate that Quentin Joyce should have attended that rally, and it was very surprising that he should do so, as William Joyce, after having acted for some time as Mosley's deputy and propaganda chief, had parted with him after a bitter dispute in which Mosley's supporters, if not Mosley himself, freely accused William Joyce of embezzlement. Perhaps Quentin Joyce's deep grief made him feel a need for keeping company with those who, like his brother, were at war with society, and his simplicity failed to guess what scruples were in the mind of the lawyers and the public, just as his social isolation prevented him from hearing any rumour of them. But once his name had appeared in the newspaper as a guest at Mosley's party, it would have been a very brave government indeed that granted William Joyce a reprieve.

On the last day of the trial the press and the Fascists no longer had the Royal Gallery to themselves. It was thronged with Members of Parliament, a comradely and self-assured crowd, happily gossiping on their own stamping-ground and much less respectful to the ceremonics of the place than the press and the Fascists had been. They had to be pushed off the carpet by the attendants when the Mace and the Lord Chancellor went by, so busy were they exchanging comments on Joyce which were not meant inhumanely but sounded so, because they themselves were in such good health and so unlikely, if things went on as they were going, to be hanged: "They say he isn't here today," "No, if he were acquitted, it would be awkward. They'd want to arrest him immediately on defence-regulation charges, and nobody can be arrested within the Palace of Westminster. They'd have to let him go down into the street, and he might get away." "Perhaps he's chosen not to come today. Shouldn't blame him." "He's very plucky. I saw him at the Old Bailey." "So did I. What a queer little fish!" Joyce's brother was standing beside the last speaker, but he seemed not to hear. Both the Fascists and the pressmen were all preoccupied with the need to dash up into the gallery the minute the signal was given, because the announcement of the verdict would take only a few seconds and might be over before they had climbed the stairs.

The Lord Chancellor and the four Judges were sitting around the table at the bar of the House, as they had done every day, but now the red benches were fully occupied, the House was crowded with peers; there seemed so many it was remarkable that nobility had kept its distinction. As the press and the public took their seats in the gallery, the Lord Chancellor rose and stood in silent handsomeness till the place was still, and then said, "I have come to the conclusion that the appeal should be dismissed. In common with the rest of your Lordships, I should propose to deliver my reasons at a later date." Then the four old Judges rose in turn and gave their opinions. While the first was saying, "I agree," Joyce's brother and his friends got up from their seats beside mine in the second row of the gallery and clambered down to some seats in the front row which had been assigned to newspaper agencies and were not now occupied. Suddenly one of the suave attendants was standing behind them and was saying, in a tone of savagery the more terrifying because it was disciplined and was kept low so that the proceedings should not be disturbed, "You get out of there and go back to the seats where you belong." This seemed a most brutal way of behaving to men who were listening to a judgment that doomed one whom they loved; for all the Judges except one were saying "I agree," and that meant that Joyce must hang. But on the face of the attendant, and of others who had joined him, there was real fear. However innocent Quentin Joyce and his friends might have been at that moment, they had become associated with the idea of violence, and from the front of the gallery a violent man could have thrown grenades into the court.

Meanwhile the ceremony went on, affecting in its beauty and its swiftness. The Lord Chancellor moved backwards down the floor of the House, superb in his black robe and curled white wig, the only figure in a historic dress in the assembly, the symbol of the continuing rule of law. He halted at the Woolsack. He stretched out his hands to the peers on each side of the chamber and bade those vote who were content with the judgment. This was the last sad stage of the outnumbering of Joyce by the law. Now scores of judges faced the dock, and he was gone from it. The peers nodded and murmured and raised their hands. At this point a young man with hollow eyes and pinched nose and a muffler round his scrawny neck, who was sitting on the public bench of the gallery among the Negroes and the Hindus, cried out some words which some among us could recognize as Scottish Gaelic, and then proclaimed in English but with a strong northern accent that William Joyce was innocent. Attendants formed a wall around him, but did no more, for fear of interrupting the proceedings. The Negroes beside him expressed horror with rolling eyes; the Hindus looked prim. Joyce's brother and his friends threw a glance at him which was at first startled and then snobbish. The interrupter was not one of their sort of Fascist. Meanwhile the Lord Chancellor bade those peers who were not content with the judgment to vote, and there was silence. He declared, "The contents have it," and strode from the chamber. The peers streamed after him. The place was empty in a moment.

Quentin Joyce and his friends ran down the stone staircase into the street. They did not look so upset as might have been expected. The man who had shouted made his way out of the gallery without being touched by the attendants, who looked away from him, having taken his measure. In the lobby outside, crowds of pressmen gathered round him and questioned him and took down his answers, which he delivered with the gasping haste of the evangelist who knows he never keeps his audience long. The elegant general who was in charge of the attendants murmured to the Superintendent of Police, "I say, do we want this sort of thing, or don't we?" The Superintendent said he thought that the man would probably go away of his own accord if he were left alone. So the madman held an audience in the House of Lords, the very considerable crowd that were coming in to take part in the debate on the American loan neatly dividing to avoid disturbing him and joining again, until the pressmen left him, having insufficiently appreciated the remarkable quality of his utterances. A young reporter asked him, "But don't you think it mattered that William Joyce betrayed his country?" and he answered, in the accents of Sir Harry Lauder, "William Joyce didna betray his country. Ye canna say a man betrays his country when he goes abroad to better himself. Millions of people have done that and nobody's accused them of betraying their countries, and that's what William Joyce did. He had a fine poseetion waiting for him in Germany, and he just took it." Surely this was a mind as fresh as Shaw's.

Down in the street, Quentin Joyce and Angus MacNab and MacNeill Sloan were waiting, eager to speak to the press, eager to give praise to their martyr. That was why they had not looked so very greatly upset when the appeal was dismissed; they were like the people who, leaving a death-bed so painful to them that they could not have borne to contemplate it for another instant, find relief by flinging themselves into elaborate arrangements for the funeral. Angus MacNab, in his easy and gentlemanly but hollow and eccentric voice, was telling a reporter how calm William Joyce had been when he saw him in prison during the week-end. "He was in excellent spirits," he said, his eyes gleaming mystically behind his spectacles, "and he was discussing, quite objectively, and with all his old brilliance, the psychology of the four Judges. He was wonderful. . . . But I must leave you now and go and tell my wife what has happened. My name? Angus MacNab, and please do not spell it M-c-N-a-b. The correct spelling is M-a-c-N-a-b." And Quentin Joyce was talking freely in his careful voice, which, without being mincing, was more gentlemanly and more English than any English gentleman's voice, because this ambitious and Anglophile family consciously ironed out the Irish brogue from their tongues. Some reporters were asking him to write an article or make some statement about his brother, which he was refusing to do, evidently out of loyalty to some code of family relationships. "I cannot do that," he was saying primly. "It is for my sister-in-law to tell that story when she comes out of prison. A wife is nearer than a brother. It is her story." It was plain that he and all his family of conspirators and revolutionaries had felt themselves not less but more disciplined than the rest of the world, solid upholders of order. He went on to speak of some demonstration the Fascists would make against the sentence. "And believe me, there will be plenty of us," he kept on repeating, while, at the threat of trouble, Mac-Neill Sloan nodded, pallid with esurience. "Yes, believe me, there will be plenty of us."

But there were not plenty of them. There were not anything like plenty of them—even outside Wandsworth Prison on the morning of January 3, when William Joyce was hanged.

Wandsworth Prison lies in a shabby district in South London, so old-fashioned that it begins to look picturesque to our eyes. It is a mid-Victorian building with a façade of dark stone, derived from misunderstanding of Florentine architecture, and it is divided from the highroad by some cabbage patches and a dispirited nursery garden, planned whimsically, with thin streams trickling under toy bridges and meandering between the blackened stems of frosted chrysanthemums. The prison looks across the highroad to a monster of a school—built in the style of a Burgundian château and set in the midst of a bald and sooty park—which during the war housed the institution ironically known as "the Patriotic School," where persons who escaped from the occupied countries were detained, often for dreary weeks, until they had satisfied the authorities that they had not been sent over by the Germans. An avenue runs between the cabbage patches and the nursery gardens to the prison's great doorway, which is of panelled wood, dark green, with a heavy iron grille at the top, set in a coarse stone archway. A small notice board hangs on this door; and on it was pinned an announcement that the sentence of death passed on William Joyce was to be carried out that morning. On these occasions there is nothing whatsoever for a spectator to see except at one moment, when a warder comes out of a smaller door which is cut in the large one, takes down the notice board, and replaces it after two other notices have been added to the first: one a sheriff's declaration that the prisoner has been hanged, the other a surgeon's declaration that he has examined the prisoner's body and found him to be dead. But about three hundred people gathered to see that minute shred of ceremony.

They gathered while it was still dark and the windows of the cells were yellow in the squat utilitarian buildings which stretched away from the Italian façade; and they waited through the dawn till full daylight, stoically bearing the disappointment that the hour of the hanging was at the last moment postponed from eight to nine. Some of those who waited were pressmen, lamenting that there was no story here; straining figures on the roof of a yellow Movietone truck set up a tall camera to focus on the notice board, certain that there would be nothing anywhere else in the scene worth recording. Others were people drawn by personal resentment. An old man told me that he was there because he had turned on the wireless one night during the V-1 blitz when he came back from seeing his grandchildren's bodies in the mortuary and had heard Haw-Haw's voice. "There he was, mocking me," he said. There were many soldiers who had strolled out for a little after-breakfast diversion from a nearby demobilization centre. As time went on, all these people danced to keep their feet warm on the frozen earth.

There were some who did not dance. Most of these, however, were not particularly interested in William Joyce. They were opponents of capital punishment, who would have stood and looked disapprovingly outside any prison where anybody was being hanged. The most conspicuous of these were two plain and oblong Scandinavian women dressed in black, who indulged in silent but truculent prayer. Quentin Joyce and his friends were not there; they were attending a memorial service. It is possible that this particular spring of trouble may flow into the Church and there be lost, for during William Joyce's imprisonment he became reconciled to the faith in which he was born. But there must have been many Fascists who would not attend that service,

either because they were not Christian or because they were not
close enough to Joyce's family to hear of it; of these only a handful waited outside the prison, and of them only one grieved
openly, standing bareheaded, with no effort to hide his tears at
the moment of Joyce's hanging. Three others slipped through a
gap in the trees of the avenue and stood in the nursery garden,
where some rows of cabbage-stalks veiled with frost flanked a
rubble rockery, naked with winter, and at that moment they
practised a highly tentative reverence. Their bodies betrayed that
they had had no military training, and they wore the queer and
showy sports-clothes affected by Fascists, but they attempted the
salute which looks plausible only when performed by soldiers in
uniform. It was the poorest send-off for a little man who had
always loved a good show and done his best to give one; who, so
the prison gossip went, halted on his way to the scaffold, looked
down on the violent trembling of his knees, and calmly and cynically smiled.

3

DURING the trials there had flowed into the mind of the
community a conviction that Joyce had not been guilty of
any offence against the law. This was in part due to the inadequate reports of the proceedings which were all that the press
could find space to publish because it was starved of newsprint.
This restriction had been obviously a necessity during the war,
but it was suspected that the Labour Government was prolong-
ing it for political as well as economic reasons; for, as most newspaper owners are Tories, a check on the size of the paper amounts
to a check on Tory propaganda. That the Labour Government as
a whole nourished this intention cannot be believed, for it must
have realized that its accession to power had been not only
not hindered but actually helped by the election campaign of
the Tory press. But the idea had a flavour which accords with
the popular idea of Sir Stafford Cripps: it perpetuated a depriva-
tion, it showed legal art, and it might have been a shy consequence of admiration for the Kremlin's short way with the

liberties. If it were he that was responsible, he had not realized that political propaganda is the least effective feature of the newspaper. It is the presentation of the facts that matter, the facts that put together are the face of the age; the rise in the price of coal, the new ballet, the woman found dead in a kimono on the golf links, the latest sermon of the Archbishop of York, the marriage of a Prime Minister's daughter. For if people do not have the face of the age set clear before them they begin to imagine it; and fantasy, if it is not disciplined by the intellect and kept in faith with reality by the instinct of art, dwells among the wishes and fears of childhood, and so sees life either as simply answering any prayer or as endlessly emitting nightmare monsters from a womb-like cave.

The English public read almost nothing about the Joyce case which was not so disjointed as to be unintelligible. The news-editor had day by day to compress what could hardly be compressed at all until the trial was over and the legal arguments were grasped as a whole. The argument that was most easy to quote was the answer of the defence to the first indictment, which was the impossibility of convicting Joyce for the crime of being a British subject and adhering to the King's enemies, when in fact he was an American subject. The subsequent arguments, that Joyce had acquired a temporary allegiance to Great Britain, and had taken his obligation abroad with him to Germany by taking a British passport, were much more complicated to set down, and in any case were not liked by most of the journalists —using "like" in a purely gustatory sense, as it might be applied to a person's reaction to bananas or a film star. They were, to begin with, sympathetic towards William Joyce's lawyer, Mr. Slade, who has indeed a manner that invites sympathy, for he always appears to be making a magnificent fight for a hopeless case. Whether this air is always what an accused person is fortunate enough to find in his defender is doubtful, but it immensely exhilarates the spectators. The journalists' attentions thus won, they soon conceded that the case was not so hopeless. In the course of Mr. Slade's defence he put forward certain simple negatives which were far more quotable than the complicated positives by which the prosecution established the existence of temporary allegiance to the Crown as a recognized conception, and the nature of a passport; and his own more complicated propositions were so complicated that they could not be quoted at all. He figured, therefore, in the minds of many journalists as a plain blunt man gallantly putting himself about in an attempt to save an underdog hunted down by the lawyer chaps. Though the press obeyed in the letter and in the spirit the rule which forbids comment on cases under trial, their selection of what to publish of the proceedings and what to suppress conveyed their version of the story to a public that had been ready to listen to it long before it began. "Of course he can't be guilty of treason," it was said in all the London pubs. "He's a dirty little bastard, but we've no right to hang him, he's an American." "A miscarriage of justice," said the clerk in a government office, handing out a legal document concerning Joyce to an inquirer some months later, "that's what that verdict was. I hold no brief for the little man, though he was a wonderful speaker. I'm no Fascist but I always used to listen to him when he spoke up our way by the Great Northern Hospital; but it stands to reason that giving an American a British passport can't change him into an Englishman. A miscarriage of justice, that's what that was."

The legal discontent with the verdict was also, to a degree found startling by the laity, a reflection of the inadequate press reports. Treason is not a common offence, and people do not often pretend to be British when they are really American; so many lawyers were quite willing to believe that a trial involving those two elements would bring to light a great deal of law which was new to them. They therefore accepted the reports without reservations, and were as much misled as anybody else. "I see," said such a one, "that Joyce's appeal in the House of Lords is going well for him." His reason for thinking thus was a remark addressed by the Lord Chancellor to Mr. Slade: "Surely the proposition is elementary that allegiance was only due from an alien while he was in this country." Heard, this sentence conveyed with brilliant crystalline peevishness that Mr. Slade was hammering home the obvious, and it was followed by the statement, "The question, surely, is whether there are any exceptions to this rule." Read out of its context, it sounded like an encouraging invitation to pass on after a point had been proved. But the lawyers' objection to the Joyce verdict had profounder roots than misapprehension. Like the journalists, like the public, they felt a distaste for any attempt of the law to lay 'hands on Joyce which proceeded from the emotions and did not consult the intellect until it was asked to furnish an explanation for its own vehemence. They felt it more sharply and personally, because it was their mystery which was being profaned: and as they, as all of us, are forced sometimes to doubt whether the mystery of the law is not itself a profanity, since we live in the New Testament world, and justice has been blown upon by mercy. This reluctance has now forgotten its cause, since we are no longer Christian. Hence it remains as an arbitrary awkwardness about inflicting punishment, which is the more passionate by reason of its puzzled ignorance of its origin, and which reverts to the fiery prejudices of the Old Testament without regaining the caution which is characteristically patriarchal. One cannot live to be a patriarch without being careful as well as violent.

This complicated reaction is manifested very clearly in the vehement preface contributed by Mr. J. W. Hall, the well-known law reporter, to the volume on Joyce which he edited for the Notable British Trials Series. He cannot tolerate a single step of the process by which the state strove to disarm its enemy. It was unjust, he thinks, in every part, starting with the procedure of the trial:

When Joyce was arrested on the 28th May, 1945, and it became apparent that it would be necessary to bring him to trial, he was deliberately kept on the Continent, where he had been in hospital as a result of the wound he received at the time of his arrest, while Parliament quickly passed the Treason Act.

The implication is that Joyce could not have been touched under any existing law when he was arrested, and that Parliament rushed through legislation that met his case. That is not at all what happened. The Treason Act, 1945, was in fact introduced in the House of Lords in the middle of May, something like ten days before William Joyce was discovered in Germany. It had been designed long before to meet the possibility that a number of traitors might have to be tried, in which case the legal traffic would have been held up for months by the antiquated procedure imposed by the old act, which insisted that every person accused of treason must be tried by three judges and a jury, after having received a copy of the indictment, a list of the witnesses and a copy of the jury panel, at least ten days previously, and enjoined other technicalities obsolete in purpose. The new act aimed also at removing the provisions concerning evidence contained in the old act which, in fact, amounted to special protection for traitors, for no man could be found guilty of treason unless two witnesses testified that they had seen him commit an overt act. Under the new act the procedure in cases of treason is made the same as the procedure in cases of murder, which has never struck anybody as noticeably unfair. It is because the United States did not alter its law concerning the evidence in treason trials that it has been unable to prosecute its traitors, who include some very nasty Fascist agents. So, far from this very reasonable piece of legislative reform having been pressed on by the government with unseemly haste and venom, it was left about as a bill till it narrowly escaped oblivion. For it scraped into existence only in the last hours of the Churchill Government. It is true that Joyce was flown to England only the day after the act received the Royal Assent, but he had been less than three weeks in custody, during which time he had had to recover from a leg-wound; and after all it was very natural that he should not be hurried back to England if the result would be that he would have to be tried by a form of trial which Parliament had already commanded to be superseded.

He should not have been tried as he was, according to Mr. Hall; nor should it have brought any harm on him that he held a British passport. A passport, Mr. Hall explains, means nothing. Listen to his argument, for the doom of our time is woven through it. A passport, Mr. Hall explains, means nothing. It has been different things at different times: sometimes a soldier's leave pass, sometimes a license to leave the country, sometimes a permit to pass through it, sometimes a certificate of character required from the traveller by the country he visited. But every institution in England has at one time been something else; in the courts what must be considered is what it is today. Mr. Hall considers Lord Alverstone's judgment that a passport is a document issued in the name of a Sovereign on the responsibility of a Minister of the Crown to a named individual, intended to be presented to the governments of foreign nations, and to be used for that individual's protection as a British subject in foreign countries, and Mr. Hall deduces only "that the protection of the bearer is the object of a passport, but not that the right to protection springs from the passport." That is obvious, but irrelevant. A man receives a passport on the understanding that he has a right to protection; it is a certificate that he has such a right. But, Mr. Hall argues, no inference against Joyce can be drawn from his possession of a passport, because he had obtained it fraudulently. He compares his position to a person obtaining a certificate of marriage when he has married someone who was married already or who was within the prohibited degrees; as soon as the illegality is discovered the certificate is "displaced" and has no further legal effect. But a marriage certificate is, except in certain unusual circumstances, a static object. If a man obtains control of a dynamic object, such as an automobile, and uses it to the danger of the community, he is prosecuted, even if he obtained that control fraudulently. Moreover, the possession of a passport, when it is fraudulently obtained, does not make a man a British citizen if he is not one. But it may be evidence that he intends to continue enjoying British protection. A stolen or forged railroad ticket gives a man no contractual bond with the railroad company; but it is very strong evidence that he intends to travel to the place mentioned on the ticket, in a train owned and controlled by that railroad company. Finally, "it is worthy of passing comment that the Home Secretary, before allowing the law to take its course, did not think it necessary to wait and see whether any passages in their Lordships' opinion might afford some ground for the exercise of clemency." Mr. Chuter Ede is well known to be one of the most humane and conscientious Home Secretaries who have held office. He is here reproached for not having postponed Joyce's execution for nearly a month, until the Lord Chancellor and the four Lords declared their reasons for the judgment which they had announced on December the 18th. This judgment had been against Joyce's appeal by four to one: and what effect such an adverse judgment would have on inclining the heart of the Home Secretary to clemency is not apparent.

So Mr. Hall pecks at various legal aspects of the case; and also

attacks the whole problem of punishment. It is his opinion that
Joyce should not have been hanged, and obviously his offence
was not comparable to other iniquities usually visited with capital punishment. According to this curious quantitive consideration, it would be impossible to punish anybody at all for any
minor offence such as riding a bicycle on a footpath, either by a
term of imprisonment or a fine. For if death (which one may
take as involving the total confiscation of a man's means, though
he may leave them to his heirs) is to be reserved for the obscure
extremes of malefaction, and punishment is to be scaled down
to accord with the fine diminishing gradations of guilt, then all
the small sinful fry must go free, for there are more such gradations than there are years in our lives or pennies in our pockets.
Only machinery can measure to the millionth of an inch. The
mind seeking justice envies such measurement, but must content
itself with erecting on the edge of the abyss signboards crudely
warning of disaster. But, says Mr. Hall, there was no excuse for
even putting up a signboard here. In an appendix to his volume
he quotes reports compiled by the B.B.C. on the effect of Joyce's
broadcasts in England and the Empire, which suggest it was
negligible. But Joyce was not tried because he had succeeded in
recommending German National Socialism. He was tried because he had filled space with his statement: "I am a traitor. Why
are you not so too?" It does not matter how his question was answered. The offence was that it should have been asked, that the
Judas hidden in a man's bosom should have been shown coming
out of his hiding and pretending to prophesy.

In the last two paragraphs of Mr. Hall's preface he speaks
truly:

If it be said, "There would have been a public outcry if Joyce had
been reprieved," my answer would be that the first function of a legal
system is to substitute the reasoned and dispassionate judgment of the
law for the clamour of popular prejudice. It may, however, be doubted
whether there would have been any popular clamour, for very much to
my surprise I have found an almost equally universal feeling, shared by
lawyers and laymen, servicemen and civilians, that (with the utmost
respect to the eight out of nine learned judges) the decision was all
wrong, and that an unmeritorious case has made bad law. The feeling,
and it is, I believe, strong and widespread, is not so much that Joyce,

having been convicted, should have been reprieved, but that he should not have been convicted.

If one treats the sensation mongers who stand outside a prison during an execution with the contempt they deserve, it is, I think, fair to say that the conviction and execution of Joyce have caused more disquiet than satisfaction.

It is true. But that disquiet was no sign of mercy or any other sweetness on the part of the age; rather was it a sign of its sourness. The people were saying, "William Joyce was a vile man but he should not have been hanged," and they smiled as they said it, calling themselves gentle and unrevengeful. But they were hypocrites, and were avoiding admission of the truth for a base reason. They should have admitted that William Joyce was not a vile man but should have been hanged, and they refused to make that admission for a base reason. They had cast their eyes on the conception of the law with a new and dishonourable intent. The law is a force which has never yet been finally analysed. To make laws is a human instinct that arises as soon as food and shelter have been ensured, among all peoples, everywhere. There have been yellow people who have flashed on horseback across continents, apparently too mobile to form customs, apparently preoccupied with slaughter and destruction; there have been black people who have squatted on their thin haunches unchangeably through the centuries, their customs drooling to superstition round them. These have been thought by men of other kinds to be without law, but it was an error. Both societies had reached a general agreement as to how to order their lives, and ordained penalties against its violation. But neither they nor any other society could define exactly what they were doing when they were making that agreement and ordaining those penalties. Demosthenes came as near as anyone to a definition when he said that every rule of law was a discovery and gift of the gods, and he added that it was also an opinion of sensible men. This seems a paradox, for assuredly men are not gods, and the last thing a god could fairly be compared with is a sensible man. Nevertheless, nine hundred years later the great Justinian saw that that definition was reasonable and prefixed it to his *Digest of Laws*, only changing "gods" to "God." Pagan and Christian alike realized that the law should be at once the

recognition of an eternal truth and the solution by a community
of one of its temporal problems; for both conceived that the
divine will was mirrored in nature, which man could study by
the use of his reason. This is the faith that has kept jurisprudence
an honest and potent exercise throughout the ages, and still
keeps it so, though the decline in religion has made many find
other names for what is written in nature and has to be deciph-
ered by such men as wish to be good: such as the service of
humanity, the rights of the state, the sovereignty of intelligence
or moral sense.

The Englishmen who thought that Joyce should not have
been hanged had wholly lost this conception of the law. They
do not believe in the divine will; they do not believe, either, in
the service of humanity, the rights of the state, the sovereignty
of intelligence or moral sense, to the extent of imposing penalties for treachery to the sought social end; which means they do
not believe in it at all. They wish the law to be purely arbitrary:
a transparent chessboard laid over life, as an addition to its hazards, and even as a disguise for its real hazards. If the law be
thus, then the individual proceeds from the place of his origin
to the place where his ambition will be realized, taking care to
tread always on the white squares of the superimposed chessboard and never on the black. The judgment passed on the
whole journey will depend solely on the fidelity with which this
last, almost physical, condition is observed. Now, this is not
always a faulty judgment in practice. These Englishmen who
are endeavouring to make a new use of the law have to use the
old law as their instrument, and this, since it was devised by men
who sought to serve the divine will or the public good or intelligence or morality, usually denounced as crimes acts which were
in fact threats against the survival of the community. Therefore
a man who treads on a black square does as a rule not only of-
fend against the letter of the law but against the spirit, and truly
deserves blame and punishment; and conversely, a man who
treads on the white squares is as like as not truly innocent.

The debasement of the situation lies in the uses to which the
inevitable time-lag of the law is put. For the law, like art, is
always vainly racing to catch up with experience. Life is always
unpredictable. At every turn of history it presents the citizen with

new obligations, and renders dangerous the exercise of his liberty in some sphere by suddenly rendering that exercise an affront to the liberty of others. It is the task of judges and legislators to alter the law that it may cope with these capers of time. By a gross inappropriateness judges and legislators are described always as sitting, the one on the bench, the other in the House of Commons or the House of Lords; for in fact they run, they run fast as the hands of the clock, reaching out to the present with one hand, that they may knot it to the past which they carry in their other hand. There are always lapses in time when the present and the past are not joined, and it is these which Englishmen such as wished Joyce to live love to exploit. They enjoy exaggerating this inability of the law to adapt itself immediately to the age; they attribute to it an absurdity actually found most frequently in regulations framed by the civil service and by local bodies, which have to deal with material objects with the aim not of defining them exactly but of prescribing action of a highly artificial nature in regard to them. It amuses them, in fact, to imagine a state of society in which it is possible to travel through life with a criminal purpose and yet never, because of this legal time-lag, leave the white squares of legal innocence; and they feel a laughing, winking admiration for the rogues that achieve this journey. A vast number of English people were ready to cheer the cold shark Horatio Bottomley, because he had exploited the unforeseen situation created by the existence of a popular press, edited and owned by men who cared nothing for their repute among generally respected citizens, and read by a public which had a certain amount of investable capital and was ready to invest it without taking advice from any generally respected banker or stock-broker. It touched them neither in the heart or the sense of self-preservation that most of Bottomley's victims were people like themselves, whose savings were their sole shield from actual want. Simply they derived pleasure from thinking of him as drinking three bottles of champagne a day and keeping a racing stable on the proceeds of crime which, till his physical and mental forces were alcoholized into impotence, he managed to keep unimpugnably distinct from the illegal. It opened to all of them the prospect that one day they might find some such opportunity of gain easier than honest, and unpunishable, and it gave them an actual and immediate dispensation from a tedious duty. For if men are regarded as chessmen, who can but lose or win a game, they cannot be loved; they can only be assured of fair play within the rules of the game. The public who cried out that William Joyce should not have been hanged wanted the perverse satisfaction of seeing a man whose crime it knew by the testimony of its own ears go unpunished, thus being assured that life was moral nonsense. They hoped too to reward the impudence in him, which they had rightly judged to be as remarkable as Bottomley's; but they felt no interest in any other of his attributes. They would not love him. Yet there was certainly much to be loved in William Joyce.

4

THERE is no sight more touching than a boy who intends to conquer the world, though born in all probability to be its slave. Young William Joyce was such a boy, and took the first step towards conquest; for he was brave. Perhaps he really lay deep in the heather that he might tell the Black and Tans whether the three men left the farmhouse in the fold of the hills; perhaps he only pressed in on the Black and Tans with childish information that was of no service to them; perhaps he did no more than dream of either action. But such actions and such dreams depend for their origin on a resolution to die rather than live if death should prove nobler than life. That William Joyce was mistaken in his estimate of where nobility lay in his situation is not a great count against him. A boy of sixteen cannot be expected to be politically wise, but he might have already chosen to live as long as he could, no matter what the price. And behind William Joyce's political folly was a grain of wisdom, a degree of preference for the things that must be preferred if humanity is to survive. He liked the scarlet coats of the English garrisons; but it was Mozart himself who asked in one of his letters if there was anything in life finer than a good scarlet coat, and all scarlet coats take up a common argument. They dissent from the dark earth and the grey sky, they are for pride, they

teach the bodies that wear them a good carriage, they are for
dance and drill, for measure and discipline. It was not to be
held against the boy that he preferred the straight-backed aliens
in scarlet coats to his compatriots who slouched with hats crushed
down on cowlicks and collars turned up round unshaven jaws
on their performance of menial toil or inglorious assassination.
His family—and he was loyal to his own blood—cultivated that
preference. That the smart soldiers created the slouching assassins,
that imperialism creates slavery and unendearing slaves, he could
hardly have been expected to work out for himself at that age.
He was indeed isolated from his age in a dream of astounding
obsolescence, wholly alien from the society in which he believed
himself to be at home. It was in a town in Lancashire, where
rationalism is temperamental, in a period when the emotional
attitude in which men stood easy was cynicism, that he wrote
his letter to the University of London Committee for Military Education. From 86, Brompton Street, Oldham, in August
1922, he sent forth that message which was read in court: "I can
obtain testimonials as to my loyalty to the Crown. I am in no
way connected with the United States of America, against which,
as against all other nations, I am prepared to draw the sword in
British interests. As a young man of pure British descent, some
of whose forefathers have held high positions in the British army,
I have always been desirous of devoting what little capability and
energy I may possess to the country which I love so dearly." No
absurder letter can ever have been written from 86, or 85, or 87,
or any other number in Brompton Street, Oldham; but the little
creature was not quite absurd as he licked the stamp and the
flap of the envelope and hurried with a swagger along the black
street to the pillar-box, taking his first step toward the conquest
of England. It was going to be of no consequence at all that he
and his family had had to leave Ireland. He would take the
larger island instead.

In October 1922 he sent in the completed enrolment form to
the Officers' Training Corps from Number 10, Longbeach Road,
S.W. 2, where he was staying when he began his studies for his
science degree at Battersea Polytechnic. Joyce's destiny drew him
to South London; he crossed the Thames only to meet disaster.
This is to say that his destiny led him away from London: from

the London where England can be conquered. For South London is not London. It even calls itself by a vague and elided locution that leaves out the name of the capital. "Where do you live?" "South the river." The people on the other bank never speak of their landscape as "north the river." They may go down east, or go up west, but they move within London, where the Houses of Parliament are, and the Abbey, and Buckingham Palace, and Trafalgar Square, and the Law Courts, and Somerset House, and St. Paul's, and the Mansion House, and the Bank, and the Mint, and the Tower. The house where William Joyce first took up his dwelling on the other side of the Thames stood in one of those streets which cover the hills round Clapham Junction like a shabby striped grey counterpane. Longbeach Road is a turning out of Lavender Hill, that drab highway which follows the crest of a ridge running from Clapham Junction towards Vauxhall, grimy but genial, so genial that passers-by, asked the way, cry, "First on the left, dear." Its humble heights look down the sharp declivities of its northern side-streets to the railway tracks of the Southern Railway, streaked with metal as with water, the tree-tops of Battersea Park, and the spires and towers and embankments of the other London. The house itself was one in a line of those tiny houses which astonish by their lack of size, for their bow-windows suggest a sitting-room hardly large enough to permit an armchair on each side of the fire, and by the profusion and artlessness of their ornament. There are panels of coloured glass in the front door, and the porch is lined with strips of tiles moulded in fat patterns, such as one sees in old-fashioned dairies; the roof of the porch is converted into an unusable balcony, and the front of the house is picked out with plaster encrustations, representing chains of leaves. Some builder had loved beauty, but had neither individual taste nor command over a tradition. It was a poorer and less pleasing house than any other ever inhabited by William Joyce, and indeed he was there only as a lodger; he had left Ireland, alone, in December 1921, his family staying there until 1922, and then making their home in Lancashire until 1923. The solitary youth, filling in the O.T.C. enrolment form, was careful to state his claim that he had already seen military service, having served with the Worcestershire Regiment for four months. Such service must have been completed

by the time he was fifteen years and eight months old. The innocent and ugly little house, through its small lodger, was becoming involved with those of whom it was said long ago that blood
is their argument, and was making its first link with the events
that were to leave it one day surprised at its wholeness in a bomb-
shattered district.

When Michael Joyce came south in the following year, he became, with superb adaptability, a grocer; and he took the step,
unlooked-for in a dazed immigrant, of establishing his family in
a house that was as delightfully situated as any in London. Allison Grove is a short road of small houses which has been hacked
out from the corner of the gardens of a white Regency villa in
the greenest part of Dulwich, a queer cheap insertion in a line of
stately properties. It has its own great sycamore tree and many
syringas, and the most agreeable surroundings. Not far off is the
remarkable pleasantness of the Mill Pond, still a clear mirror of
leaves and sky, and beyond it is Dulwich College amidst its groves
and playing fields. To the south a golf-course makes a wide circle
of mock country, bounded by suburbs rising on round hills,
which, cleansed by being seen through the unusual lens of smoke-
less air, shine bright as the villages in the background of Row-
landson water-colours. To the north, behind the line of mansions
into which Allison Grove intrudes, lies the handsome Victorian
formality of Dulwich Park, with its winding carriage drives and
its large sheet of ornamental water. An Irish family that had to
come to London could not have more cleverly found a part of
London more spaciously and agreeably unlike itself, and their
house was cleverly found too. One side of Allison Grove had
been built in Victorian times; the harsh red brick had been piled
up in shapes as graceless as outhouses and to heights obviously
inconvenient for the housewife. But the houses were amply
planned for their price; and one of them gave room enough for
the Joyce parents and William and his two younger brothers and
his little sister. Nothing could have been handier. There was a
railway station a few hundred yards away, and the spry little
William used to run up the steps every morning on his way to
the Battersea Polytechnic, leaving the house feeling empty, no
matter how many of the family were left in it; and ran down
them again in the evening, and filled the house again. The

neighbours, who thought the Joyces outlandish but likeable, though curiously arrogant, all noted that William was the apple of the family's eye, and they could understand it, for the boy had certainly an air of exceptional spirit and promise. But, if William always left his home and returned to it like a conqueror, during the day, at Battersea Polytechnic, he must have suffered many defeats, being tiny, alien, and ineradicably odd. In 1923 he was to experience the crushing defeat of failure in two subjects in his Intermediate Science examination.

His reaction was characteristic. There was nothing disgraceful in his failure, he was only seventeen, his schooling had been much interrupted by civil war and change of country, and he could have tried again. But he immediately abandoned his intention of becoming a Bachelor of Science and turned his back on Battersea Polytechnic. It is interesting to speculate just what effect this step had on his destiny. His ambition was very strong; and it just might have happened that if he had become a Bachelor of Science he would have recognized the easy and brilliant future which this age offers to the Communist scientist, and would have ended as a colleague of Professor Haldane on the *Daily Worker*. As it was, he went to the Birkbeck College for Working Men, which is a part of the University of London, a physically sombre institution though intellectually vigorous, hidden in the dark streets between Holborn and the Law Courts, and studied the English language and literature and history. He made an excellent though odd student and passed with first-class honours, though for the first two years of his course he was subject to a new distracting influence. In 1923 he joined the British Fascists. This was an odd instance of his inability to get the hang of the world he meant to conquer. Mussolini had come to power in 1923, and warm admiration was felt for him by numerous persons of influence in England; and a young man might well have sincerely shared that mistaken admiration and at the same time have wished to liven that admiration into a means of personal advancement, but joining the British Fascists was not the way to make that advance. They formed a body which was never numerous and had few links with the influential admirers of Mussolini, and whatever its intentions may have been, it appeared less mischievous than eccentric. It was promoted by an elderly lady, member of a military family, who was overcome by panic when she read in the newspaper that the British Labour Party was sending a delegation to an International Conference in Hamburg. It was patronized by a certain number of retired army men and a back-bench M.P. and an obscure peer or two; but the great world mocked at it, and it had as aim the organization of amateur resistance to any revolution that might arise; it was a charade representing the word "barricade."

If William Joyce wanted either to hold a commission in the Regular Army, or to teach, or to become a journalist, membership in this universally unfavoured movement was certain to be prejudicial to his hopes. It may be said that he was still young, but many a boy and girl of seventeen, determined to rise in the world, has cast a canny eye on such strategical pitfalls. But from first to last he had none of the clairvoyance normally given by ambition. He was the very opposite of Balzac's Lucien de Rubempré, who in his progress from a cheap boarding-house to the palaces of the Faubourg St. Germain had only to stare at a door to know how to behave behind it. The proof was later to be laid before the ears of all of us. Though William Joyce divested himself of almost every trace of Irishry he never acquired anything that resembled any English accent, and, indeed, had only to open his mouth to betray that he was not a member of the traditional English governing class. It was partly this obtuseness that led to his membership in the British Fascists, but there were more positive factors at work. The party, as well as holding meetings of its own, made a practice of interrupting and breaking up the Communist meetings which were being held in London, especially in the East End, often with the aim of explaining and defending Bolshevik Russia. Joyce, according to a tutor who coached him at this time, took these affrays with extreme seriousness. He spoke of the Communists with real horror: as, in fact, Orangemen would speak of Sinn Feiners. There was working in him a nostalgia for the Irish situation. Later in the air raids, we were all to learn that danger is a better champagne and brings gaiety until the pain and fatigue are too great. William Joyce had experienced that gaiety outside its true context; the luck that shelters youth had spared him more pain and fatigue than he could bear. Hence he enjoyed, with a constant driving esurience, street-fighting. No sport could be meaner. The thin boy wearing spectacles is cut off from his friends, he is hustled into an alley, his arms are twisted, his teeth are knocked in. But the sport was recommended to William Joyce by the memory of his courage in its springtime, and the excessive deaths in Russia gave him his excuse. He was led into temptation.

In 1925 he left the British Fascists. This may have been because he became involved in certain internal dissensions which appeared, inevitably enough, in the movement; dog of a certain sort is always eating dog. Or it may have been because he feared to fail in his arts course as he had failed in his science course, and sacrificed his hobbies. But before long he passed into a sphere of a much more urgent distraction. His passion for violence did not spare himself or those he loved. A week after his twenty-first birthday, on the 30th of April, 1927, he set fire to the whole of his personal life as he had lived it till that date. He married a girl of his own age, a chemist's assistant, the daughter of a dentist, who was remarkable for her pleasant good looks; and because she was a Protestant, he, the son of Irish Roman Catholic parents, married her at the Chelsea Registry Office. Few young men celebrate their coming of age by as wide a gesture of independence. He, the little man, who might well never have got a woman at all with all the tall men about, won a woman who was desirable; he stood up straight and shook off the hands of his parents; he struck the Pope of Rome across the face. It would be easy to pretend that all his subsequent errors and misfortunes followed from this rupture with his Church, but in truth his religious revolt was merely one link in a chain of dissents which it was his life work to forge. It is the weakness of imperialism that in a country occupied by a strange power no man can know the sweetness of conformity, can marry his will to the common will for happy ends. If he be at one with his fellow-countrymen he must be a rebel against the conquerors; if he be at one with the conquerors he must rebel against his fellow-countrymen. Whatever road Michael Joyce had taken, he was bound to be impaled on one horn or other of the dilemma, and his son, if his soul were of the stuff that can be stamped with ideas, would be bound to be a perpetual and instinctive rebel. That was what he was, and what he liked to be; and he could handle the material consequences of his rebellion with zest and vigour.

By 1933, when this phase of his life ended, he had as much reason for pride in his achievements as most young men of twenty-seven. He had no difficulty in supporting his wife and himself, for he had already, as a student, joined the staff of a tutorial college, which regarded him as one of its best teachers. After he had taken his degree he continued his studies in a post-graduate course in philology, and later began a course in psychology at King's College. He also found time to pursue his political ambitions, and worked for the Conservative Party, not only practising his speaking but learning the technique of organization. It must be remarked that all these achievements brought him not an inch nearer any position of real power. He could never by any chance have been invited to join the staff of any school or college of conventional academic prestige, for in spite of all his studies there clung to everything he did or said a curious atmosphere of illiteracy. Only uneducated people accepted easily the fact of his education; educated people were always astonished to hear that he had been at a University. Even his handwriting, which was spiky and uneasy, suggested that he rarely took up his pen. (It casts a light on what being tried on a capital charge does to the most courageous of us that the notes William Joyce passed to his counsel from the dock were written in a script which, though clear and steady enough, differed in many respects from his normal handwriting.) It is inconceivable too that the Conservative Party, or, for that matter, the Liberal Party, or the Labour Party, should have admitted William Joyce to anywhere near the inner circle of operative power, even if that circle was drawn widely enough to dilute that power far below Cabinet strength. It was not only culture in the sense of book-learning which was inaccessible to him; it was also culture in the sense of the life of the people. A police officer who had known William Joyce for many years and had liked him said hesitantly, for he was speaking a few days before the execution, that sometimes Joyce had reminded him, even in the days before the war, of a real criminal, of the sort that make lags. It was not that he had then committed any crime, but because he, like the lags, "did not seem to fit in anywhere."

Between 1930 and 1933 his enthusiasm for the Conservative Party flagged, and during this time he renewed his connections with British fascism, which had now much more to offer him and his special case. A number of obscure people in London were at that time conscious that a disaster was overhanging Europe. Those who foresee the future and recognize it as tragic are often seized by a madness which propels them into a course of action certain to accelerate the approach of the tragedy; so it was natural that some of these should join with the young men who were gratifying a taste for street-fighting under the plea that they stood for order and fascism, while others joined with the young men who were gratifying a taste for street-fighting under the plea that they stood for order and communism. Both were undermining the period of civilization which gave them power to pursue these curious pleasures. Even so the Fascists had destroyed order in Italy and enabled Mussolini to seize power, and the same process was then being extended to Germany. The Fascist wing of this British movement would have existed without Sir Oswald Mosley. He was its follower rather than its leader. It had sprung up because people who, living in an established order, had no terror of disorder had read too much in the newspapers about Mussolini and Hitler and the Bolsheviks; and if it had not arisen spontaneously it would have been fomented by foreign agents. It was a dynamic movement with roots that went deep and wide, and it did not impinge at any point on the world inhabited by the existing executive class. With the people that controlled politics, or commerce, or the professions, it had nothing to do. It grew beside them, formidable in its desire to displace them from that control, but separated from all contact with them as if a vast plate-glass window was between them. To no movement could William Joyce more appropriately have belonged.

It was Sir Oswald Mosley's peculiar function to give false hope to the British Fascists, to seem to lead them out of limbo and to introduce them into the magnetic field of national power. Ill-informed about all conspicuous persons, they did not know that he was a homeless one, like themselves; he also had been born outside and not inside his environment. He had been born into the old governing class of the Tory aristocracy, but had never been liked or trusted by any of his fellows; and he had penetrated into the new governing class of the Labour Party to the extent of holding office in the first Labour Government, but had formed no tie of liking or trust which would prevent it from preferring any other of its members to him. It is probable that William Joyce, with his incapacity for drawing any social inference whatsoever, was as blind as the rank and file to the qualities of isolation and failure inherent in Sir Oswald.

Within two years after Sir Oswald had founded the British Union of Fascists, William Joyce became his Director of Propaganda and Deputy Leader of his party. He lived then in a home which, though cheap and unfashionable, possessed its picturesque distinction. He had taken a flat in a road clinging to the lip of the escarpment just under the Crystal Palace, the strangest spot in the strangeness of South London. At this distance from the river the tameness of town has overspread heights which, though insignificant in elevation, are wild in contour; and if it covers them with the tame shapes of houses it has to stack them in wild steepness. But above this urban precipice the buildings themselves were wild, and that with the extreme wildness exhibited by wild creatures who think themselves tame. Outside the front door of 41, Farquhar Road, two glaucous towers ran up into the sky and between them the torso of the Crystal Palace looked at one and the same time like a greenhouse and a Broad Church cathedral. In summer-time the night behind this didactic architectural fairy tale was often sprayed with the gold and silver and jewels of Messrs. Brock's fireworks, while a murmur of oh's and ah's and cheers rose from the crowds that walked in the gardens among the cement prehistoric animals that had been placed there in the mid-nineteenth century as illustrations to some argument about the inevitability of progress and the usefulness of knowledge. A little way up the road was the Crystal Palace railway station, the most fantastic of its kind in England, so allusive, particularly in its cast-iron ornamental work, to uplifting Victorian festivity that it would not be surprising to find its platforms thronged by a choir singing an oratorio by Parry or Stainer. The windows on the other side of the house where Joyce lived looked down on the whole of London, across the Thames, over the imperial city, up to the green hills of Hampstead and Highgate. The view reveals an astonishing number of parks, moderate in size, unvisited save by the people who live around them, un-unified populations scattered over London, therefore easy to deceive, meet victims for Fascist propaganda. At night the lights of London make a spectacular theatre, and it is said that keen eyes can distinguish the light which burns under Big Ben to show that the House has not yet risen. It was from this flat, on the 4th of July, 1933, that William Joyce addressed his application for the passport which cost him his life. He needed it to travel to the Nuremberg Rally.

It was a consciously illegal act. Or was it not quite that? The statement makes it appear that he had never been sure about his nationality—which is to say that he never made sure about it, that he never paid the visit to a solicitor which would have told him everything. He took a gamble on it. He took another gamble on standing for Shoreditch as a Fascist candidate in the municipal elections of 1937. Two thousand five hundred and sixty-four people voted for him, and 2,492 voted for another Fascist, out of a total poll of 34,128 at Shoreditch, which is a two-seat constituency.

He took another gamble when he gave rein to his passion for street-fighting in his new post and in cold deliberation and with burning appetite applied himself to the technical problems of creating disorders; for a conviction might mean deportation, if he were discovered. It was about this time that Michael Joyce, who had long been reconciled to his beloved first-born, tore up his American passport and all documents relating to his American citizenship before the round astonished eyes of his son Quentin, muttering his secret and commanding that it should be kept a secret, clairvoyant in his perception of the existence of the awful danger threatening his blood, but wrong, as clairvoyance nearly always is, concerning its precise nature and the point in time and space where that danger waited. He thought it was to be a common exile of his family across the sea, and must have seen it near at hand, about eighteen months after William Joyce took his first post with Mosley, when he and his chief, together with the Fascist officer for Sussex, Councillor Bentinck Budd, and a ranker named Mullan, appeared at Lewes Assizes on a charge of riotous assembly at Worthing. They were acquitted after a trial that lasted for two days, and disclosed the sickness that was rife among the obscure.

The incident at Worthing had followed a rhythm by which the normal course of life in provincial towns of England, and even in London itself, had been disturbed again and again during the past few years. First the local Fascists would announce well in advance that Sir Oswald Mosley was coming to hold a meeting in the largest local hall. Truculent advertisements and parades would prevent the town from forgetting it. The idea of violence would suddenly be present in the town. The proper course for those who were anti-Fascist was to abstain from all action on the day of the meeting, to stay in their houses and ignore it; but the idea of violence would enter into them also and they would feel under a compulsion to attend the meetings and interrupt and provoke the stewards to throw them out. Then relatives and friends would know what they were thinking, and would grow tense with dread. On the day of the meeting Sir Oswald Mosley and his party would arrive in a town already in the grip of hysteria, and would bring with them all the paraphernalia of competently conducted civil war: a complete counterfeit of all necessary preparations for battle, except the explosives. There were men in uniform carrying weapons, truncheons made of shot-loaded sections of hose-pipe sealed with lead; armoured cars; ambulances complete with doctors and nurses—making a picture that meant danger, that aroused fear, that provoked the aggression which is sick fear's defence. The anti-Fascists, who had at first expelled the idea of violence from their minds and then reluctantly readmitted it, gathered, unstrung by these mental conflicts, round the hall in which the Fascist intruders were holding their meeting, spinning out words to cover the emptiness of a programme that contained nothing but anti-Semitism and an intention to establish dictatorship against the general will. When the Fascists came out they paraded in front of the crowd, bearing themselves insolently, until they provoked hostile demonstrations. Having provoked these, they assaulted the demonstrators, who struck back; and the civil order which generation after generation of Englishmen had insisted on creating in despite of tyranny and the lawlessness of their own flesh, lay dead in the street; and the life of liberty, which depends on civil order, was threatened, and all future researches into reality, which depend on liberty, were in danger of never coming to birth. A torch was held to the foundations of civilization by the people who had abandoned themselves to a fruitless lechery, a drunkenness without laughter.

At Lewes this foolish and horrible story was told once more. The meeting had been over at ten. A hostile but inactive crowd had been waiting outside the hall. Mosley and his lieutenants came into the street, bearing themselves in the jack-booted way, with elbows bent and clenched fists swinging. They began to speak in offensive tones to the people standing by. One paused in front of a boy of seventeen, a post-office messenger, and said something to him. The boy did not answer, and the Fascist asked, "Don't you understand English?" The boy, looking at the Fascist's black shirt, said, "I don't understand Italian," and the Fascist hit him. At Lewes Assizes, Sir Patrick Hastings, while cross-examining this boy, asked him, "Can you think of anything more insulting than what you did say?" It is of course a barrister's duty to get his clients out of the dock, and Sir Patrick was defending the four Fascists; and he had the right to ask any question he thought proper. But it is interesting to remember that Mosley had visited Fascist Rome not long before and had taken the salute with Mussolini at a review. He was no doubt encouraged by the atmosphere of the court. There were sound reasons why this should not be wholly unfavorable to the defendants. It was obvious that the Fascists could not be regarded as solely responsible for the riot. That the anti-Fascists had sinned as well as being sinned against was shown by the number of tomatoes they had thrown at Mosley and his lieutenants; these could hardly have been found lying about the streets of Worthing at ten o'clock at night. There was, moreover, a witness for the prosecution who, though an interesting personality, provocative to the imagination of the novelist, raised certain misgivings. He was a red butler. This might be the name of a species of butterfly, and indeed he appeared to be highly peripatetic, for since he had retired from the service of the rich he had joined the New Fellowship, an anti-Fascist body considered by many to be Communist, and had travelled round the country selling anti-Mosley pamphlets outside Fascist meetings. Sir Patrick, cross-examining this witness on the contents of these pamphlets, asked him, "Do you believe a word of this rubbish?" though he had quoted at least one sentence from them which was unimpugnable in its accuracy: "Mosley is receiving money from nobody knows where and open support from Mussolini and Hitler." Mosley did not publish a balance-sheet, and he had been the guest of both the dictators. But the pamphlets certainly contained a great deal of nonsense. They implied that Mosley had promised Malta to Mussolini and parts of the British Empire to Hitler, and, as it would have been impossible for either of them to give Mosley effective help to seize power in England, and as once he was the dictator of England he would have been their superior in resources, it is hard to see why he should have made any such commitment. The evidence of this witness made it appear possible that some of the anti-Fascist organizations were providing an opposition hardly less irresponsible and professional and dangerously itinerant than the Fascists.

The atmosphere of the court was, however, even mellower towards the defendants than any of those considerations could have made it. Some considerations, impossible to identify from the bald newspaper reports, seem to have affected the conduct of the case by Mr. Justice Branson. We are unable to guess why, to mention only one perplexing point, he should have intervened with such astonishing grimness in the cross-examination of a witness for the prosecution who affirmed, when questioned about an incident in a certain street, that "the whole affair seemed to be a joke on the part of the crowd." This statement made Mr. Justice Branson request: "Tell us one of the jokes. I am always interested in good jokes." The abashed witness replied, "They were singing 'Mosley's got the wind up' and that sort of thing." Mr. Justice Branson majestically inquired, "Do you call that a joke?"

He was even more severe with the police. It appeared that the defendant Budd and his wife, who lived in Worthing, had sent several passionately apprehensive telephone messages to the police station before and during the meeting, which might well have been regarded as part of the Fascist war on the communal nerves. The last was a message from Mr. Budd from the hall where the meeting was being held. "Tell Superintendent B—— to send some men down to restore order. If it is not done I shall go out and take the law into my own hands." Mr. Justice Branson commented severely on the failure of the constable who took the message to take any action; but he obviously had no need to take action, for his superior officers were already on the spot outside the meeting. His severity was even more extreme and perplexing when it came to the examination of an unhappy sergeant who gave a picture of the debauch of savagery with which the police force of this sea-side town had had to deal that night. In a typical passage the witness described how he had seen Fascists rush to the doorway of a chemist's shop, had followed them, and when they had run away had found a person lying on the pavement unconscious, and then had turned round and seen another person, who was one of the witnesses in the trial, lying in the road, also uncon-scious. Mr. Justice Branson interrupted this witness to say: "I understood you to use the phrase, 'The crowd which first chased down South Street.' Was there a crowd which chased down South Street?" The sergeant answered, "There was a large number of people." Mr. Justice Branson asked, "Why do you change your language? One expects in these cases that the police will give their evidence fairly and frankly. Just bear that in mind in an-swering the rest of the questions."

It was not surprising that William Joyce was acquitted at Lewes. There was no evidence to connect him with the riot that had taken place, and it was said by Sir Patrick Hastings that his name did not appear in any of the depositions. The other three defendants were also acquitted. At the close of the case for the prosecution the Judge said he must take the responsibility of telling the jury that it should find a verdict of not guilty. As the jury expressed its full concurrence with this direction, and an-nounced that it had been its intention to request that the evi-dence for the defence should not be heard, since the prosecution had failed to make out its case, and as the cases of assault which had been brought against some of the defendants in the local courts had been dismissed, the effect of the trial on William Joyce must have been intoxication. It is of course certain that the Judge conducted the trial with perfect propriety, and the jury obviously carried out its duties as conscientiously. Nevertheless,

Mr. Justice Branson may well have exercised a powerful influence on William Joyce's determination to travel the road that led to the gallows. Indeed, the courts of law, civil as well as criminal, provided considerable encouragement for the ambitious Fascist at that time. But in the civil courts it was hardly the lawyers who could be held responsible. Virtue has its peculiar temptations, particularly when it is practised as a profession. The good are often so well acquainted with the evil intentions of the wicked that they report the speeches of the wicked as if these candidly expressed their intentions instead of, as is customary, veiling them in hypocritical dissimulations. This has on many occasions led to the award of heavy damages against the good in cases brought under the laws of libel and slander by the wicked. The anti-Fascist press was not mindful enough of this danger when they dealt with Mosley, whom they considered to be wicked. In one libel action Sir Oswald Mosley won, and rightly won, a verdict entitling him to five thousand pounds damage, and his costs. It must have seemed to William Joyce that society had gone a long way towards certifying that fascism was not incompatible with its institutions, and it must have seemed to him that the opposition was unscrupulous and antisocial.

The daily routine of his work must have encouraged him in this delusion that he and his kind enjoyed the acquiescence, even the fondness, of society. It was unfortunate that the police liked him. They did not show him this favour because they shared his faith. It is a mistake to think that the police favoured the Fascists over the Communists—as they certainly did—on political grounds. Their preference was based on several considerations, some simpletonish, some shrewder than the findings of the contemporary intellectuals. There were policemen, as there were generals and admirals, who were deceived by the Fascists' use of the Union Jack and slogans about Britain into thinking them conservative patriots instead of international revolutionaries. There were others who regarded the Communists as bloodstained Bolsheviks, and admired the Fascists as their enemies. But there were many who thought, and both common sense and wisdom was with them, that if the Communists had ignored the Fascist meetings and refrained from interrupting them, the Fascists would have been checkmated, since they would not then have been able to exercise violence and plead that they were defending the right of free speech. They would then have had to attack Communist meetings or make unprovoked assaults on Jews in order to get their street-fighting; and in that case policemen who arrested Fascists would have been able to get them convicted. As it was, the police were constantly forced by the Communists' actions into arresting Fascists who were discharged by magistrates because they pleaded that they acted under provocation; and there is nothing a policeman likes less than seeing the charge against a man he has arrested being dismissed. This is partly, though not entirely, a matter of pride. It also concerns his promotion. If there is any blame to be attached to the men involved in these proceedings, it should not fall on the police but on the magistrates, who were so very often satisfied that the Fascists had been provoked. They were responsible if there was engendered in the police a mood of cynicism which rendered them less lively than they might have been in their duty of protecting all citizens, irrespective of their kind and attributes, from violence. If a citizen went to a meeting held by a party which advertised its loyalty to King and country through every material and spiritual loudspeaker, and which was notorious for its easy resort to violence, and that citizen remained seated during the singing of the national anthem, the policemen present felt a disinclination to concern themselves with what subsequently befell that citizen. They were of course wrong. Their business was to suppress violence, however it had been provoked. But such citizens, and all those who played the Fascist game by accepting their challenge, were as irritating masochists as any that have appeared in Europe since the Andalusian martyrs who, during the Moslem conquest, forced the hands of their tolerant conquerors by proclaiming Christ within the mosques themselves.

If the police liked Joyce, it was because he persuaded them he was alleviating this ugly situation. He was a fine disciplinarian. His men were truly his. On them he now could play all the tricks of charm that take in young hero-worshippers; the recollection of a previous meeting, stated with a suggestion that an ineffaceable impression had been made, a permanent liking engendered; the sternness broken by a sudden smile. He had also learned the trick of turning his puniness into an asset of terror; a little man can be terrible when he outstares a taller and stronger subordinate who has been insolent to him, and coldly orders another subordinate, still taller and stronger, to inflict a brutal punishment on him. "Joyce really had his men under control," said a member of the police force, "and he was always fair to us. We could never come to an understanding with the Communists; if we saw the leaders it was hard to get on terms with them, and if we did persuade them to alter a plan they didn't seem able to make their men carry out the alteration. But if I went to Joyce and told him that his men were doing something that wasn't fair on the police, trying us too hard or interfering with our time off, he'd have his men right off that job in half an hour, and there'd be no grumbling. And he always kept his word, we found him very straight." This officer—and he spoke for many of his colleagues—thought Joyce a far abler man than Mosley. It is possible that William Joyce was, at that time, a person of real and potent charm offering the world what Blake said pleased it most, "the lineaments of gratified desire." He saw his path to greatness clear before him. He experienced the sharp joys of public speaking and street-fighting nearly every night, and every month or so the more prolonged orgy of the great London or provincial meetings. Moreover, the routine of fascism freshened and liberated the child in its followers. Mosley had taken a black old building in King's Road, Chelsea, formerly a training college for teachers, where he housed his private army of whole-time members of the B.U.F.; and there life was a boy's dream. Uniforms were worn that were not really uniforms, that at once claimed and flouted authority, as adolescence does; there was discipline savage (and therefore sadistically sweet) while it lasted, but perfectly eluctable, not clamped down on a definite period of time by the King's Regulations; corridors were patrolled by sentries beetling their brows at nothing, executive officers sat at desks laden with papers alluding to mischief as yet too unimportant to be checked; dead-end kids that could call what was dead alive and the end the beginning only because they knew no better, innocently and villainously filled rubber truncheons with lead. There is nothing like infantilism for keeping the eyes bright and the skin smooth.

At this time, too, Joyce must have been intoxicated by new experiences of several kinds. He went to Germany, to the long, sterile orgasm of the Nuremberg Rally: where, on the great barren place which had been several farms, crowds, drunken with the great heat, entered into union with a man who was pure nihilism, who offered militarism and defeat, regulation and anarchy, power and ruin, the cancellation of all, the primary peace. That was a deep pleasure, surrounded by shallower ones: the drives through the entrancing country, scored with the great public works which German Joyces had ordained by a wave of the hand, the visits to the fine villas which German Joyces had made their own and stuffed with works of art, the eating and drinking from the Gothic and Renaissance tables of German Joyces where the heavy goblets stood on Genoese velvet. In his own country he frequented now, for the first time, the houses of wealthy English people, and there perhaps knew not the absolute enjoyment Germany could give him. Few of the upper-class supporters of Mosley were intellectually distinguished in any way that induced the relinquishment of social prejudice. Only an eccentric, equally distinguished as a physicist and a steeplechaser, and a peer whose enthusiasm for fascism was part of his passion for the grotesque and wholly conditional upon its failure to realize its objects, come to mind as probably unbiased by class feeling in their response to charm; and of what they would consider charm William Joyce had none. It would be impossible to exaggerate his lack of any attractive distinction. He had his wit; everybody who met him in England or Germany agrees that he never talked for long without putting a twist on a sentence that surprised the hearer into laughter. He had also the quiet pleasantness that was remarked on so often by the officials who had charge of him during his last days. But there was ingrained in him a dusty commonness, a puny coarseness, that was bound to repel the fastidious. The other upper-class supporters of Mosley were for the most part professional soldiers and sailors, usually in their fifties; and of these some asked William Joyce to their houses out of a sense that they should recognize his services to the movement. He was to them, nevertheless, like an officer risen from the ranks. Awkwardnesses occurred. One week-end he was a guest at the country house of an army man who kept a large stable; and on Sunday morning the host let his guests try some of his less valuable horses. William Joyce, who had learned to ride as a boy in

Mayo and Galway, handled his horse so well that he was allowed to try another one, a fine and difficult thoroughbred. The host's father, an old gentleman so deaf that he could not tell whether he was shouting or whispering, stood among the other guests and watched. "How marvellously Mr. Joyce rides!" a lady bawled into his ear. "Yes!" he bawled back. "But not like a gentleman." Nobody was sure whether Mrs. Joyce had heard.

When a man's social horizon widens, his sexual horizon rarely stays where it was. There was a rackety recruit to fascism, a wealthy young man who had suffered the initial handicap of being expelled from an ancient school, not for perversity but for precocity induced by the enterprise of an American actress, who took a cottage for the summer in the district. He invited Joyce to a shooting party, where he met the sister of an Irish peer and was profoundly impressed by her. She felt no corresponding emotion and probably never knew of his. It may have been such disturbing encounters which first suggested to William Joyce what might not have occurred to him if he had stayed where he was born, that he need not always stay married to the same woman. From the beginning, it is said, his life with the girl he had married when they were both twenty-one had been a cycle of romantic ecstasy and vicious quarrels and impassioned reconciliations; he would turn anything into a fight. During his time of service with Mosley his relations with his wife grew more and more purely quarrelsome, and in 1936, although they had by then two little daughters, he again outraged his family traditions by being divorced.

On a visit to Lancashire, where he was always at home, since he had known it as a child, and where he had had some of his greatest successes as a speaker outside London, he met the woman who was to be his second wife, a pretty and spirited girl, the daughter of a textile warehouse manager and an enthusiastic member of the B.U.F. She was obviously, like William Joyce, a person whose ambition was at war with her physique. She was a trained dancer, who often performed at cabaret shows given at festive gatherings of North Country Fascists; and there are photographs which show her in costumes that show a time-lag in taste, recalling the metal bowler hats and serviceable Jaeger veils Maud Allan wore when she danced Salomé's Dance of the

Seven Veils about 1912, and in poses which are pathetic in their desire for grace and their failure to attain it. Though Joyce's second marriage was to follow the same pattern of ecstasy and dissension and reconciliation as his first, there was apparently a deep and true love between him and his wife which was to endure to his death. There is indeed to be recognized in the commonplace prettiness of her face a certain not commonplace solemnity and submissiveness, as if she knew she should bow to a great force when it visited her; and it appears certain that she believed William Joyce to be that great force. But she was coincident with his ruin. To be her husband, he crossed the river.

He left South London, that had been his home since he was a boy and used it as his base for his first steps toward conquering the world; that was still the home of his father Michael Francis Joyce, who had bequeathed him a certain mystery, and Queenie, Joyce's mother, and his two brothers and his sister; that was his appropriate home. Where the drab rows and the complacent villas shamed their builders by losing their drabness and their complacency because they were set on hills, which, under bricks and mortar, retained the wild shapes of nature: there should always have lived this mean and coarse little man, who was the theatre for the desire of glory and an irresistible impulse to death. But he moved to the north side of the river, but not to imperial London. Till he left for Germany, he lived on the flat lands, which, being unable to defend themselves against the town, have been violated by the mean architecture of the time of their violation. These lie in the south-west, inland from Chelsea, at the foot of the slope that falls from Hyde Park and Kensington Gardens, and they house the underlings of imperial London. When he married his second wife he was living in Fawcett Street, one of the dreariest spots in the dreary parallelogram contained by the Brompton Road, the Fulham Road, Redcliffe Gardens, and the walls of Brompton Cemetery; a place where the cats limp and have mange, and the leaves bud brown in the spring. It was the first of his London homes that was dull and characterless; he might have chosen it when he had ceased to care whether the routine of life was pleasant because he was so preoccupied with the crises of the future. The ceremony to which he went forth from this grey home was at the Kensington

Registry Office. He could have been married by a priest if he had wanted; since his first marriage had been civil, neither it nor the subsequent divorce existed, in the eyes of the Church. But he was still at war with the traditions of his family; and was perhaps at that moment a little confused in his attitude towards them, for he caused his father to be described in the register as "of independent means," a phrase hardly applicable to Michael Francis Joyce, builder and grocer. One of the witnesses came later to know Joyce's family very well: Angus MacNab, then and forever after a worshipper of Joyce, who was to sit with Quentin through all three trials.

5

WILLIAM JOYCE'S second marriage brought him north of the river. Perhaps it had a direct effect on what he was ultimately to do there; on his decision to desert Mosley and become an agent of Nazi Germany. It is true that a number of factors unconnected with Joyce's private life were driving him towards that decision. Chief among these was his relationship with Mosley. Joyce was nobody's fool, and never weak in self-esteem. If he had ever looked up to Mosley, which is doubtful, he very soon came to look down on him, and that at the very same time that he was satisfying himself as to his own unusual powers as a speaker and organizer and leader of men. It can be taken as certain that, if the police thought him more able than Mosley, he held the same opinion with some intensity. Moreover, it is impossible that Joyce was blind to the firm stand that Mosley took on his social relations with Joyce and the rest of the toughs, quite indubitably not gentlemen, who formed the brains and guts of his movement. The wife of one of the few Fascist leaders who were in the inner ring with Mosley was asked, "Did you and your husband ever ask Joyce to your house?" She answered in horror, "Oh, no, never. That was the great thing that worried us all, about what we were to do after Tom"—as Mosley was known to his familiars—"had become dictator. We didn't know how we were going to get rid of all these dreadful common people we had had to use to get power." It is unlikely that the sentiments behind the remarks would have remained hidden from the cold eyes of William Joyce, and that he would have missed the political implication behind them. He may have recognized that the purge of June 1934 was inherent in all Fascist movements; and he may have asked himself just why Mosley had chosen him as Deputy Leader of the Party. It would have seemed more natural that the position should be filled by one of the army or naval high-ranking officers who supported the movement, some of whom were able and personally impressive men, rather than by an insignificant little man with no social influence, for whom Mosley had no personal liking. William Joyce was tough enough to put the question in that form, and shrewd enough to answer it by admitting that his charm for Mosley was the obvious unlikelihood that he would set up as a rival for leadership of the movement.

There was also a difference between their outlook on policy, which became more marked as time went on, and in which the advantage lay with Joyce so far as honesty was concerned. Mosley had started his movement before Hitler came to power; Mussolini had been his inspiration. But very shortly after 1933 the emotional interest of the British Fascist movement shifted to Germany. This was in every sense natural, for what makes every Fascist movement go round is the pickings for the boys; and the boys in Italy had never had anything like the swollen and novel pickings that came to the boys in Germany. It might be that the Pontine Marshes swung level with the Autostradas; but, against the quite original fantasy of Berchtesgaden and Goering's hunting-lodges and Goebbels' garden in the heart of Berlin, Mussolini had nothing to show but a number of sets for *La Tosca*. Moreover, many Fascists like William Joyce were seduced in a way not at all dishonourable to them, by the innocent face of the world's enemy; pine-woods on little hills, grey-green and glossy little lakes, fields striped with the different stitches of cultivation neat as embroidery, russet-roofed villages with headlong gables and church steeples that have swallowed pumpkins—all the setting for fairy stories about millers' sons that make fortunes and buy the world. There was also the refreshment of meeting other young men and swimming with them in a bath of infantilism, of showing off and being shown off to, of boasting and believing boasts and boasting again, of making vows to meet next year and bathe again in these waters that are fresher and wash off the dust better than the waters of adult life, which are themselves dusty.

Mosley would feel such influences less than his followers, for he was travelled, was used to luxury, had some taste, and had the full dose of infantilist indulgence which is permitted and even required from a young man of means. But he seems, like many people, to have believed that Hitler was a man of supreme ability, and perhaps felt some personal liking for him. That he married his second wife in Hitler's presence may have signified either real affection for Hitler or a desire to build up an alliance by intimacy. While William Joyce was cold but naïve, Mosley was hot-headed but sophisticated; he could argue with his own passions in defence, not of the truth, but of his own ends. Hence Mosley could bear to proclaim the Nazi doctrine of a totalitarian and anti-Semitic state without overt propaganda for Hitler. His line was to admit admiration for Hitler and Mussolini, but to deprecate any excessive interest in Continental affairs and profess belief in isolationism. "Mind Britain's Business" was his slogan; and he assured the public that if Hitler were given a free hand in Europe and were returned his mandated colonies, and we at home suppressed the Jews, the peace of the world would be guaranteed, and the British Empire would be immune from attack. But he was careful to say that if Hitler should ever attack the British Empire, its peoples would of course defend themselves, and would be victorious. William Joyce wanted to preach acclamation of Hitler as the saviour of the world on such unconditional terms that by implication it must be the duty of every good Briton to resist any British government which took up arms against him.

Both these policies would work out to the same result. If Great Britain pursued an isolationist policy and let Hitler conquer Europe, he would have no reason to hold back from crossing the Channel and setting up what government he pleased; and there the matter would remain, for it would be extremely difficult for America to come to the aid of an invaded Great Britain which had acquiesced in the invasion of all the rest of Europe. In these circumstances it would seem certain that it would be the Fascists from whom Hitler would draw his quisling government. On the other hand, if the Fascists devoted their cause to the proclamation of the greatness of Hitler and the beauty of his state, and preached collaboration freely and frankly up to the declaration of the war and afterwards (within the limits set down in the law of treason), then again it would seem certain that the Fascists would furnish the quislings. Of the two policies Joyce's frankly admitted the international character of fascism, which makes a man ready to be traitor to his country, his county, his town, his street, his family, himself, and loses its dynamic power if it does not act by and through this readiness for treachery. Moreover, it was designed on the plane of heroism, and for that reason, had England been defeated in 1940, might have been more corrupting, for there would have been less shame in going over to the quislings if they had shown themselves brave men.

But policy was not the only subject of disagreement between Mosley and Joyce at this moment. Joyce was, for the first time in his life, troubled about money. He had been brought up in a household where there had always been enough to maintain the simple satisfaction of all needs. He had supported himself and his first wife adequately on his earnings as a tutor, which he had been able to stretch by taking on extra classes. His tastes were not extravagant, and for his pleasures, which were public speaking and street-fighting, he did not pay but was paid. Now, however, he had to make a home for himself and his second wife and pay alimony to his first wife, and Mosley was paying him a small but inelastic salary. He needed an increase in pay just at the very time when Mosley was least likely to give it. He was in genuine financial difficulties. He was spending nine-tenths of his income on the cause, but that went nowhere in maintaining a private army of anything from twelve hundred to two thousand, together with a greater number of subsidized hangers-on. It is true that he was subsidized by some industrialists, and by some City firms, even including one or two who by reason of their origin should have been most careful not to compromise themselves in this direction. But these industrialists were not the great magnates who were persistently rumoured to be contributing to Mosley's funds; they were for the most part old gentlemen at the head of minor firms who had only moderate means at their disposal. If the City firms were sometimes more generous they were also more canny, and both alike were beginning to be less forthcoming. They had contributed because they had believed Mosley to be a stabilizing force in society. But do what he could, he could not prevent his movement from looking what it was, revolutionary. The increasing brutality of the street-fighting with Jews and Communists was betraying the nature of its inspiration.

Also, the movement was unable, whatever Mosley did, to find recruits who did not, if they were eminent at all, approach the freakish. The only distinguished men that ever joined the B.U.F. were Major-General John Frederick Charles Fuller, the most brilliant writer of our time on the art of war; Roy Campbell, a poet of undoubted genius; and Sir Arnold Wilson, an extremely able colonial administrator. Another writer of some standing and much charm supported the party, but it was too generally recognized that he had not been sober for thirty years for his political opinions to carry much weight. There should have been some appeal to the Kipling tradition in an officer who was the author of a best-seller about army life in the East, but he was unnegotiable by reason of his devotion to Oriental mysticism in its quainter manifestations. About this time a Fascist leader was driving a banker who was regarded as a possible convert back from a week-end which had seemed very profitably spent, when he realized that they were passing the home of this officer-author and suggested that they should stop and call on him. The banker was delighted. But the butler repelled them. The major was in, and the butler would take a message to him, but he could not possibly be seen. The Fascist persisted, and finally the butler, who was a traditional butler, for this was a traditional home, broke down and said, "It's no use, this is the day he spends sitting on the roof with his Yogi having his perpetual enema." The Mosley movement did hardly better with its aristocratic supporters. One of these bore a title founded by a historic personage of the first order. If anybody alluded in his hearing to "the great Duke of ——" his brows would contract and he would supply a correction. "The first Duke of ——," he would say huffily. Later he was to give his life nobly in the war against fascism, and this anecdote relates to a superficial oddity and not to the sum of him.

It is worth while recalling only to explain the difficulties that Mosley was having in creating an impression of normality. Even with his numerous service members he had his difficulties. He had to handle these with care, lest possibly an officer of personal attractions and gifts for oratory and administration should dispute his leadership. But all the same, it was a pity that his most active admiral should be stone-deaf. It is true that deafness has more than once played a decisive part in our great island story. Our pro-Bulgarian policy, which has so disastrously endured for generations, was largely the work of a *Times* correspondent who travelled through the Balkans ceaselessly but without being able to hear a word that anyone said to him. But all the same, too many of the characters on Sir Oswald Mosley's stage were too farcical for him to enjoy having on his hands an admiral who was so obviously the stock deaf old gentleman of farce.

Naturally enough, the pillars of society wondered whether Mosley and his friends really fitted into the structure it was their function to uphold. So Mosley was short of subscriptions and he could not pay Joyce more money; and Joyce was left in a state of insecurity and with a feeling that Mosley had failed to fulfill the promise he had seemed to make to his obscure followers, the promise that those outside should find themselves at last inside, that the powerless should find themselves as equals among the powerful. Some time in the beginning of 1937 a police officer who knew Joyce found himself alone with him in a compartment in a late train from the Midlands which had a breakdown. For a time they talked of impersonal matters, then, as the delay lengthened, fell into silence, which the police officer suddenly found himself breaking with the question: "Joyce, what do you really think of Mosley?" He had no idea why he asked that question; he had heard nothing of any breach between the two. The little figure, which had been huddled in fatigue, now fixed the police officer with eyes cold as ice. He was famous among the British Fascists for his power to curse, and for the next ten minutes, quietly and steadily, he used it, then sank back into apparent slumber. The police officer paid him the classic compliment of saying that he never once repeated himself, and that "there was nothing ordinary in it," and he summed up its content as an opinion that "Mosley was letting them down by doing his job so badly." A few weeks later it was announced that Mosley had dismissed Joyce from his post as the Director of Propaganda and Deputy Leader of the Party, for the reason that he was under a necessity to cut down on his salaried staff.

There were certainly two interacting forces leading to this breach: Joyce's need for money and his determination to preach supernational instead of national fascism. Very soon it was being said that Joyce's need for money was the real cause of the dismissal, and that because it had pushed him to an extreme step. He had been detected, it was said, in embezzling the funds of the Union. This does not seem probable. The Joyces were a very respectable family, "the sort of people," as a neighbour said, "who went to evening classes"; nourished in the night of revolution though they were, there was that in them which carried some daylight with it. He must have had a bias towards honesty which was unlikely to stop functioning when he, an ambitious man, saw every possibility of realizing his ambition still open before him, and when he must have had a very good notion of where he could get money for the asking. Joyce himself told a version of the story which is quite credible, though not a complete explanation of the breach. He said that he had told Mosley that he must have more money, and was going to raise his own salary and take the increase from certain funds; that he had believed that Mosley had realized that he was speaking seriously; and that after he had made this adjustment for some time Mosley had sent for him and, forgetting or pretending to forget their earlier discussion, had raged at him as an embezzler. Apparently the administration of the B.U.F. was so chaotic that this story may well have been true. Yet it does not cover all the facts of this breach. If Mosley had discovered that Joyce was robbing the till, he would have found the situation no novelty, for he had been long recruiting men for their aptitude in violence, and the violent are often thieves as well. One would have expected Joyce to leave the Union quietly, as others had done before him. On the contrary, the breach was ostentatiously public and clear-cut. It may have been that Mosley had discovered that Joyce was making affiliations of the very sort he was particularly anxious to avoid.

When Joyce left the B.U.F. he took with him another conspicuous member, John Beckett. This was a man much older than himself, who was one of those pathetic casualties of the Labour Party whose failures have been due not so much to their own demerits as to the temptations besetting Members of Parliament belonging to a political party long in opposition. He had started life as a shop assistant, was disabled in the First World War, and had emerged in the first years of peace as a popular speaker on Labour problems, largely owing to his attractive physique and his abundant vitality. In 1924 he was elected to Parliament and shortly afterwards made a spectacular protest against the government's neglect of the problem of unemployment, seizing the Mace and threatening to throw it down on the floor. It was one of those gestures made by bad actors, which they imagine fraught with complex significance but which the audience sees simply as their farewell to good fortune. It was right to cry out against unemployment, and doubtless this man's heart was in his cry, but all the same it was the wrong cry, as Sassoferrato's cry over the sorrows of the Virgin, which are most pitiable, is the wrong cry. He was in Parliament for only six years, while every year the possibility that he might follow any profession other than politics became more remote. He passed over to the Independent Labour Party, organized Mosley's New Party, followed him into the British Union of Fascists. He married a beautiful actress somewhat older than himself and was later divorced; he went bankrupt; he had other troubles connected with the courts. In 1937 he was the editor of the B.U.F. official organs *Action* and *The Blackshirt*, being an able technical journalist. It must have been inconvenient for Mosley to lose both Joyce and this man at one and the same time, but he, like Joyce, received a very definite and final note of dismissal.

Within three weeks of leaving the British Union of Fascists, Joyce had founded his British National Socialist League; and very soon afterwards he had an office in London, a shop in Bristol (which sold daggers, rubber truncheons, and knuckledusters) and an official organ, *The Helmsman*. This was quick work; it also cost money. It is true that it did not cost much money, but then Joyce had almost none. He had gone back to his work as a tutor, and was doing well, but not so well that he could earn much more than would support himself and his wife and pay his alimony. The B.N.S.L. could never boast a membership that was more than a fraction of the strength of the B.U.F., and never pretended to live on its subscriptions. The only subscriber to B.N.S.L. funds who has been identified with any certainty was the old Scottish stockbroker whose sister was later to visit Joyce in prison, and he gave generously, but nothing that went into thousands. Joyce himself declared that he was financed by certain industrialists, but it seems most unlikely that any industrialist shrewd enough to have maintained his business would have thought it worth while to subsidize this lone little man who, however great his gift for organization, had now only a handful of followers to organize. It is significant that on one occasion, when pressed on this point by a pretended convert, William Joyce gave him in strict confidence the name of a North Country manufacturer who, he said, was his chief backer; and that inquiry showed this manufacturer to survive on this earth only as the nominal owner of a business which had for some years been administered by a bank. There was, on the other hand, a great deal of German money lying about in England at that time, to be picked up by anybody who chose to take a certain amount of trouble.

How little that trouble needed to be, how that money could petition to be picked up can be illustrated by the case of the two young women with strong right-wing views who thought it would be amusing to write and publish a news-letter. After a couple of numbers appeared they were approached by a man holding a teaching position in a certain University, who told them that he would finance their news-letter to the extent of two or three thousand pounds, provided only that they published a certain amount of approving references to Hitler. If William Joyce accepted money from such sources, he was breaking no law. In the United States it is a crime to take money from the representative of a foreign power without registering as a foreign agent, but in England such an act can be performed with impunity, and it would be easy to name a number of English persons on the right and the left who have benefited by transactions with Continental governments anxious to have friends in England. The United States law is, however, rendered useless by the power of bribery to take forms other than cash payments. There, as in England,

publishing houses specially founded for the purpose can commission propagandist works, the management of societies for friendship towards specific countries can offer well-paid jobs, a Continental government can buy whole editions of books or subscribe
for thousands of issues of a journal. If William Joyce was taking
money from Nazi agents he was doing nothing uniquely shameful. We can judge that he was taking such money from certain
recorded actions of his which show him trying, in his curious
scrubby, spirited, ugly way, to be honest and give good value
for his bribe, to be logical and not shrink from committing an
act of treason in time of war, which he rightly believed to be no
worse than a similar act committed in time of peace in the hope
of provoking war.

When Joyce received the first demand that he should make
payment for his payment, he and his wife had moved to a very
pleasant home, the most expensive home he occupied in his whole
life: the top flat of a doctor's house in that soberly agreeable
street, or group of streets, Onslow Gardens, in South Kensington.
It would never have been let to him had he presented himself as
the prospective tenant. But it was taken by Angus MacNab,
whose obvious good breeding and gentleness impressed the doctor and his wife very favourably. He explained to them that he
was setting up in business as a coach in partnership with a friend
named William Joyce, and at a second interview brought with
him Mrs. Joyce, whom they thought not so attractive as he was,
but still pretty and agreeable. On these samples of the household
they concluded the transaction, and were disconcerted when its
third person arrived with the removal van, which contained a
prodigious amount of books and some poor sticks of furniture,
and proved to be a queer little Irish peasant, who had gone to
some pains to make the worst of himself. The wearing of uniforms by private persons was by then illegal; so he and MacNab
always wore black sweaters of a shape calculated to recall the
Fascist black shirt. Joyce's suit and top-coat were deliberately kept
dirty and shabby in imitation of Hitler's turn-out; he cropped
his hair in the Prussian style and never wore a hat; he always
carried a very thick stick; and he bore himself with a deliberate
aggressiveness. The doctor and his wife instantly took a dislike to
him, which they never lost, though afterward it coexisted with

some liking. One cause of their dislike lay in their affection for his wife, whom he treated with mild tyranny, overworking her and giving her no thanks, in the peasant way. He was tiresomely exigent about his meals; and not only had she to cook them, but had to wash up afterwards, and then run off to help at the League office in the daytime, in the evenings at meetings. But the doctor and his wife had to admit that she adored him and that he evidently made her very happy.

They had other complaints against him. Their new tenants were indubitably noisy. They banged doors and stamped about when they came in excited from their meetings, and sometimes gave rowdy parties. To one of them they invited the doctor's wife, who happened to be alone that evening. She was not reassured. Most of the guests were wild Irishmen—the same that attended his trial. These were for the most part from families with the same roots as the Joyces, who had been supporters of the British occupation of Ireland and who had had to leave the country for safety's sake when Home Rule was granted. One among these was the son of a man who had performed an act of charity towards a man he found dying of gunshot wounds beside the road without inquiring his political affiliations, was consequently victimized by his neighbours till he was obliged to take refuge in England, and there died in poverty, leaving his family aggrieved because they had received no adequate compensation from the British government. The doctor's wife was unaware of the pathetic antecedents of these merrymakers, but she was disconcerted by the vehement quality of the merriment they made, and she came to her own conclusions when she met a gentleman with long hair who was wearing a scarlet cloak and a pectoral cross, and who introduced himself as the King of Poland; it was not revealed to her that he had once been sentenced to a term of imprisonment for the publication of obscene poetry, but she felt there was something a little odd about him.

Nevertheless the doctor and his wife did not attempt to terminate the lease. They were moved to this forbearance partly by their kindly feeling towards Mrs. Joyce, who they foresaw would suffer greatly in one way or another through her marriage. They also liked MacNab, who was amiable and fantastical. Once when Joyce had gone off with the key to the flat and a pipe had burst inside it, MacNab, explaining that he had been a leading member of the Oxford Alpine Club, swarmed up the back of the Kensington house, by pipes and window ledges and gutters, till he found a window open on the fifth story. But the doctor and his wife developed more serious reasons than these for tolerance. One of their sons was taken ill and had to miss a term or two at his boarding-school, and during this period MacNab and William Joyce coached him, the one in Greek and mathematics, the other in Latin and French. The parents found the boy was getting better teaching than he had ever had in his life; and they discovered that these two strange men really cared for the things of the mind, really possessed unusual intellectual capacity. After that they sometimes asked their tenants down to their sherry parties, and they noticed to their surprise that though William Joyce was so obviously odious in so many ways, so vulgar, so pushing, so lacking in sweetness, many of their guests found his conversation interesting and amusing and even charming. They were baffled. They did not know what they themselves wanted to do; but if they had known, the doing of it might not have been easy. The rent of the flat was paid with perfect regularity. It would have been difficult to break the lease except on very contestable grounds, and contest was certainly not out of Joyce's line.

So it seemed as if this exile was to lose his rootlessness in a place that asks roots to grow, and promises the grown plant pleasantness. Joyce's flat looked down on a communal garden which runs the whole length of one of the sections of Onslow Gardens; the houses which back on them have their dining-rooms built out into this garden. In summer-time the ladies of these houses often sit with their friends among tubs of flowers on the flat roofs of these dining-rooms, taking tea and looking down on their well-schooled children, who play on the lawns below. In late summer-time, in the year 1938, William Joyce sat in his pleasant home and applied for the renewal of his passport. It may be assumed that he had been sent for by someone who wished him to go abroad. It may also be assumed that he had not expected this summons, for he had let his passport expire without applying for its renewal. It had run out on the 6th of July. This was September the 24th: five days before the Munich Agreement was signed. Nothing is gained by the postponement of an application for the renewal of a passport. At whatever date the application is made, it is renewed from the date of its expiry. It is possible that William Joyce felt no exultation at all while he was filling in his application form. He had said that he had faced danger as a boy, but that was nearly twenty years ago. Ever since then he had lived cradled in the safety of the civil order of England which he and his Fascist friends and Communist enemies were vowed to destroy, and safety becomes a habit. He must have liked the green dignity of this gardeny part of Kensington; he would not have chosen to lodge there if some part of him had not remembered the home of his boyhood, that was also green, that was also London, in Allison Grove. He must have liked the setting of his life, and its core. He liked teaching; he had his meetings; and he was still deeply and romantically in love with his wife. If his ability to live in that home depended on his undertaking to leave it at any moment, then he must daily have known a real anguish.

That time Joyce did not have to give value for his bribe. The hot wind of danger blew and fell again; and immediately after Munich, Joyce lost his colleague Beckett, the former editor of *Action* and *The Blackshirt,* who severed all connections with him and started a pacifist organization of his own, which followed an ineffectual course and landed him safely in internment in 1940. It was as if he had caught some intimations of the end to which Joyce's policy was to lead him, and recoiled. At that time too, Joyce began to lose the friendship of his landlords; and the German radio sounded too loud through the house, the hiccoughing piano achieved the Horst Wessel song too often. The breach widened when Hitler walked into Czechoslovakia; the doctor and his wife were standing in the hall aghast at the news when Joyce came in, and asked him, "Now what do you think of Hitler?" Joyce said, unsmiling, "I think him a very fine fellow," and went on his way up to his flat. MacNab came in a little later. The doctor and his wife pressed him for his opinion; and he too approved. The curious friendship between the two households, so unequal in social background and in character, faded from that moment; though the doctor and his wife still showed kindliness to Mrs. Joyce.

Joyce, working alone, worked frantically. He spoke to every

society that would let him inside its doors, in the warmer weather he had an open-air meeting every day, and sometimes several in one day. It was as if he were trying to leave an impression on the public mind that could be counted upon to endure; and indeed he partially succeeded in this aim. An enormous number of people in the low-income groups heard him speak, some during the years when he was with Mosley, and even more during the period when he was his own master. Many people in the higher-income groups had also their contact with Joyce, but they did not know it. Anybody who was advertised as a speaker at a meeting appealing for funds or humane treatment for refugees from Nazi persecution would receive by every post, for many days before the meeting, threatening messages, couched always in the same words, and those words always so vague that the writers of them could not have been touched by the law. They were apt to come by the last post, and the returning householder, switching on the light, would see them piled up on the hall table, splinters from a mass of stupidity that might not, after all, be finite and destructible, but infinite and conterminous with life. Their postmarks showed they came from Manchester, Bristol, Bournemouth, Bethnal Green, Glasgow, Colchester. All over the country there were those who wished that the stranger, being hungry, should not be fed, being naked should not be clothed. Goats and monkeys, as Othello said, goats and monkeys; and the still house would seem like a frail and besieged fortress.

This device was the invention of William Joyce. The people who heard him in the streets sometimes saw this alliance with crime displayed. A number of his meetings were provocative of the violence he loved; he was twice tried for assault at London police courts during the year preceding the outbreak of war, though each time the wind that sat in so favourable a quarter for Fascists blew him out with an acquittal. But at many others of his meetings he used all his powers, his harsh, sneering, cajoling, denatured, desperate voice, his quick and twisting humour, his ability to hammer a point home on a crowd's mind, to persuade the men and women he saw before him of the advantages of dictatorship, the dangers of Jewish competition and high finance, the inefficiency of democracy, the greatness and goodness of Hitler, and his own seriousness. His audiences were not much interested in his arguments and were shrewd enough in their judgment of him. Many remembered him seven years afterwards. Only a very few said, "I liked him." Most said, "He has the most peculiar views, but he really was an extraordinary chap," or some such words. "Extraordinary" was what they called him, nearly all of them. This impression might not have served Joyce so ill had the days brought forth what he expected. If the Germans had brought him with them when they invaded England and had made him their spokesman, many Londoners might have listened to him with some confidence because he was a familiar element in a scene that conquest would have made terrifying in its unfamiliarity; and they might have felt awe, and perhaps, still more, confidence, because there was something of the wizard in the little creature.

William Joyce's paymasters issued their second summons to him eleven months after the first. During that time his circumstances changed. In July he had left his agreeable home in Onslow Gardens, at his own instance. In June he had suddenly written to the doctor saying that, with much regret, he must confess himself unable to carry out his three years' lease, which had still another year to run; the number of his pupils had, he explained, suddenly showed a sharp decline. The doctor answered, possibly not without some feeling of relief, that Joyce was at full liberty to sublet the flat, and this Joyce undertook to do. One day, before they left, the doctor's wife met Mrs. Joyce on the stairs and, with the extreme sweetness and generosity this couple always showed their strange tenants, paused to tell her how sorry she was that their connexion must end for so sad a reason. She said, "All our fortunes vary, you know, one goes up and one comes down and then one comes up again, so you mustn't worry if things are bad." To her astonishment Mrs. Joyce burst into tears, flung her arms round her neck, and sobbed out, "You do not know how bad they are, you have no idea how bad they are." About this time a strange visitor appeared. A man who, like so many of the British National Socialist League, was Irish, rang the bell marked "Joyce" that was beside the doctor's bell at the front door. Joyce came down, opened the door, looked at the visitor, slammed it, and went upstairs again. The visitor went on ringing, and began to pound on the knocker. MacNab came down, white-faced, and opened the door, parleyed with the visitor, but like Joyce re-treated. Out on the porch the visitor rang the bell and hammered on the door and began to shout. The doctor's manservant went out and tried to send him away, he cried out that he must see William Joyce, no one else would do. The door was shut, he re-mained outside, crying out in accusation, in imploration, in panic, as one who knew a great shame was to be committed and could not stop it. The police would have been fetched, but at that moment the doctor arrived, a tall, authoritative man, and took him by the arm, and turned him round towards South Ken-sington Station, and told him to follow the road to it. He went off, mumbling about a catastrophe. What is significant is that Joyce, ordinarily the most voluble of men, did not give his land-lord an explanation for this incident.

Paying their rent up to the last minute, leaving no tradesmen's bills unsettled, Joyce moved with his wife to a lodging as poor as any he had known since he had left Longbeach Road as a boy. It was an area flat in Eardley Crescent, a short street of dreary and discoloured houses, mean in size, which lies on the Warwick Road side of Earl's Court Station. Over their roofs, making them more dwarfish, looms the stadium, in inchoate heights, more senseless than anything sculptured by unsentient forces, morbid with the sick pallor of concrete; and at the end of the street is the wall of Brompton Cemetery, panelled with openings covered by wire netting, which disclose the sparse tombstones lying askew among the long grasses on the cemetery's edge, and the distant white crowd of stout Victorian dead round the central avenues. This was not only a melancholy home for Joyce, it was minute, no broader than a henhouse. It might have been chosen by a man who believed himself about to start life again at the beginning, without a penny behind him; if William Joyce had had to go back to tutoring as his sole means of livelihood he might have found it hard to re-establish himself. Or it might have been chosen by a man who believed himself about to go on a long journey and to need no more than a place to keep his clothes and his baggage till the time came to pack the one inside the other. It was probably chosen by a man who held both these views of his future. Human beings are mercifully so constituted as to be able to conceal from themselves what they intend to do until they are well into the doing of it. William Joyce must have been sure, in the summer of 1939, that there was going to be war, for we were all sure of that. And with half of his mind he knew what part he was going to play in it, but with only half; for again he let his passport expire. He did not apply for its renewal until the 24th of August; and that date destroys William Joyce's last claim on our sympathies. For it is one day after Hitler signed his pact with Stalin. Then this man who all his adult life had hated Communists must have known that his leader was an opportunist and not a prophet: that he himself was apostle of a policy and not a religion: that there was nothing in the cause to which he had devoted his life that was equal in worth to the ancient loyalties, which will not forswear themselves, which do not blaspheme themselves and kiss their enemies upon the lips. Now he should have seen what was on the underside of the banners stamped on the overside with the swastika that hung between the sky and the stadium at Nuremberg. Now he should have recognized that the words he had been saying since 1927 were "Evil, be thou my good." But he would not open his eyes or unstop his ears, and in that darkness full of colour and in that silence full of cries and cheers he stood fast and chose damnation. It is here his happy marriage helped to contrive his doom. He had made his decision to go over to Germany with the knowledge of his wife. To have gone back on it would have been a confession that he had been unwise when he made it; and he may have feared that such a reversal might have looked like a failure in courage. There are risks the most loving will not take with the beloved.

This damnation was not simply sought. For William Joyce did not go to Germany on the eve of the war on an off chance, and offer his services, and find that they were accepted. That there was a long and complicated and illicit series of events behind his appearance in Berlin in September 1939 is proven by the recollection of one who, in that year of doom, was a schoolgirl. One summer evening she was walking in the Fulham Road with her uncle, a young man who was a member of the British National Socialist League, when they met William Joyce, who was well known to both of them. He seemed strangely excited, and he told them, laughing extravagantly, that when he had been driving a car on the previous day he had been pulled in by the police for a trifling breach of the traffic regulations. The schoolgirl and her uncle were puzzled by his emotion. The uncle said, "But this is nothing. All sorts of people get run in for motoring offences." Joyce answered, waving his hat and clapping it back on his head, "Do you call this a motoring offence? I would call it a holding offence!" and went on his way. A "holding offence" is a device often used by the English police. When the police suspect a man of a serious crime but cannot prove him guilty of it, perhaps for the very good reason that he has not yet committed it, they watch him to see if he does not commit some minor offence, such as a breach of the traffic regulations. If they are lucky and he acts according to their expectation, then they can serve him with a summons, and until he has faced his trial can exercise a certain amount of control over him. During this time they can prevent him from leaving the country. Late in August 1939, in a street near Queen Anne's Gate, William Joyce met an acquaintance who had long ago been his neighbour in East Dulwich, and they halted and had a chat. When they parted, Joyce's acquaintance noted that he turned into the building beside which they had halted, and realized that this was the Passport Office. Even before that the name of William Joyce must have been posted at every port; and as soon as he fetched and had in his possession a renewed passport the warning signal should have been repeated. But a few days afterwards the police were searching for him all over the country; the old lady in Sussex, the stockbroker's sister, was questioned, and her house was watched. William Joyce had found a port where there was either a breakdown of routine fantastically fortunate for him, or where there was another traitor, working with him on the same pattern of treachery.

6

IN GERMANY autumn is not as it is in England, a sweet time of sleep; when, if the senses are sharpened by the blue frost of the morning, wakefulness has faded by the misty golden noon, and is forgotten under the thick eyelids of the brown and grey afternoons. It is not as autumn is in America, a cold forest fire, that fills the eyes with flames, and the veins with a gay ice; all seasons in that continent bring unrest, but this is the happiest restlessness of the four. But in Germany it is as if a beautiful burgess matron, it being no longer lawful that she should remain flesh, were turned to gold, before she turns to marble. For there autumn stands still like a statue, and is not grand, but is magical, and hard as metal. On the lakes the images of the dark pines and the yellow birches lie bright as themselves, and the morning mists have sharp edges. Virginia creeper clothes the little villas with redness like the glow from an elfin foundry. On the paved terrace above the swelling and darkened river, where the townsfolk walk on Sunday afternoons, the horse-chestnut trees shed leaves like spread hands in some substance just sallower than gold. The tiles above the gables are always autumn-colour, so are the pumpkin bulges in the church steeples: they are red-brown. The air is like iron; those who sail up the waterways which run all the way from the Wannsee to the Baltic find their lips seared, though they may not feel very cold, by the air which has come the same way, and farther, from the cap of the Arctic. The country keeps its integrity of form under the approach of winter; and the blood of those who live in this country, which was designed for simple happiness, is not thinned.

Into this season, which is one of Germany's particular graces, William Joyce was brought directly by his treachery. One day his little feet twinkled up the area steps in Eardley Crescent; and at the top, no doubt, he paused to put his arm round his wife's waist and give her a hug. His eyes must have been dancing. No matter what his misgivings might have been, the risks of the adventure must have enchanted him. It must, indeed, have been intoxicating for him to go through London, where he had never been of any importance, where he was at best a street-corner speaker better known than most, and realize that, if he won his gamble, he would return to it as the right hand of its conquerors. There would be then no building he would not have the right to enter, bearing with him the power to frustrate its existing function and constitute another. There would be no man or woman of power, in the degree and kind which he respected, whom he would not see humiliated, even to the point of imprisonment and death. The first should be last, and the last should be first, and many would be called and few would be chosen, and he would be among those that were chosen. He left the damp and the fog which would soon close in on London, and the obscurity which had closed in on him ever since he was born, and he went out to the perfect autumn of Germany and the promise of mastery. Very soon he was established in a home in the splendid modern suburb of Berlin, Charlottenburg, where there are broad streets and wide-windowed flats, and the handsomest civic intentions made manifest. He lived in the Kastanien Allée—Chestnut Avenue—where the trees shed their hand-like, metal-like leaves in great numbers down a handsome vista.

William Joyce must have been happy during the first weeks of the war. He had reason to feel proud of his escape from England to Germany, as an achievement in the *Scarlet Pimpernel* vein, and as the result of a firm act of the will, which, as month passed month of "the phony war," seemed justified. It must have certainly appeared to him that England, decadent in its democracy, was going to fall into Hitler's hand so soon as he chose to try it on its stalk. He must also have enjoyed the amenities of Berlin, the opportunity to practise every sport; he was still only thirty-three, and he had never had enough time to play. His career is not encouraging to those who say that Satan finds work for idle hands to do; from his middle teens he seems to have worked nearly all his waking hours, and to have slept little. He must also have enjoyed speaking German, a language which he had studied with a great deal of pleasure. And he enjoyed the fellowship of the Nazis, whom he believed to be about to inherit the earth because they were not meek. On the 18th of September, 1939, exactly fifteen days after the outbreak of war, he joined the German radio as an announcer of the news on the English service, and had very soon become a reader of the news.

His voice was very soon recognized by the doctor and his wife in Onslow Gardens, who had already begun to wonder about their former tenants. When an officer of the National Fire Service had come to examine their attics for combustibility they had found an inexplicable addition to their home. In a cistern loft, accessible only from the flat the Joyces had occupied, a bed had been put up and was there with its bedding. There was plenty of room to put up a bed in the ordinary rooms of the flat; the loft could be entered only by a very small trap-door, and it must have been very difficult to get the bed up through it; there was almost no space to spare round the bed. It must have been put up there during the Joyces' tenancy, for somebody who had to be sheltered without the knowledge of the doctor and his wife. Obviously, strange and furtive things had been going on. That chapter was finished. William Joyce had lost a friendship which he had found it hard to win, and of which he had been proud. And he cannot have fulfilled his duties very long without wondering just how competent his new Nazi friends were. They underrated his remarkable powers as a broadcaster, and gave him nothing to do but read news bulletins. But he was used to being thought little of by people when he first met them. That the news he was broadcasting was often fatuously untrue, and rendered all German propaganda suspect by its untruth, was probably unknown to him. When he told England that in September or October 1939, long before any bombs had fallen on the British mainland, Dover and Folkestone had been destroyed, he may well have believed it. It is worth while noting that this period of Joyce's service to the Nazis was given an interest in England which it lacked for him. The local details by which Joyce was supposed to show that he had a direct channel of communication with England, such as allusions to stopped town-hall clocks and road repairs, are not in fact found in the records of his broadcasts. They were invented as part of a whispering campaign designed to weaken public confidence, which was carried on by Fascists, most of whom, if not all, belonged to organizations other than Joyce's British National Socialist League. Ignorant of the inaccuracy of his broadcasts, and the use that was being made of them, Joyce may have been bored with his work. But he cannot long have felt such a passive emotion about the conditions in which he worked.

Indeed, he must very soon have looked round the office of the English section of the Rundfunk in panic. It is said that the Duke of Wellington, on seeing some troops for the first time, exclaimed, "I don't know if these fellows frighten the enemy, but, by God, they frighten me!" So might William Joyce have exclaimed when he first saw the colleagues who had been artlessly assembled by Dr. Goebbels' propaganda machine. The only one of any definite personality was Norman Baillie-Stewart, who had been tried for selling military secrets to Germany in 1933 and then had been sentenced to five years' penal servitude. But for a reason which William Joyce must rightly have thought absurd if he divined it, the Germans made use of Baillie-Stewart only with extreme caution. The rest were inglorious odd-come-shorts. The most sympathetic among them was an elderly lady called Miss Margaret Frances Bothamley, who before the war had founded a body called the Imperial Fascist League and run it from her flat in the Cromwell Road, a brownstone quarter of London. She was in a state of extreme confusion. She had brought with her to Germany photographs of the King and Queen and the Princesses, with which she ornamented her flat; and she asserted that in her youth she had made a secret marriage with a German music-master named Adolf, whom she appeared to identify with Hitler. During the first months of the war Joyce was forced to recruit a member of Miss Bothamley's organization, who had been spending the summer in Germany: a colonel's daughter who was a member of one of the most famous literary families in England on her father's side and was related to a most exalted peer on her mother's side, but who had, through a series of unhappy accidents, found herself in her late forties lost in less distinguished worlds. She began by being an enthusiastic pro-Nazi, but, being fundamentally not without honesty and decency, turned against the regime, and annoyed Joyce by sitting about in the office and doing knitting with an air of silent criticism.

There was also Mr. Leonard Banning, who must have been a disappointing colleague for William Joyce. He was just under thirty, and he had a long history behind him of inextricably confused idealistic effort and paid political adventure. He had at one time been a member of the British Union of Fascists, but had left it and had later been a paid organizer in the service of the Conservative Party, while at the same time—which was odd —carrying on pacifist agitation. Then he went abroad and taught English at various branches of the Berlitz School of Languages, and was so doing in September 1939. It was his story later that the day before war was declared he went down to the station and tried to buy a ticket to England, and found they would not sell him one for German money, and, as he had no foreign currency, went home. Few of us do not know the mechanism employed. He had wanted to stay in Germany. A certain softness of the voice and sinuousness of gait suggested, while there were indications that his sexual habits were orthodox, a gentleness of disposition which might find relief and inspiration in the forthright masculinity of Nazi society. Therefore, in making that move towards departure from Germany, he behaved like all of us who have had to contemplate a morally desirable departure from the pastures of satisfaction. He said, "I ought to go and see about that today. But tomorrow will do just as well. I have a lot to do now. I will go tomorrow." He did that until one day, when somehow it became possible to put aside all engagements and take the necessary steps; and on that day it happened that those necessary steps could no longer be taken. Then he returned home saying, "Well, I have done all I could. Nobody could have told that today it would be too late. It is not my fault." And at the back of his mind a voice must have said with cold cunning, "Yes, I will be able to tell them that, if things go wrong and I am called to account," while another voice said, "Look, you Nazis, I have stayed with you." Few of us, except the people who are in fact intolerable nuisances by reason of their incapacity for compromise, but have at some time or other behaved according to this formula. William Joyce, having just abandoned this formula at the great crisis of his life, was unlikely to feel sympathy with Leonard Banning or other recruits of his type.

He owed the presence of Banning in his office to the activities of a certain Herr Albrecht, whose business it was to see what Englishmen stranded in Germany would do for their hosts. He sent for Mr. Banning and a friend of his called Mr. Smith and questioned them as to their readiness for co-operation. Mr. Banning went home and wrote Herr Albrecht a letter with both the hands of his mind. "Dear Herr Albrecht," he wrote, "I write to make it perfectly clear that I have not offered to work for the Gestapo. I would never think of doing that, and I absolutely refuse to sell my country. There is a certain price I will not pay. The most I would do is radio propaganda." And he ended with a postscript which bears a significance beyond his intention. "Mr. Smith," he wrote, "will not even do radio propaganda." Mr. Smith, using that term in its generic sense, did not even do radio propaganda. Only a small proportion of the civilian internees or prisoners of war turned traitor; and of those that did, many found themselves too noble to be the instrument of their own ignobility and went back to their camps, where some of them were punished till they died, and all suffered grave torment. They were not many, the men who could split their minds in two and pretend that while they were serving Germany they were making contact with anti-Nazi elements and sabotaging Nazi activity, which was the defence that nearly all of them kept at the back of their minds and produced at their trials. All such men hated William Joyce, who did not split his mind, who desired to make England Fascist, and, to procure that end, was ready to help Germany to conquer England, and never denied that desire or that readiness, either during the war or after it.

He sat among the hatred of these poor silly creatures, and knew a more humiliating hatred from some others who worked in his office. A certain number of Germans had been drafted into the office, men who had a special knowledge of the English language and English life. As such men had usually acquired their knowledge through having English relatives or having been educated in England, they were for the most part anti-Nazi. They despised Joyce as a traitor to his own country and an enemy to their own country, the true Germany; and they were gentlemen, and cruelly knew he was not a gentleman. But there was another painful element in the office, which must have cut William Joyce far deeper. The Nazis were prone, in all sorts of circumstances, to make a peculiar error. When one of their enemies became their friend, they went on treating him as an enemy. However ready he might be to serve their interests, however much they might need his help, they continued to savage him. The great historic example of this curious trick is their treatment of the Russian soldiers and civilians who, by tens of thousands, gladly surrendered to them as they invaded Russian territory in 1941 and 1942. These people who might have been their most valuable aids then and forever after, they packed into cattle trucks and sent off to camps where they were starved and tortured. Later they were fetched out and invited to fight alongside the Germans, but by that time their enthusiasm was not what it had been, and the treatment they received in training and at the front failed to revive it. The Germans acted on the same perverse principle towards the British broadcasters, who were all favourably disposed towards them to start with, and, having burned their boats, had every reason to remain firm in the faith. But at the head of the British section, which they had as if in mockery called the Concordia Bureau, they placed a certain Dr. Hexler, who was so much of a brute as to be for all intents and purposes a maniac. Throughout the war he exercised every sort of ferocity on his wretched staff, English and German.

Two Germans were to tell a British court what Dr. Hexler had been, in evidence that was disinterested and, indeed, unaware of its own portent. When Mr. Banning was tried at the Old Bailey early in 1946, the prosecution called as a witness one of the German technicians who had recorded his talks. He was an S.S. man, a lank and hollow-cheeked young man, who might have been carved in wood in the thirteenth century, and he spoke a peculiar wooden German which might come to be natural in a man who had been drilled all his youth by tyranny and then marched along a straight road for many years in the direction of defeat. He was called Krumpiegel; surely one might as well be called Rumpelstiltskin. As he gave evidence there stood beside him the interpreter who is one of the chief glories of the Old Bailey, a slender and distinguished old gentleman of Spanish Jewish descent, very courteous to the defeated barbarian but plainly savouring a certain satisfaction as, in his silvery voice, he translated the comic expressions used by barbarity. "Did Banning look happy when he was at the Concordia Bureau?" asked the defending counsel. Mr. Salcedo translated: "He says that he does not consider happy (*glücklich*) an appropriate word to use in connection with Banning's personality, but for the greater part of the war he could fairly be described as contented (*zufrieden*)." The defending counsel continued: "But did Banning seem to be contented in his relations with the head of the Bureau, Dr. Hexler?" Krumpiegel looked more wooden than ever; he folded his arms behind him, said some words, and looked blank as an ill-treated child that has told the truth about its tormentors and does not believe that it will not be punished for it, whatever the grown-ups say. Mr. Salcedo translated: "He says Dr. Hexler's relations with his employees were never a source of gratification." There came later to give evidence for Mr. Banning one of the anti-Nazi Germans who had worked in the Concordia Bureau. This young man wore an air of desolation more usually presented by places than by persons. There used to be a derelict factory on the New Jersey marshes which had the same air of not having, anywhere in all eternity, a possible use. His evidence gave Mr. Banning little help in proving his innocence, but absolved him from mockery. A question made allusion to Dr. Hexler. The anti-Nazi paused before answering. In accomplished, springless, exhausted, pedantic English, he said, "Dr. Hexler was . . . the *prototype* . . . of the Nazis." Both Banning and this young German had been battered by huge irrational waves, tides obeying the moon of Hell.

It would be interesting to know whether these waves ever battered William Joyce. At no trial did any evidence emerge that threw any light on his relations with his employers; and on the American correspondents who alone of the outside world saw him during this period he left only an impression of laughing, cursing, story-telling garrulity. The little creature was, as we were to see later, so tight-lipped that we cannot construe this as evidence that he was not savaged like his colleagues. But, whether he suffered this violence himself or not, he must have observed its infliction upon others; and that would be his first experience of the real suspension of civilization, the real reversion to barbarism. If a rebellious Fascist was beaten up in the cells in the barracks of King's Road, Chelsea, if a Jew was chased up an alley in Bethnal Green, this violence might be valued by persons with peculiar tastes, as a pearl; but a pearl has to be formed within a shell, and civil order was the shell in which an act of violence could preserve its exciting quality. A world where violence was the shell as well as the pearl was new to William Joyce, and it cannot have been an easy conception to accept. But there must have seemed, as 1940 went on, not much need to worry about what were obviously only temporary conditions. When there were gathered in as Nazi harvest first Norway, then Denmark, then the Low Countries, then France, there was nothing on earth to prevent the fall of England; and all the poor misfits in the Concordia Bureau must have had their heads stuffed with infantilist dreams. In these dreams a fast car, long as a bus, would have been sent down to Dulwich to pick up the family and bring them to Joyce's office: which would have been in Buckingham Palace, or in the War Office, or Downing Street, or wherever.

It would, in fact, have been in none of these places. Inexorably the law that to him that hath it shall be given would have come into operation again; there would certainly have come forward as quislings after the first few days of the German occupation this popular historian and that expert in foreign affairs, this civil servant and that leading Communist, and these would have been given precedence over William Joyce, who would have found himself fulfilling just the same subordinate role in the new dispensation as in the old. But that he would not have suspected. He must have imagined himself saying to his father and mother, smiling, "Well, this is my room. Do you like it? And the next one is mine, too, that's where my three secretaries work." He would have talked his young brothers and his sister into taking good jobs, and would have found admiring Angus MacNab, whom he released at once from internment, a post that would keep him close to him. In the evening his wife would have worn fine new dresses, like the wives of Goering and Goebbels, in a home he had no doubt long since chosen as he passed it in his little car, on the way back from a meeting. Mr. Banning had friends at Brighton, and, in his daydreams, would have extended his protection to them. They were afterwards to put up bail for him. Miss Bothamley, no doubt, would have explained the beneficent intentions of the invaders to Queen Elizabeth and the Princesses; and the colonel's daughter, who was a kindly creature, would have looked after the interests of her former husbands. No expert has ever been able to explain just why the situation in which these dreams might have known a partial realization did not materialize. It must have been a sickening blow to the inhabitants of the Concordia Bureau when weeks and months passed, and the Nazis still did not invade Britain.

There came the air raids, and the apotheosis of William Joyce. So perfectly did the circumstances of his outer life mirror the dominant fantasy of his inner life that it was as if he were not a real man but the hero of a legend told about his kind of man. He was a revolutionary, and a revolutionary blows both hot and cold: he hates order and he loves it. He wants to overthrow the order which exists and which may be the only order capable of existing. But he risks the annihilation of all order only because he believes he can evade that disaster and can substitute for the existing order another which he believes to be superior. This may be an absence of order which, by a mystical logic, he has proved to be more orderly than the presence of order. But perhaps the revolutionary is not really treating order as an end in itself, but is using it as a means to an end. Perhaps he is really preoccupied with the establishment of a balance of forces within the sphere of his being: that balance which alone can restore nothingness to a world so obstinately created, so irretrievably stuffed with things. One cannot destroy this world, these things. But one can temporarily destroy them by an act which is permanently futile. All the available energy of the will is poured out into the destruction of a system which has come into existence not at the behest of that finite force, the human will, or any number of human wills, but as the result of the interaction of innumerable forces, some invested in man, some diffused through earth and air and fire and water, not combined in man but in their purer forms. Not in a short time is the nature of man modified; so the human interests which profited by the system survive after it has crashed. The changes wrought by science on earth and air and fire and water proceed as slowly; so when the will and earth and fire and water set about to make a new system, it is bound to be like the old. In revolution there is a vast explosion of the creative powers, and nothing is created; nothing is even altered. So the appetite for death that is in us all is immensely gratified.

The French Revolution has given pleasure to all subsequent generations because it was an outstanding event which afterwards proved never to have happened. A number of revolutionaries arose and overturned the monarchy of France because of its tyranny and its financial and economic inefficiency, in order that they might substitute a republic which should give its people liberty, make them equal, and join them in fraternity. When the dust settled, France was ruled by a self-crowned emperor who wielded power more absolute than any French king had ever been given by the priests that crowned him; and the society which reconstituted itself after his fall conferred on its people increases of liberty and equality and fraternity no greater than were won by other nations untouched by revolution. The Russian Revolution, which is plainly going to be a source of still greater satisfaction, achieves a more perfect balance; for, with an enormously greater expenditure of blood than France ever saw, it slowly reconstituted the Tsardom it destroyed, identical in spirit, and reinforced in matter; so that the waste of the revolutionaries' creative effort is manifestly more extravagant. William Joyce was among those who were setting their hands to the Nazi Revolution, which, with an infinitely greater expenditure of blood than either France or Russia had seen, was to tear down Europe and leave it in ruins, as it is today and shall be until our souls and earth and air and fire and water make it again.

Therefore he must have known delight as the German planes went out to destroy England; and anguish too. For though the revolutionary's love of death finds joy in what he does, his love of life knows it to be criminal. That is why he contrives that the drama of the revolution shall develop so that in the end he shall pay for his crime with his life. The scaffolds of Paris took, in the end, all those that set them up; and of the actual engineers of the Russian Revolution, all but a handful were hoist by their own petard. So when the German planes went out against England, William Joyce must have been inflamed with joy because they were to scatter death on the democratic civilization he detested, but he must also have been eaten in his bowels with a sense of guilt, burning not less fiercely than his exultation, with the peculiar passion of his revolutionary kind, which is to the normal state of man as lightning is to the calm sky behind it. That passion burns so fiercely, it is said, because it is lit from the primal fires of our nature, our first loves and hates, sprung from the first contact of our flesh with the flesh from which it was formed, with which it was formerly mingled, which surrounds it with tenderness, with odious compulsion. The mother gives the first warmth, the first food, the first protecting strength; the father gives the first superb revelation of a strength greater than hers. But they put the child down when it wants to be taken up, they will not go on giving food till the limits of greed are reached, they sometimes move it into colder airs; and for these hostile acts they are hated, each time with a final and desperate hatred, because the child has not enough experience to know that the hostility will not continue forever. At that stage the parents are the environment, they are authority; and the conceptions of environment and authority are coloured throughout our adult lives with the unrestrained emotions of cooing and squalling infancy. Most parents and children contrive to gentle their relationship by tolerance of each other's wills so that it serves them well, and most citizens make the claims of the state and their individualities balance on their books. But there are those who never persuade the love and hatred they feel for their parents to sign a truce; and these often find themselves compelled to spend their lives in love and hatred of the society of which they are a part, striving to make it more beautiful and noble, but insisting that the prerequisite of its reform is its destruction. The extreme case is the revolutionary, who clothes his desire to establish a nihilist balance of forces, which is the most abstract of lusts, the most metaphysical of murders, with the dedication of the whole being seen in a baby sucking a nipple or kicking and howling when its mother lifts it from its cot.

Now William Joyce, the sublime example of this extreme type, stood in Berlin at the microphone, conspiring to replace the complex social organization of Western civilization by a system which was not a system, which had not an idea in its head but to set people who needed work to do some work, it did not matter what, and to shut up people whom it did not like in concentration camps, and which was now to press home its negativism by making a useless war. But there stood also at the microphone the son of Michael Francis Joyce and his wife Queenie, whom he had flouted by renouncing their Church and their social traditions, the husband of the girl whom he had married in their first youth and betrayed in her early womanhood, the father of the two children whom he had deserted. He had done all that was possible in the framework of normal life to throw contempt on the ties which bound him to these people. Now, as he used the ghastly facilities of this crisis in history, he played out that drama a second time. He appeared before them when he was not there, a sport till now reserved for phantoms, and those drawn from the faithful rather than the faithless. His father and mother, his first wife, his children, must have remembered all he had ever been to them. He sent out threats against their safety, speaking of the planes that were being sent out against them so that they should be burned to death, of the hundreds of thousands of "gross registered tons" (a phrase he always enjoyed reading) of their country's shipping that were being sunk so that they should starve. It was given to him to cancel their relationship not once but twice, the first time on the realistic plane, the second time on both the realistic and the poetic plane.

Very early in the battle of Britain a bomb fell on Michael Francis Joyce's house in Allison Grove. Nothing remains of it now save a hole in the ground beside the remains of a neighbour's basement; a fine tree, long grasses, and lilacs and syringas grown wild-branched for lack of pruning give the scene a certain elegiac beauty. The family lost all their possessions except a trunk full of old papers and a few pieces of furniture, and they went to live at a rest centre until they were found another house. To strangers they seemed arrogant and unmoved by the shame of being kin to Joyce, who by now had been identified by many people, particularly in this district, as the news reader on the German service known all over England as "Lord Haw-Haw." But when a worker in the centre came to Mr. and Mrs. Joyce and told them that she was a friend of the doctor and his wife who had been Joyce's landlords in South Kensington, and that she herself had met Joyce, the old man and his wife broke down. William had always been the difficult one of the family, they said, but they had never thought he would be led away into doing anything so terrible as this, for he had always been a good boy at heart. It was perhaps his trouble, they pleaded, that he was too brilliant. They were ultimately found a house, a characterless little modern villa in an uninteresting part of Dulwich, which must have been too small to hold a family of such numbers and such strong individualities. It is not easy to understand why Michael Francis Joyce, who was by then over seventy, and his wife, who was growing very frail, did not go to the country under the evacuation scheme. But there was no real reason why Lear should have wandered on the blasted heath instead of taking shelter from the storm. Men sometimes feel, however, that if a certain hammer falls it is their part to act as anvil. Michael Francis Joyce lived among the amazement of the news and the bombs until he died five months later, on the 19th of February, 1941.

It is not known whether Joyce heard of the destruction of his family's home and the death of his father at the time of these events; but it is not impossible that he did, however loyally his relatives kept their obligation not to communicate with him, for the Joyces had connections and friends in both Eire and the United States. In any case the tide of his joy was on the turn. It had risen to its height in that same time when the house in Allison Grove was bombed, when his father and mother were dependent on strangers for a hearth, when he, for no discernible reason but to curse the true facts of his birth, became a German citizen. But the mind makes its own inexorable justice. It commits the crime, it furnishes the appropriate punishment; and in the life of Joyce what happened within his skull was painted with great brush-strokes on the earth and sky. He had dismissed remorse for his sins against the natural loyalties along with all the rest of conventional morality, knowing a trick worth two of that; and the planes England sent against the Nazi revolution dropped their bombs on sham cities, doppelgänger Berlins and Hamburgs and Essens, laid out on fields with lights, where mock fires were started to make the raiders believe they had hit their targets. At such failures William Joyce sneered over his radio. But justice knew tricks worth three of that; and in time the Berlin night above William Joyce's head was sprayed with such gold and silver and precious stones as he had seen when he had stood with his young wife at the windows of his flat by the Crystal Palace, watching the fireworks displays. But these bore real fire; and after the flames came worse: the sound of doom. An American correspondent who broadcast from Berlin up to the time of Pearl Harbor has described how one night he could not leave the Rundfunk building because of a fierce R.A.F. raid, and took shelter in the company of William Joyce and his wife, and how Joyce served out a stream of amusing and inventive oaths against the raiders. He smiled as he blasphemed; but his was true blasphemy, a railing against life, the way things grow, the way things happen, reality itself. Now he tried to break the one link his egotism had maintained with any real object outside himself. That he and his wife loved each other deeply cannot be doubted, but as the war went on his treatment of her became noticeably unkind. When a child is moved to hatred by some action of its parents and screams at them and beats them with its little hands, and its rage wears out, it feels guilty, it sobs, it devises means of punishing itself, it goes and stands in the corner of its own accord. William Joyce, aware of the offence he had committed against the intimates whom he had addressed over the air to tell them that they were less than strangers to him, aware that the strangers whom he preferred to these intimates had destroyed the hearth of his father and driven him out to die under an unloved roof, felt guilty, and tried to punish himself by making a stranger of his wife, the one intimate left to him. The reality of the love between them would not permit him to make the sacrifice, but his sense of sin egged him on to it during those years when the city he had chosen as his, because it promised to be his accomplice in all his meditated violence, altered and assumed the character of an accuser. The nights came with these new dangerous fireworks and the new thunder that kept its threats; and in the morning more of the huge houses where brutal people lived in the pride of their unkind flesh had been purged by fire, and were hollow as skulls, and told Joyce to remember death.

During these years his work in the Rundfunk became more degrading in nature. From the beginning he had been engaged in the unhandsome business of recruiting announcers and speakers in the camps of British civilian internees; but a gloss could be put on its unhandsomeness. If among the internees there were many like the sturdy Mr. Smith who were Britons in fact and sympathy and conveyed to the Gestapo that they would "not even do radio propaganda," there were others like his friend Mr. Leonard Banning, who had come to work in Germany because of a deep affection for the country, and the colonel's daughter, who was a member of a British Fascist society and had been caught by the war when she was paying her annual visit to renew the ecstasy she felt when she saw Hitler. There were other internees who were British only from a legal standpoint, such as people who had been brought up in Germany since childhood or who were the children of mixed marriages; and of these a number, and probably the greater number, were sincerely glad to have an opportunity to perform any service asked of them by what they considered as their real fatherland. But as the war went on William Joyce was obliged to do more and more of his recruiting among prisoners of war, first drawn from the mercantile marine, then from the regular services, the army, the navy, and the air force. In only a very few cases could Joyce have the slightest reason to suppose that the men he was approaching would have any ideological bias towards fascism. What he was doing was to seek out men who as prisoners of war were undergoing an extreme physical and mental ordeal, and to bribe them by promises of freedom and food and drink and the society of women into sacrificing their honour: which was no empty phrase in this connection. When they went to the microphone with William Joyce, they broke their oath of allegiance to the head of their state and cut themselves off from their comrades for reasons that were apparent and contemptible, and they committed in little such an act of cruelty to their kin as Joyce had committed to his, on his own grand scale; they transferred their loyalty to the people who were dropping bombs on their parents and wives and children. It was an ugly business and it grew uglier in the handling.

At first very few prisoners yielded to temptation. The British authorities had foreseen the situation and had made provision for it. Members of all services were warned before they left England that the Germans would ask them to broadcast, putting it to them first that they would thus be able to reassure their families regarding their safety, and they were ordered to refuse in any and all circumstances. The British officers who were put in charge of prisoner-of-war camps under the German staff constantly warned all ranks of the attempts that would be made to seduce them, and kept an eye on those who seemed likely to succumb to seduction. Moreover, certain men, mostly non-commissioned officers, were put through a course of training before they went abroad which prepared them for the ordeal of accepting the German offers and serving as spies while they were serving as broadcasters. One of them, a quartermaster sergeant of the

Gunners named John Henry Owen Brown, who has since retired to a villa called The Wee House in a Thameside suburb, resembled a Homeric hero in his courage and his cunning. Few of these spy-broadcasters came into action at once; so that all the Germans got for some time was an odd prisoner or two who, dazed by shock or by natural imbecility, consented to be interviewed before the microphone regarding the circumstances of his capture. They did not take serious steps to improve their position till 1942, and the big drive they made did not show its results until 1943 and 1944. There were never many traitors, but there were some, and this was inevitable, because the number of prisoners of war was so large that it was bound to include a few representatives of the Fascist minority in Great Britain, and rather more than a few rogues and madmen. Moreover, some sane men were losing their balance under the pressure of the terrible conditions peculiar to the life of a prisoner of war, the worst of which is the uncertainty concerning the duration of his imprisonment.

The most interesting example of the sincere Fascist traitor was a pilot officer in the R.A.F., a man of forty, who joined the S.S. and wrote broadcasting scripts for Joyce. He uttered a revealing remark when a court martial, with the irrationality characteristic of courts martial when trying serious offences, sentenced him to ten years' imprisonment for an extreme act of treason which might well have cost him his life. He said indignantly to his lawyer, "This just shows how rotten this democratic country is. The Germans would have had the honesty to shoot me." The Nazis made curiously little use of this honest and lettered fanatic or any of his kind. They seemed more at ease with the rogues and the madmen and the sane men off their balance, whom they took great trouble to procure, almost more trouble than one could think would have been necessary. They established holiday camps, at which the conditions were comfortable and even, to the eyes of many privates and ratings, luxurious; and the German welfare officers in the ordinary prisoner-of-war camp approached men whom they had marked down as likely prospects and told them that, as they had of late been working specially hard or seemed to be in poor health, it had been decided they should go for a month to one of these special camps. It would very often be true that these men were overworked and ill, and therefore the invitation seemed to them a welcome sign of humanity in their captors, and when their own officers told them not to accept it, the advice seemed a sign of their inhumanity. Most of the men thus tempted kept their heads, but some did not. These were exposed during their sojourn in the holiday camp to gentle propaganda, and at the end of the month were returned to the normal discomfort of their original camp. After they had had a few days on which to brood on the change, Joyce or one of his agents paid them a visit and suggested that a permanent return to comfort might be arranged if only they would read some scripts before the microphone. It would be explained that these broadcasts would be extremely pro-British and would simply aim at the affirmation of German good will towards Great Britain, and this was often true, for this was the early radio policy of Dr. Goebbels.

This was a cleverly designed procedure, because it gave the men a pretext to get out of the prisoner-of-war camp and retain a show of self-respect, but most of the men on whom the promise of comfort reacted were not greatly interested in their self-respect. As a typical broadcasting traitor there may be taken Francis Dale, a New Zealand Commando, who was captured in Crete in 1941 and in a couple of years fell into the Nazi net, for reasons he disclosed with pathetic candour in his statement. "After coming out of the various prison camps in Germany, where we had, to say the least, lived a rather rough life, coming into this villa, furnished as it was with every luxury, completely shattered us. We did not know what to think of it. The food was nothing special, but the place was so comfortable." In 1946 this man appeared at the Old Bailey, in the course of a curious exploration of the possibilities inherent in the criminal law of England. He had been court-martialled under the army act and sentenced to ten years' imprisonment, and he had come out of jail to give evidence against one of the four traitors charged with high treason; and now he was emerging again to give evidence against six merchant-seaman traitors, which he offered quite without malice and indeed attempted to cancel by several artless efforts to convince the Court that he and they, united in a common state of nobility, had all committed acts of sabotage against the Germans. But his appearance alone prejudiced his claim. His breadth of shoulder was more than human, and every now and then he sucked his teeth or sniffed as a pig grunts, just to register the continuity of consciousness. Everything about him spoke of simplification on the scale indicated by a sentence in a well-known American book on the care of dogs: "After a dog has had a love affair, it puts on its hat, goes away, and doesn't write." The seduction of such a person would not have been difficult; and it was hard to understand why the Germans took such pains over it, or why, when their aim was accomplished, they made such a fatuous use of him. For he was employed to deliver such stuff as this:

"Once more I say, people of Great Britain, just think for a moment and you will realize how much we are losing, individually and as a nation, as a whole. The sooner we stop this senseless slaughter and come to our right senses and furthermore kick the Jews out of our country, the sooner we shall be able to secure peace for ourselves and for the rest of the world and, above all, shall we secure a return to the high British standards of living that are so dear to us all. Let them remain, and we shall find ourselves sold to everlasting Jewish bondage and our children will only be able to turn round and say that we delivered the Empire to the Jews."

The only words in this broadcast which might have riveted the attention of English listeners were its last sentence, which was, remarkably enough, "United we fall." By this time the English, who had for ten years housed a large Jewish population who had had to flee for its bare life before persecution, were unlikely to believe in the international power of the Jews, and were even less likely to believe, after having suffered the blitz and passed through the severest phase of the food shortage, and had their hearts jerked out of their breasts again and again by the North African campaign, that they had more to fear from the Jews than from the Germans. It is not easy to believe that William Joyce, who was no fool and had a long experience in propaganda, could have believed that the broadcasting of such stuff was politic. He was certainly a passionate and sincere anti-Semite. Every time he spoke of those whom he called, in a drawled, sneering dissyllable, "The Jeeoos," his acquired accent cracked and fell away and his strong native Irish had its own way. But it was the line of his cunning to suppress his immediate passions for the sake of the ultimate victory; and it might have been expected that he would at this particular juncture have broadcast messages that pretended a German passion for tolerance, and readiness to let bygones be bygones and race be race. It would seem probable that he was not in any real degree his own master in determining the policy of the Concordia Bureau, which he was supposed to direct; and it is to be noted that people who were accustomed to hear Joyce speak in public and talk in private in England declare that they could not recognize the substance of his broadcasts as characteristic until late in the war; some put the date as late as D-day.

In 1943 he was still obeying orders; and the man whose efficiency was respected by the metropolitan police must have thought those orders fairly silly. He must have marvelled over the fuss that his masters made over Mr. Walter Purdy. This young man, the son of a widow living in Barking, was twenty-two when he was captured at Narvik, where he was serving as a junior engineer in *H.M.S. Vandyke,* and he suffered from a psychological form of St. Vitus' Dance. He had always to be committing some action, whether or not it bore any relation to any he had committed before or was to commit afterwards, and his reasoning self spent most of its time trying to pull these unrelated actions into some sort of coherence. Though his family were good simple Barking stuff, his anxiety to bring his disordered self safe through these storms it raised had given him a nervous glittering smartness; and he had a glittering eye, too, as he told his stories. He was an Ancient Mariner who had never made the trip with the albatross. Yet if he had not been on the journeys he described he had been on others even stranger. The circumstances in which he told his lie add up to a story as improbable as any of them. His entry into the Nazi service began when he had been a prisoner of war for three years and had got into a certain amount of trouble, having been sentenced by the German authorities to ten days' imprisonment for having struck a superior officer of the camp. At this point he bought from one of the German officers a copy of a book by William Joyce which was called *Twilight Over England* and consisted of his collected broadcasts, and got him to send it up to Berlin with a request that he should autograph it. His excuse for doing this was that he intended to take the book home and sell it, and that Joyce's signature would raise its value. But he had a link with Joyce, for he had met him nine years before when for a brief period he had been a member of the Ilford branch of the British Union of Fascists; and three weeks after he sent Joyce's book to Berlin he left for one of the holiday camps. Before he went he gave a fellow-prisoner a letter addressed to the Senior British Officer, with directions that it should not be given to him until the camp was broken up at the end of the war. This letter contained a statement that he intended to disregard the instructions forbidding co-operation with the Germans which had been issued by the authorities, if any opportunity arose to persuade the Germans to repatriate him to England or a neutral country.

This letter was plainly a form of insurance policy. If the Germans won the war, then he would be on the right side, and his friend would never have the opportunity to give up the letter. If the Allies won, then he had this letter to prove that he had disobeyed orders and broadcast for Joyce only because he hoped to get back to England. It must be noted that practically all the traitors defended themselves on the ground that they had gone over to German service in order to get opportunities to escape and to do what they could to sabotage the German war effort. This defence was so invariably raised, and by men of such different types, that it seems probable that it was suggested to them by the agents who recruited them. "After all, you can always say that you thought you would have a better chance to escape once you were out of the camp, and that you meant to send messages home over the air, or put sugar into the petrol tanks of our vehicles, and so on. Nobody will be able to say you did not."

The first part of this suggestion Walter Purdy had dealt with by his letter; on the second part he brought to bear his peculiar proliferating ingenuity persistently during the remaining two years of the war. He worked well for Joyce, broadcasting violent anti-Semitic propaganda. At the same time he conducted an immense and animated correspondence with his family in London, suggesting in veiled terms that he was incorporating in his broadcasts information to the Royal Air Force about the weather. In these letters he used the term "Eric's boss" for the R.A.F., because he had a nephew called Eric who was a sergeant in that force; at one time he wrote that "the instructions I gave were concerning weather or not my cash to them had been received, and weather they have been able to invest it in the securities I previously mentioned in my letters," and he summed up his instructions in a little poem—"When it is just good night, There's not a flight of birds who'll take the sky, But when the moon is bright, On a good good night, There's many a man will try. A good night all is just the call, For brave men good and true, But a good good night to everyone, Is the best good night of all." This, of course, alleged a special significance in the ending of his broadcasts. The originals of these letters were destroyed by a flying bomb during the last months of the war, but there is no doubt that they existed, for his family, highly respectable and well-meaning people, gave them to an official of the Red Cross, who forwarded them to the proper quarters. Walter Purdy stuck to the story he told in these letters right to the very end. Only when he was under cross-examination in the dock of the Old Bailey did he realize that the British authorities knew, as he had known, that his broadcasts were not direct but recorded, and that the recordings were not always used the same day they were made, and that in consequence his warnings must always have been valueless, and that he must have been well aware of this. For all the intelligence and crazy creativeness of his scheme, he lacked the something in his brain which would have warned him that, once the war was over, the British authorities would have no difficulty in acquainting themselves with the routine of the Rundfunk.

While Walter Purdy was carrying on this deception, which must have taken up a great deal of his time and put him to much trouble, he was living through adventures of a cast peculiar to his experience. At one point he was arrested by the Gestapo and taken away from Berlin to a British prisoner-of-war camp at a place called Colditz; and he claimed that this was because the Germans had discovered various deeds of daring which he had committed, including two attempts to murder William Joyce. It is to be noted that the trial at which he told this story began on the same day that the House of Lords was disallowing William Joyce's last appeal against his conviction for treason. A very good reason for doubting this story is the fact that at Colditz there was working the superb John Henry Owen Brown, fulfilling his function as an Intelligence agent in communication with England from within a German prison camp; and about this time the Germans had become suspicious of him. When Purdy got to Colditz he met an officer with whom he had been imprisoned in another camp, a dentist who had apparently become distraught through prolonged separation from his drill; for though Purdy arrived at the camp alone, which was always considered a suspicious circumstance, he asked Purdy what he thought of Brown, and when Purdy disingenuously replied that Brown was quite a nice fellow but too friendly with the Germans, he assured him that he was mistaken and that Brown "was doing very good work, and he has to appear to be friendly with them." They then went to look for the postal officer, and the fate which was presiding over the occasion led them to the entrance of an escape tunnel, the existence of which was not known to the dentist. Later Purdy was present at a reading of B.B.C. news, which, of course, revealed that there was a wireless hidden in the camp. As soon as he arrived at the camp he had to submit to interrogation by several of the senior British officers, who had to collect information which might be helpful to prisoners intending to escape, and to these he told a not implausible story of having escaped from a holiday camp, of having been sheltered in Berlin ever since by a woman, and of having been recaptured because he had lost his fake papers in an air raid. But suddenly he told them the truth, accusing himself in terms of complete self-abasement, crying out that he had behaved like a rat and a traitor. He expressed himself with a fantastic honesty which carried a double threat for himself. His confession was couched in terms that would have cost him his life if the Germans had heard him; but when he was asked by the Senior British Officer, "Suppose the Germans allowed you to go back to this woman who I understand you are living with in Berlin, would you then give away what was going on in the camp?" he answered, "I am afraid I would." He explained that he was very much in love with the German woman who had befriended him, and wanted to marry her, and for that reason he would have to give the information if the Germans promised him his freedom in exchange for it.

The Senior British Officer then said, "In that case there is nothing I can do except to try to get rid of you," and he ordered him to be put under close arrest, which is to say that two English

officers were continually with him, and requested the German
Camp Commandant to take him out of the camp. This was done
very shortly afterwards. It was a morally mysterious incident. For
not only would the Germans have shot him if the British officers
had repeated in detail what he had said to them, ill might have
befallen him in the camp once he had refused to give a pledge
of secrecy. Discipline did not prevent some very unpleasant things
happening to prisoners of war whose comrades believed them to
be informers. But we do not know how long that Dostoievsky
mood lasted. Within a very few days the Germans entered the
camp and went straight to the tunnel to which the unfortunate
dentist had unwittingly led Mr. Purdy, and they also searched for
the secret wireless set and found it; and Quartermaster Sergeant
Brown was interrogated by a number of German officers, and by
a Major Heimpel, a counter-intelligence officer, and Dr. Ziegfeld,
a Foreign Office official, with both of whom Purdy was in frequent contact. Brown was then regarded with such suspicion
that he had to lie low for the time being. It was, however, the
opinion of the Old Bailey jury that these events were unconnected
with Purdy's sojourn in the camp, and he was acquitted on the
charge arising out of them.

It is pleasant to learn that Quartermaster Sergeant Brown
returned to work not very long after Purdy brought this trouble
on him, having convinced the Germans that he was a trustworthy
traitor, and in November 1944 carried out a characteristic operation. He sent four prisoners of war who were working under his
orders to do a job of housecleaning in a villa in Berlin belonging
to the German Foreign Office, which was now shared by Purdy
and another traitor. Untroubled by German supervision, they
searched the house and found in the wastepaper basket, that
ancient focus of international interest, some correspondence
deeply compromising to Purdy. But the net was to do nothing so
simple in Purdy's case as to close in on him. When Germany
crumbled into defeat there began for him the nightmare that all
the traitors knew at that time. They were treated like unloved
children whose parents are doing a moonlit flitting: stuffed into
the van and told to hold their noise or else. Purdy was sent in
November 1944 to act as interpreter at Kampen, a town near
Duisburg between the Rhine and the Dutch border; and he was

sent back to Berlin in March 1945, when the Allies crossed the Rhine at Remagen. For two months he waited there, and on April the 7th, when the Americans were nearing Hanover, two S.S. men in plain clothes called and told him to pack a bag and come with them. They put him on a train for Italy with a mixed bag of traitors, and there they were taken from place to place until he and a Dutch broadcaster stole a motorcycle and rode towards the German front lines. Finally they were captured by Italian partisans, who handed them over to the American army, where they were interrogated. Just after the end of the war he was repatriated to England, and there he was interrogated, four days later, by Inspector Davis and Inspector Edwards, two Scotland Yard men who had been lent to the War Office and had done distinguished intelligence work. They took an immensely long statement from him, in which he told the whole story of all he had done for the Germans, claiming that he had been moved at times by a desire to serve Great Britain, and sometimes by the fear of death. And no proceedings were taken against him.

This was natural enough. No evidence had then come in from the officers of the camp at Colditz; and most people who met Purdy thought him insane, an impression which was confirmed by the extraordinary nature of his statement. At that time the authorities had too much on their hands to bother overmuch about a lunatic who had certainly strayed into the Rundfunk but who had been more trouble to the Germans than he was worth. The matter might have rested there had not Purdy continued to be himself, to create his unique and suicidal experience. A few months after he had entered the Nazi service he had met in Berlin the manageress of a pastrycook's shop, Margarethe Weitemeier, with whom he had fallen passionately in love, so passionately that at the camp at Colditz he had exposed himself to considerable risk for her sake. He had wished to marry her, and had remained closely associated with her till the break-up of his life in Berlin. Very soon after he arrived in London, however, he fell deeply in love with a young typist; and his emotion had the curious effect of making him write a complete account of everything he had done in Germany. It is interesting that this account, which was many thousands of words long, was almost the same, sentence by sentence, as the statement he had given to Inspectors

Davis and Edwards, weeks before. He put this in an envelope and gave it to the typist, telling her she was to send this to a solicitor if he was arrested.

He was not sure himself why he did this. Sometimes he said it was because he was afraid that if the police arrested him after all, he would not be allowed to consult his solicitor and supply him with the true facts of his activity in Germany; and sometimes he said that he wanted people to read the statement after he had been hanged and understand what sort of man he had been. His next step was one that many much less intelligent men than Purdy would have recognized as unwise. He abandoned his sweetheart before he had recovered the envelope. She opened it and read its contents, which were a complete surprise to her. From motives not so much of greed as of anger, she told him that she would take the letter to the police if he did not give her a sum of money large enough for him to find it hard to raise. This threat, as the letter was practically a replica of the statement Purdy had made to the police, need have amounted to very little. But Purdy thought it right and proper to go into the nearest police station and, in a dramatic monologue delivered with great force and brilliance, appeal to the law to protect him against this attempt to blackmail him. He told his full story without the slightest reserve; and when the dazed constabulary appealed for guidance to headquarters, the result was positive. By now the reports from the officers who had been at Colditz had come in, and if Purdy was well enough to be going about London in an active state he was well enough to stand judgment for his crimes.

So it happened that he was arrested and charged with high treason, not with the milder crime of an offence against the Defence Regulations, for the reason that such acts as the betrayal of the secrets of the camp at Colditz, of which he was then believed guilty, were precisely those which the authorities wanted to see punished. He was prosecuted on three counts; and on the two counts arising out of his broadcasting and the preparation of leaflets for a propaganda branch of the S.S. he was found guilty, but on the third indictment, arising out of his activities in Colditz, he was found not guilty. He was sentenced to death, and returned to Wandsworth Jail, where William Joyce was awaiting his execution, and was put in another condemned cell; but hardly noticed it, being rapt in a new interest. The police like no crime less than blackmail, which indeed is the iciest sin, far further from love than murder. As soon as they had Purdy's case well under way they prosecuted the typist who had betrayed him for demanding money from him with threats. Immediately Purdy became inflamed with a desire to give evidence in her favour. It seemed mean of the girl to deny him his last opportunity for an exhibitionist display by pleading guilty; but that she did, at a trial where a kindly judge, realizing that she was a satellite caught in the extraordinary orbit of a fated person, gave her a sermon and bound her over. It is probable that this frustration clouded Purdy's satisfaction when, after his appeal had been rejected, he was reprieved. There were two considerations which made this reprieve inevitable. He had been acquitted of the one charge out of the three which was really serious enough to merit death; and everybody who had been able to form any impression of him, including the lawyers, who had been fascinated by the bright, mad ability he had shown throughout his trial, was of the opinion that if he could not be certified insane, as he certainly could not have been, it was only because his brand of disorder was peculiar to himself and therefore could not fall into a recognized category of madness. It is distressing to think of this unhappy creature, whose only law was activity, who was an existentialist without knowing it, condemned to the numbness of life imprisonment.

One of the most curious features of this curious case was the enormous number of Germans with whom this odd but unimportant person was in contact. It had taken an elaborate machine and a welfare officer and a Foreign Office official (*Gruderführer*) and William Joyce to recruit him. Once he was inside the system he received the attentions of an army of men, often with titles that indicated the holder of a University degree—Dr. Springbern, Dr. Kurt Eggers, Dr. Menzel, Dr. Ziegfeld, Dr. Adann, Dr. Heferkorn, Dr. Minzel, Dr. Wansche, Major Heimpel. These persons, who were presumably highly trained and maintained by the German government at considerable expense, spent a great amount of time and energy on interviews and correspondence with this uneducated and ill-balanced person, and at least two S.S. agents (including one bearing the delightful name of Herr Wockenfuss, Mr. Distaff-foot) seem to have followed him about

for long periods. The net return for this expenditure was some
unimportant information about a tunnel in a prisoner-of-war
camp—as most escaped prisoners were caught after a few days of
liberty—some even less important information about a wireless
set, and some information about John Henry Owen Brown,
which would have been important had they not disbelieved it;
and a number of broadcasts of the familiar and ill-advised type:
"Next time you travel by train or bus and one of your companions
is obviously a Jew, I want you to observe his actions. You can
hardly mistake their dominant characteristics—their coarse,
greasy hair, their greasy foreheads, their negroid lips—but their
actions betray their race more than their appearance," and so on.
It is, moreover, more than likely that Purdy did not even com-
pose these broadcasts, but received them from Joyce and read
them.

It is hard to avoid suspecting that the organization of British
treachery had become a racket, and that a number of Germans
were exploiting it to find themselves easy and remunerative jobs
at a safe distance from the front. It is hard to avoid suspecting
also that German administration was not highly efficient. With all
this wealth of personnel it was discreditable that a villa used by
the German Foreign Office for its agents should have been
searched, not by one English spy, but by four English spies, who
sat on the floor round the wastepaper basket and read its contents at leisure. This state of affairs must have disgusted William
Joyce, with his pride in his brisk competence. He must have
found his office abhorrent to his sense of order and his hope of
victory. It was true that the colonel's daughter, whom he had
always disliked, had, after sitting about the Concordia Bureau
for some years knitting in a sullen manner, made her departure.
She had gathered her tattered integrity about her, sold all she
could lay her hands on to pay back to the Germans every mark
they had ever paid her, and had swept off into a concentration
camp, from which she was to emerge, at the end of the war, into
twelve months of prison and such subsequent exclusion from the
society of her kind, such bleakness and hopelessness, that one may
count her as having paid her bill.

It was true, too, that William Joyce probably had at this time a
bit of his own sort of fun. The Concordia Bureau was responsible

for providing broadcasters for what was known as the New British Broadcasting Station: a station which pretended to its listeners that it was operating on British soil. Mr. Leonard Banning, with a duplicity which would never have been suspected in one of his idealist demeanour, frequently tried to convince British listeners of this by assuming a Cockney accent and a wheeze in which he breathed, "You'll probably 'ear us tomorrow night at the same hour, but it's getting 'ard, the police are always on our 'eels nowadyes." It is unfortunately not open to us British to laugh at this ridiculous enterprise, since we engaged in similar follies. They are objectionable in principle, if only for their effect on the nationals of the power which broadcasts. Either they detect the fraud and distrust their own government, particularly in its handling of the radio; or they do not detect the fraud, and believe that there are sympathetic and constructive parties in the country they are fighting which in fact do not exist. These enterprises are objectionable also in practice: the broadcasters who have been told to disregard our common obligation to tell the truth are apt to feel that this implies the disregard of all other moral obligations, and it is conceivable that in the end there may be sent over the air such nasty fantasies as broadcasts purporting to come from microphones secretly installed in the bedroom of an enemy leader who is raping a girl. The proceedings of the New British Broadcasting Station were for the most part merely pitiful. But it presented one feature which was highly offensive on religious grounds, though not so offensive as the broadcasts which were simultaneously being emitted from the Irish station in Berlin. There educated men, some of them writers of standing, simpered pietistic sentiments combined with carneying praises of the regime which had murdered and was still torturing millions of their fellow-Catholics in Poland. Still it was fairly offensive that a speaker who called himself "Father Donovan," but who was obviously not a priest, since his chorus-boy falsetto would have led to his rejection by the broadest-minded seminary, delivered mock sermons in which he spooned out sanctimonious references to the mysteries of the Roman Catholic faith. "Father Donovan" was in fact a seaman in his late twenties called Reginald Arthur Humphries, who had been serving in *H.M.S. Royal Arthur* when he was taken prisoner; and the dirty, sniggering joy he took in his impersonation made him one of the most unpleasant yet one of the most infantile of the traitors. But those who listened to him often soon became conscious of something in his broadcasts which was apart from him and less crudely unlikeable. The substance of his talks was quite different in spirit from their delivery. They might have been written by someone who had suffered in childhood from having to listen to a great many bad sermons by Irish priests of inferior type, and was now privately getting his own back on them by seeing how easily he could produce the same stuff himself, and who found an intellectual pleasure in seeing just how far he could go in reproducing the sickly nonsense at its worst without crossing the line into obvious parody. In view of Joyce's attitude to the religion of his parents it is very probable that the talks of "Father Donovan" represent the only real fling his harsh sense of humour was allowed to enjoy during these dolorous years.

There was no end to their dolours. The staff he was given became more and more terrible. It was bound to be poorer than the staff of Germans whom the B.B.C. employed to broadcast on its German service, for we could draw on an army of refugees who were many of them men noteworthy in both character and intellect and who understood the case against fascism; but the Germans need not have given Joyce the really extraordinary subordinates with whom he was burdened. Purdy was only an extreme example of their general undesirability. A fair sample were the two broadcasters who were sent him from the Channel Islands. One was an eccentric and passionate Salvation Army officer who, knowing either less or more about Eva Braun than we do, believed that the personal purity of Hitler was about to redeem the sinful world. The other was a young and beautiful school-teacher whose philosophy was very different. This unhappy girl, a stepchild who had never got on with her family, had fallen in love with a German officer during the occupation of Jersey. For three years she had worked for German contractors who were erecting military and naval establishments on the island, and when her lover was ordered to Germany in 1943 she accepted his offer to take her with him. When she got to Berlin her lover, who seems to have been as thrifty as he was libidinous, found her a post in the Rundfunk. As she had discovered that he was on excellent terms with his wife, from whom she had expected him to get a divorce, with the view of marrying her, she started work in no cheerful state of mind, and as the shadows deepened over Germany she became more and more lugubrious.

So too did Mr. Banning. His life had not been without some causes for brightness. He had written a novel with a Fascist-cum-pacifist message, representing the Nazis as comely young men devoted to athletics who would never have thought of fighting if the uncomely and unathletic democracies had not forced war on them. This novel was published by the Nazis, who distributed it widely in prisoner-of-war camps and in neutral countries. It is doubtful whether any work by Mr. Banning would have found an enthusiastic publisher in any other circumstance than this convulsion of history. Mr. Banning might have said, like Peer Gynt when God marooned him on a desert shore because his yacht was going to be blown up, "God is thoughtful—but economical, that he isn't." He had also formed a beautiful friendship with an American cabaret dancer named Frances who had been caught in Germany with a troupe at the time of Pearl Harbor: a lustrous creature on the turn of twenty, with chestnut-gold hair, and a complexion like an advertiser's allegation, and legs that surprised because they were still better than perfect, and an air of slight (and not unlovable) disorder about her appearance which revealed her as the girl, to be found in every travelling show, whose stage clothes (and hers alone) get left behind in St. Louis. They met while attending the American Church in Berlin; and after some time he helped her to get back to America under an exchange scheme. But these two sources of satisfaction cannot have outweighed the factors in the situation which must have distressed Mr. Banning.

He was having a worse and worse time at the hands of the Nazi head of the Bureau, Dr. Hexler, the inflamed and frantic bully. At his trials he tried to make capital out of these attacks, and to represent them as disputes in which he defied Dr. Hexler as a representative of the Nazi tyranny and defended the interests of the Allies. But it was not successful. Mr. Banning's lawyer questioned the exhausted and hopeless anti-Nazi who had come to give evidence for his client on this point. "Did you ever see Banning showing signs of disagreement when he was talking with Dr. Hexler?" he asked. "Yes," said the anti-Nazi, "I saw sometimes that while he was talking to Dr. Hexler he was tapping on the desk." "You mean, don't you," said Mr. Banning's lawyer hopefully, "that he was beating the desk—hitting it?" "No," said the anti-Nazi, thoughtfully, "he was tapping on the desk with a pencil." From this disconcerting answer Mr. Banning's lawyer rushed on to his next question: "And when did this happen?" The anti-Nazi replied with the same deadly thoughtfulness and conscientiousness, "In the autumn of 1944 and the spring of 1945." That was too late.

The other German witness who appeared for Mr. Banning was of a very different type, but did him no more good. He had originally been a journalist. He was not an anti-Nazi, and he had served in the German Foreign Office since the year after Hitler's accession to power. He was not an attractive person, and, indeed, though he cannot have been a Jew, possessed all the features mentioned in Mr. Purdy's broadcast on the physical characteristics of Jews. Yet he recalled that well-known Gentile figure, the Vicar of Bray. He had worked for the Nazis; doubtless he had worked for the Weimar Republic; now he was working for the Allied Control Commission; if and when the next atomic bomb bursts over Europe, he will be found standing a safe distance behind the people who let it off. But with all this adaptability there was a failure to understand what one would have thought so obvious that it would have to be grasped as part of the prolegomena to adaptability. Mr. Banning had claimed that he had broadcast a great deal of pro-British propaganda over the German radio, and the prosecuting counsel had thrown some doubt on the probability of this. So Mr. Banning's lawyer asked this German Foreign Office official whether he thought this contention could be true. With a broad explanatory smile, as of one who is only to show the ignorant how the works go round, he answered that of course what Mr. Banning had said was true, for it had at first been Dr. Goebbels' policy to send out propaganda that would please and conciliate the British. It did not occur to him that an English court would like Mr. Banning no better for having been an instrument of Dr. Goebbels. But if he did nothing for the defence he opened a peephole on history.

The troubles of the Concordia Bureau were not merely internal. Though Baillie-Stewart and a small staff worked for the German

Foreign Office, the Concordia Bureau was a part of Goebbels' Propaganda Office, which was the hated rival of the German Foreign Office. The primary cause of the rivalry between these Ministries was the fact that the Propaganda Office was a Nazi creation and the German Foreign Office was full of Junker stuff whose roots had not been torn up during the Weimar Republic because they had been too deeply planted in the soil of Germany under the Hohenzollerns. The rivalry had deteriorated, as all else in German life, and had become something very like a struggle between two gangs to get the bigger share of loot in a "protected" area. Perhaps because of simple departmental jealousy, and perhaps because of the large number of jobs connected with the Concordia Bureau, the Foreign Office took more and more interest in the Bureau as the war went on; and hence Mr. Banning was able in 1944 and 1945 to appeal to the German Foreign Office for protection. When Dr. Hexler threatened to send him to a concentration camp he made such an appeal, and the people who intervened and saved his life—for it appears that Dr. Hexler was by then so maniacal that he designed the extremest persecution of this insignificant little man—were the same people who were concerned in the attempt on Hitler's life in July 1944. This was apparently the group that struggled to take control of the Concordia Bureau out of Goebbels' hands. The Foreign Office official who gave evidence for Banning stated with considerable emphasis that he knew him to be personally acquainted with the Foreign Office members of this group. Plainly he spoke from within the orbit of this conspiracy; his words built up the event before his hearers and reminded them that it had really happened, it had not merely been something printed in a newspaper, and gave it the maculate quality of reality. Some of the conspirators, of course, had been earnestly desirous of killing Hitler because they were sickened by his evil life, and they, poor souls, had certainly had their heads chopped off. But there were others. Some had had no time to waste on moral judgments but had been anxious to go on living and had struck at the hands that were dragging them down to death, and no doubt they too, careless through urgency, had not been lucky with their necks. Others again were simply rats that intended to leave the sinking ship. They, having all their wits about them, could save their lives; and could use their length of days to claim what crowns of glory are the portion of their departed fellows.

7

PERHAPS William Joyce had some contact also with this group. There is as yet no evidence available and, as under this bloody regime wise men must have made it a rule never to write anything down that can be memorized, no evidence may exist. So we cannot know the truth. But since Joyce had been unfaithful to all those dear to him, and was striking with demented hands at his devotion to his beloved wife, it is possible that he felt a need to be constant to someone, so meant not to break faith with Hitler. On the other hand, people repeat their actions over and over again. He had accepted Sir Oswald Mosley and had come to despise him and had parted from him. The presumption is that he would accept Hitler and come to despise him and part from him. Perhaps, his need for fidelity exactly balancing his need for infidelity, the nihilist sat still, his happiness exactly balancing his unhappiness. That is the state, supremely appropriate to his essence, which would have been provoked in him by a powerful stimulus; and he must have received the most powerful stimulus conceivable, a blow in his solar plexus, during the year following October 1942, when John Amery came to Berlin. That arrival must have assaulted Joyce in the areas of his greatest sensitivity: in his race feelings, in his class feelings, in his family feelings, in his intellectual pride, in his ambition, which must now have been asking itself if it was ever to mount the throne it had been promised, in his instinct for self-preservation.

John Amery was the worthless son of a distinguished Englishman, Leopold Amery, who had several times sat in Conservative cabinets and was liked as well as respected for a zest in life that had sent him, though small in stature, all over the world and up every mountain he could find time to visit, right on to his seventies. This son had packed into thirty years every kind of folly and dissipation. When he was twenty-four, in 1937, he was declared bankrupt, and left England. Thereafter he lived abroad, partly on an allowance sent him by his parents and partly on the proceeds of a gun-running business he conducted on behalf of Franco, smuggling arms over the Spanish border with the connivance of the French ex-Communists Doriot and Déat, who, like many of their kind at that date, had become Fascists. When the war broke out he remained on the Continent, still travelling between Paris and Madrid, and it is believed that the traffic which he carried on then took a reverse direction and that his Cagoulard friends now received support from Franco. It is useless conceiving him as either a mercenary trafficker or a sincere Fascist. He was another Purdy, but was at once more intellectual and more confused, and had a good many years of addling dissipation behind him. At the fall of France he fled to the South of France; but the Vichy government, which was trying to preserve its credit with the French people by dissociating itself so far as possible from the frankly pro-German Cagoulards, and which was irritated on its prudish side by his habits, treated him as an unwelcome guest. Its distaste for him increased, and at the end of 1941 it put him in prison for eighteen days and released him on condition he live in the mountainous district round Grenoble. He was at the time, so those that saw him say, very drunken, very bored with the provincial life to which he was thus restricted, and in need of money. It is not surprising, therefore, that he offered his services to the Italians, who never answered his letter, and then to the Finns, engaged at that time in an anti-Soviet war, who declined them. But the local German armistice chief, Graf Ceschi, took him under his protection. Amery said that this association was not altogether of his seeking, that the overtures came from the Graf, and in view of what happened this is not incredible. In the autumn of 1942, a German officer took him and his French mistress to Berlin. There they were received by a Dr. Hesse, who belonged neither to the German Foreign Office nor to the Propaganda Office, but to Hitler's personal staff. Thereafter, for a period of several months, John Amery was the most petted and best advertised English propagandist that had ever been put on the German radio. Immense trouble was taken to draw the world's attention to his broadcasts, which were repeated several times in an evening on one particular night in the week. He was given luxurious hotel accommodation, with a heavy expense account. He was sent all over Europe to address camps and give interviews to the local press and was photographed and filmed as if he were from Hollywood.

When Amery was tried for high treason there were eight counts against him in the indictment. In Joyce's indictment against Amery there were four. First, Amery was an Englishman, and the conflict between England and Ireland had never quite resolved itself in Joyce's mind. He adored the English, he had fought for them as a boy, or had at least performed some services which he thought of as fighting for them, and he genuinely believed that as a Fascist he was labouring to confer benefits on England. All the same it was to England that he had come as a boy and had been sniggered at as a queer little bog-trotter with a brogue, it was in England that he had been denied the power and position which he felt to be his right by virtue of his intellect; and ancient hatreds, however much they may be adulterated, often return under stress to their first purity. When William Joyce cursed the raiders who were bombing Berlin, he cursed them as an Irishman cursing the English. Now here an Englishman had come, late in the day, and was put ahead of those who had been drudging in exile for years. Second, Amery was a gentleman. He had been born on the imperial side of the river Thames, heir to every advantage for which William Joyce had craved, and he had thrown away all of them that were not physically ingrained; and his retention of these must have been a cut on the raw to Joyce. His voice was charming, it told of a secure home built on a tradition of ease, of the right school. Any listener would accept it as a certificate that this man belonged of right to the places of power, though the life he had lived had annulled that certificate again and again. To Joyce, who could not open his mouth without betraying that he had been born of the people and reared amongst them and had tried frantically to annul that destiny, Amery's voice must have been a soft pleasant taunt. It is an indication of Joyce's sensitivity on this point that when he was granted a German military passport in 1944 he described his father, who had been first a contractor and builder and then a grocer, as an architect.

Amery's life, too, was a third cause for uneasiness in Joyce.

Few could meet Amery without wishing that their own lives had kept closer to the pattern prescribed by society, so obvious was it that his departures from it had brought on himself a soft, rotten debasement and on those who loved him deep and humiliating pain. William Joyce had had trouble but it was not this; and it is the way of a guilty conscience to insist on the gulf that yawns between the offence which burdens it and other people's offences, which are always far more gross. And, indeed, he had the right to despise Amery, for, though he liked a glass of whisky at a party as much as the next man, he kept himself hard as nails for his work, and paid his debts. And, fourth, his intellectual superiority to Amery must have stung him. He had, as the broadcasts he composed towards the end of the war disclosed, a limited and avid mind of great ability, which he had cultivated to the satisfaction of London University. Words flowed from Amery's mouth in the conventional groupings of English culture, but he had no mind, only a vacancy round which there rolled a snowball of Fascist chatter picked up from Doriot and Déat. Yet here he was, installed in a suite at the Kaiserhof, while Joyce had only a flat in the suburbs, with an unlimited expense account which meant opulence compared to Joyce's unimpressive salary; and here was the German radio cupping its hands round its mouth and shouting to the whole world that it must listen to Amery's broadcasts, though they could have no propaganda value whatsoever. That he was an excellent broadcaster, that the radio, which is one of the greatest liars in the world, transformed him into a pure and eager boy, burning with sincere indignation at the moral evils of Bolshevism, was beside the point. He was known to every newspaper reader in England as the problem child of distinguished parents, who had made countless appearances in the police courts, and the sole result of putting him on the air would be to make English listeners feel sympathy with his family and a reiterated conviction that the Germans were terrible cads. Worse still as propaganda was Amery's project, known at first as the Legion of St. George. This was a body to be drawn from British prisoners of war who were to fight alongside the Germans against the Russians to save Europe from Bolshevism. This was enough to make the former director of Mosley's propaganda squirm in his seat. None knew better than he did what chance there was of raising such a legion. He knew that only a sprinkling would join and that these would be mad or bad. He knew also that a recruiting campaign conducted by John Amery, accompanied by a female companion whose appearance would be interpreted by the ordinary soldier as a call to the joys of peace rather than to the tasks of war, would make English treachery a laughing-stock; and traitors have their pride like other people. It must have seemed to him that the Germans had been stricken with the densest conceivable stupidity, and that they could never gain the victory which was necessary if he were ever to realize his ambitions, or even—though perhaps he did not push his mind so far—if he were to save his life.

Yet German propaganda was perhaps never less stupid than in the exploitation of John Amery. For propaganda has many uses beyond persuasion. Sometimes it aims at throwing up a smoke-screen. What it aimed at in this case can be deduced from the character of Amery's gospel, considered in conjunction with the date. Though Amery's speeches held a few drops of anti-Semitic poison, his real preoccupation was hatred of Russia and communism. He made it a condition that the Legion of St. George should be regarded as an exclusively anti-Bolshevist force, and should be used only on the Russian front; and there exists a leaflet, issued after his concern with the body had ceased, but expressing his views, which runs:

We are fighting with the best of Europe's youth to preserve our European civilization and our common cultural heritage from the menace of Jewish Communism. MAKE NO MISTAKE ABOUT IT! Europe includes England. Should Soviet Russia ever overcome Germany and the other European countries fighting with her, nothing on this earth would save the Continent from Communism, and our own country would inevitably sooner or later succumb. We are British. We love England and all it stands for. Most of us have fought on the battlefields of France, of Libya, Greece, in Italy, and many of our best comrades in arms are lying there—sacrificed in this war of Jewish revenge. We felt then we were being lied to and betrayed. Now we know it for certain. This conflict between England and Germany is racial SUICIDE. We must UNITE and take up arms against the common enemy. We ask you to come into

our ranks and fight shoulder to shoulder with us for Europe and for
England.

Now, in the autumn of 1942 the Germans were beginning to
feel nervous. It had appeared from the end of August that the
situation in North Africa might not end their way, for Rommel's
great defensive had been halted, and that because of his lack of aircraft. The Allies' air attacks on Germany were becoming more
and more formidable. The Japanese were not doing so well as had
been hoped. Germany was not certain that it was beaten, but then
again it was not certain that it was going to win; so it formed the
idea that it had better sacrifice some of its ambitions and get rid
of some of its liabilities. If it could stop the war with Russia which
it had so rashly initiated in 1941 it would have its energies free
to fight Great Britain and the United States. But if it was to start
peace negotiations with Russia these must be kept secret, for two
reasons. One was that if Great Britain and the United States heard
of them they might use argument and force to dissuade their
ally from the proposed desertion; and the other that, even if they
failed, they would surely cut off the stream of supplies which they
were sending out to their ally, and which would form a useful
addition to Germany's armaments if they went on to the last
moment and were taken over by her when she again joined forces
with Russia. It might throw dust in the eyes of Great Britain and
the United States if, just at the time when these secret negotiations
were opened, the Germans started a new anti-Bolshevik campaign.
They made their first overtures to Moscow; and John Amery was
fetched out of his retreat in Savoy in October 1942, and broadcast
during the first part of 1943 and began his recruiting tour of the
camps. Nobody could have drawn such widespread attention to
an anti-Bolshevik campaign. If William Joyce or Baillie-Stewart
had made these broadcasts and gone on that recruiting tour, not
a soul would have taken the slightest notice. It was the unique
and fatal distinction of John Amery to be the one person out of
the earth's population who could serve the German purpose;
and the Nazis did not mind looking fools so long as they
could create the impression that they were still actively anti-
Bolshevik.

It is to be remarked that from the middle of 1943 the fortunes

of John Amery suffered a marked decline. The negotiations between Germany and Russia had broken down. He was no longer
welcome in Berlin; and when he lost most of his personal belong-
ings in one of the famous raids which, on every night between the
22nd and the 26th of November, 1943, assailed Berlin, he was
awarded a decoration for exceptional bravery and packed off to
Paris. From there he was sometimes sent to the occupied countries,
such as Norway, Belgium, Czechoslovakia, and Yugoslavia, out of
sheer nastiness: to prove that the British were degenerate, that a
leading British statesman could have a son who betrayed his country and hiccoughed as he did it. Soon they stopped letting him do
even that, and in September 1944, with savage and indecent irony,
they sent him down next to act as confidant to Mussolini, now at
liberty and a poor figure of fun after his undignified rescue from
Allied hands. "Enter Tilburina, mad, in white satin, and her confidant, mad, in white linen." What is the sin against the Holy
Ghost? It is perhaps to deal with people as if they were things:
to pick them up and set them down, without respect for their
uniqueness, for their own wills.

In Germany, William Joyce sat and waited for the end. He
moved about; most often he was in Berlin, but sometimes he was
in Eupen and at Luxemburg, at the end he was in Hamburg;
but always there was over him the same sky, the Mitteleuropische
sky, which is clearer than the English sky and is not loaded with
its dreary fogs, but has its own nocuments, which are madness and
defeat. He was involved for the last year or so in the aftermath of
the unfortunate harvest of Amery's brain, the Legion of St.
George, known as the British Free Corps. After Amery had been
ejected from Berlin, having served the Nazi purpose, the Legion
had been handed over to the S.S., and its name had been changed
to the British Free Corps, and its recruits either were drawn from
Joyce's broadcasters or broadcast for him afterwards. It is always
surprising when rhetoric, emptyish at the time when it was
written, becomes a precise statement of fact. Fifty years ago or so
Rudyard Kipling wrote a poem that was perhaps extreme in its
excitement over its subject, which was "gentlemen rankers," the
men of the upper and middle classes who volunteered to serve in
the British army as private soldiers, and seemed most otiose in the
stanza that ran:

We have done with Hope and Honour, we are lost to Love and Truth,
  We are dropping down the ladder rung by rung;
And the measure of our torment is the measure of our youth,
  God help us, for we knew the worst too young.[1]

But those lines give a fair enough factual account of the British
Free Corps. They had done with hope and honour. They had all
left their camps after being warned by their senior officers that they
were taking a step which would cut them off from the society of
their own kind, and passed into a state of degradation which
made it inevitable that society would carry out its threat, not
from nursed intention but as a result of the natural recoil from
something that stinks. The Germans had, of course, far too much
sense to keep on with the Legion because they thought they could
raise enough men to form a fighting unit for use on the Russian
front, or anywhere else. They wanted them for quite another purpose. They put these men in villas in various pleasant parts of
Germany, and dressed them in German uniforms with flashes with
the letters B.F.C. and the Union Jack to show that the wearers
were British soldiers, and let them go rotten with idleness and
indiscipline and debauchery. Their victims did a little drill and
learned German, and, as one of them said, "otherwise did nothing
except lay around, and go into the town, where we drank and associated with women." There were never many of them. It appears
that of the hundreds of thousands of prisoners of war in Germany
only thirty-odd volunteered for the corps. But even so small a
number, split into groups and sent into the German towns,
drunken and with prostitutes on their arms, did something to
raise national morale in 1944 and 1945 and persuade the Germans that it was all true, what they had been told, and that they
could not possibly be conquered by those degenerate people the
British.

It was unsentimental truth that most of the B.F.C. had known
the worst too young. One had been a prisoner for two and a half
years since, as a boy of fourteen, he had been taken off a torpedoed
British ship by a German submarine. Another had given a false
age when he volunteered for the army in 1941, and was just
seventeen when he was captured in Italy. The one believed that

[1] *Barrack-Room Ballads.* Doubleday.

John Amery was Foreign Minister of Great Britain and had somehow been ejected from his country and was being kindly assisted to
regain his rights by the Germans; the other accepted an assurance
that the British Free Corps was six divisions strong. Some were
young and, moreover, had been troubled even before the war had
begun. Such was Ronald David, a black-browed young gipsy who
faced life with the mask of the romantic rebel: his sullen darkness at once defied society and confessed unassuageable sorrow because it had rebuffed him. He had been born in New South Wales,
was left an orphan at three weeks old, and was then adopted by an
unmarried woman too elderly for the task of rearing a boy into
adolescence. When he got into his teens he made more than one
appearance in the juvenile courts; and when he was seventeen he
went to sea. Six months later his ship was captured by the German
raider *Admiral Scheer*, and for a long time he travelled in her
under hatches, from ocean to ocean, in heat and hunger. Eventually he was landed at Bordeaux and went from camp to camp,
not settling down anywhere till he was about nineteen. Then he
stayed in one camp for some time and was seduced by a German
girl named Annaliese Muller, who worked in the camp censorship
office and who was greatly loved by him. It was his story that the
German Security officers discovered them sleeping together and
threatened to have them sent to concentration camps unless he
joined the British Free Corps. This is probably true. The Germans
certainly arranged for such seductions as a basis for blackmail; the
girls were usually privy to their intentions, but the men very rarely
suspected this. But they did not apply this form of blackmail
except to men they thought good subjects for corruption, by reason of lechery or rare compulsive thirst or sourness of disposition.
It was characteristic of this prisoner that he made an open avowal
of his intention of joining the British Free Corps to his fellow-
prisoners, quite unnecessarily, and had to be shut up in a cell for
his own protection.

Some there were who were in such deep trouble before the war
that they had stayed young when they were not. There was poor
Herbert George, who, though of medium height, had the look of
a Disney dwarf. His deeply lined skin was puckered into thin
folds in the apprehensive expression of a chimpanzee, and his
features so far departed from the normal that those who met him

found themselves looking back again and again to see if they could be as they were remembered, though the total impression was by no means monstrous, merely animal and odd. He was thirty-five, but his life had passed like a flash, too full of trouble to allow maturity to come to him. The Sheerness police court had been the theatre of his woes. Once a chicken had been stolen; then a gas-meter slot had been opened and emptied; once someone had missed a shirt and scarf. It was too much, it was really too much, flesh and blood couldn't stand the worry. On an astonishing occasion he attempted to defy the canon which Hamlet erroneously believed the Everlasting had fixed against self-slaughter. When he had served the mild punishment inflicted on him for that offence, he enlisted in the army, but was discharged as daft. This was, however, only the beginning of a military career which was to be, in the strictest sense of the word, unique. For he had always been interested in politics, and when the Spanish Civil War broke out, he volunteered to serve in the International Brigade and actually fought in Spain. He soon deserted; but the incident was purged of the sordid by the candour with which, having crossed the Pyrenees and reached the Channel on foot, he sought the London offices of the International Brigade and reported as a deserter. He then went to sea, as he had done at intervals all his life, and continued as a sailor after the war broke out. In 1940 he was an oiler on a steamer that was torpedoed off Narvik, and was in one camp and another until 1944, when he received a letter from his mother saying that his wife had just gone to hospital to have a baby. After thinking over this for a long time he decided that it could not be his baby, and was deeply distressed, and when, at about the same time, two merchant seamen who had joined the British Free Corps came to enrol recruits, he enlisted, just as a sad little dog, finding himself far from home in streets where they throw things, with rain falling and the dusk thickening, will follow any passer-by.

Such poor silly souls were easy to soak in liquor; and they all, even Herbert George, who was not obviously attractive, found obliging German girls. In that they did not differ from those among them who were not so young and who knew quite well what they were doing. Six of these, who were known as the Big Six, definitely professed some enthusiasm for the aims of the

British Free Corps; and of these, some were well-educated. One, the son of a Lithuanian merchant settled in England, had been at an English public school. It was surprising that he should have got into the British Free Corps, for he was a Jew, certainly on his father's side. He may not have known this, for he had been brought up out of contact with his father's family and had early gone to the Colonies; but the Germans must have known it if any intelligent officer had examined his papers. It is possible, however, that by this time the Germans were handling the British Free Corps in a spirit of such profound cynicism that they were willing to overlook their racial theories. In this group, though it had some intellectual pretences, there are few traces of the waking of the ideological forces that might have been expected. The Lithuanian had joined because he was distraught and activist at the same time that he was pessimistic and melancholy, and he wanted to find himself a niche in the international society which he thought would be erected after the inevitable defeat of the Allies. One of the Big Six, Francis McLardy, a qualified pharmacist, had been a member of the British Union of Fascists from 1934 to 1938, but this could not be regarded as the sole factor which had brought him into the British Free Corps, though it might have been the determining one. He had been a sergeant in the R.A.M.C. and, being captured at Dunkirk, was sent to work in a prisoner-of-war hospital in Poland. There he was caught breaking a rule, and was told that he was to be sent to the worst camp in Poland, which was famous for its abominations. There was a rumour that the starved prisoners fell on the bodies of their comrades that dropped dead and tore out their livers, their kidneys, and the soft part of the thigh, and ate them. An American prisoner who was found in the camp when it was liberated has testified that this in fact happened, though that not many people could bring themselves to do it because the bodies were so lousy. To avoid being sent to this camp, McLardy wrote to the authorities and expressed that he wanted to join the Waffen S.S. and fight the Russians. That he was moved by the desire to save himself from this hell cannot be regarded as a valid excuse, for thousands of men, finding themselves in the same position, chose to suffer the pains of that hell rather than serve the men who made it.

It is possible that McLardy's failure to reach their standard was due to the sympathy with the architects of such hells which he had been taught by B.U.F. If that is so, it was the most direct influence exerted by Mosley on the proceedings of the traitors in Germany. The other adherents of the B.U.F. who appeared among them had lapsed from membership some time before the beginning of the war, and their cases prove nothing except that silly young men were apt to join the B.U.F. in some circumstances and in others were apt to become traitors. Neither here nor in any other theatre of war was there proof that the British Fascists had issued instructions to any member of the armed forces during the war. A private in the Royal Army Service Corps named Theodore John William Schurch, of Swiss origin, who was hanged two days after Joyce for treachery committed after he had been captured by the Italians at Tobruk, alleged that he had joined the British army in 1936 under instructions from the British Union of Fascists, but if this was true, which was doubtful, those instructions related to a peace-time plan of a certain organization to spread fascism among the forces which certainly existed but seems to have been discontinued during the war.

The most obvious trace of ideological action in the camp was furnished by two priggish little negativists named Denis John and Eric Reginald. In a dingy street in North London there is a baker's shop which cheers the eye by its clean and bright and not inexpensive window-fittings, and by its well-stocked shelves, which are neatly arranged with as attractive cakes and buns and breads and gingerbreads as anybody could hope to take out of an oven in these days. The owner, a stoutish middle-aged man, serves in his shop, and from early morning to late evening is either there or in the other shop in another part of the suburb which his thrift has purchased. He has his own quiet distinction, and has, as his most remarkable physical feature, watchet-blue eyes. He is the son of a German who came to England with his young bride in the last quarter of the last century, worked as a baker's assistant, bought his own bakery, became a naturalized British citizen, and died and was buried in London. When the First World War came, his son, who had been born a British citizen, fought against the Germans, and on his return married an Englishwoman. Their son, Denis John, inherited his father's eyes and slight but real difference from the run of the mill, developed in much less favourable circumstances. His parents' marriage was not a success; and it is to be remarked that most of the members of the British Free Corps came from broken homes. The baker and his wife separated when the boy was seven years old, and thereafter he was brought up by his German grandmother, who lived in London but took him to Germany every year and finally sent him to school there. At sixteen he went home to be instructed by his father in the mystery of their family craft; but difficulties arose, partly because of the unfortunate domestic situation and partly because Denis John had grown attractive in a way which was not of much use to him. He was a Lohengrin or a Siegfried, with clear-cut features and waves of golden hair of the kind that shines as brilliantly and keeps as distinct as so much golden wire. Since Ophelia told us that the owl was a baker's daughter, it is not surprising that about Denis John, the baker's son, there was something of an owl; a lustrous, extravagantly blond owl.

He now drew to himself the attentions of some young men, born in circumstances superior to his own, who from the first, according to his family's friends, did him no good. When the time drew near when he should register for military service he felt a natural reluctance to fight against Germany, which, strangely enough, he, a German's grandson, knew and loved better than his father, who was a German's son. If he had gone to the proper authorities they would have explained to him the means by which people in his position could appeal for exemption from military service as conscientious objectors. But some of his new friends were connected with that ambiguous organization the Peace Pledge Union, which in the name of peace was performing many actions certain to benefit Hitler. They persuaded him to go to the Union's offices and ask for assistance in evading military service, and it was arranged that he should take advantage of a scheme that the Union was running which exported boys not yet of military age to do farm work in the Channel Islands. At no time during this last war or the one before it would the Channel Islands have seemed the safest possible refuge; and Denis John was sent off to Jersey on the 17th of May, 1940, seven days after the Germans had invaded the Low Countries. It is not at all surprising that by August, Denis John was working for the Todt organization, the Nazi sappers; and it cannot possibly have surprised the

Peace Pledge Union. There was not even the sense of a treasonable agreement behind these proceedings. The Germans were not prepared to accept these unhappy children, and Denis John and a number of others were dragged about Europe, from camp to camp, for five years, exposed to every sort of degrading influence, till he and Eric Reginald landed in the British Free Corps. They joined it, apparently, only because the recruiting leaflets had caused an uproar in the English prisoner-of-war camp where they happened to be, and they wished to show how superior they were to the common herd.

When they all gathered together they developed an ideology, but it was strangely different from Naziism. Its perfect exponent was Alfred Vivian, a merchant seaman, a young man in his late twenties, very black of hair and very white of skin, who was plainly fussily clean and came from some clean home. He was not a Fascist and held, he said, no political views, but professed a vague pacifism. "I am a sailor," he said, "and as such have no hate for anybody, including the Germans." He was, in fact, strongly pro-German, and it illustrates the importance of truth in propaganda that he was first led to discredit the case for the Allies because he found when he got to Germany that the accounts of German privations which he had read in the newspapers at home were not true. Also he liked the Germans, and it is to be noted that some Germans showed these unhappy and inglorious men real kindness; the sullen and black-browed Ronald David was taken into one working-class household and given real sympathy and understanding. But the two factors which drew Alfred Vivian were remote from the particular facts of the international situation. The first was that he was a very clean man, proud of his personal appearance, and that in his prisoner-of-war camp he had acquired scabies and other skin diseases, and his transfer to a private house, where he could have baths and have leisure and facilities to apply medical treatment to his boils and blains, was relief from shame. The other was an obsession with rebellion. "In our barracks at Pankow and Hildesheim as well as Dresden we had a photograph displayed on the wall of the Duke of Windsor, whom we all admired as he was also a rebel," he said. "We all recognized him as the King of England. When we had parties, we always toasted the Duke of Windsor." In other words, those members of the British Free Corps who were not falling flat on their faces in the local brothels were engaged in recreating Byronic romanticism. In the security of the eighteenth and the early nineteenth century, Byron tried to reintroduce to the universe the element of wildness of soul which had been drained off it by the attempts of modern man to make religion reasonable, and pretend that God is just according to human standards, by pretending that humanity was completely irrational. These British Free Corps men were in a not dissimilar position. They had been, as prisoners of war, rapt into an isolation from the current activities of their kind compared with which the life of a monk is snarled up with the mundane. This isolation was exaggerated when they joined the B.F.C., for they entered a smaller camp, and it even became a promise of special security, for they had deserted to the side which seemed certain to be victorious. Most of them had renounced religion and thought there was no God; when they found that life was, in spite of their isolation and their security, obstinately intractable, they attempted to deal with the intractability by pretending that it was within themselves. But they sometimes repented of this. Alfred Vivian once wrote, "I now feel thoroughly ashamed of myself. I realize now that I was a rebel and am sorry for everything that happened." So, sometimes, spoke Lord Byron.

But the rest of the British Free Corps went on falling on their faces; and was watched, at short range, with extreme distaste by Mr. Thomas Haller Cooper. This was a young man who had been born in consequence of an international situation. His father, a photographer in one of the least fashionable areas of southwestern London, had been a soldier in the Army of Occupation after the last war and had brought home a German bride, thus rushing forward and impaling himself on the next great international situation. When he was nineteen his mother took him back to Germany, as a woman taking her child to present him at the temple, herself returning to London. The year was 1939. A short time after war broke out he joined the Adolf Hitler Division of the Waffen S.S., and served in Poland, and then in Russia, where he was wounded. When he was convalescent he was recalled to do traitor's work, visiting the English prisoner-of-war camps and talking with the prisoners and giving them corrupting literature, and finally was made an N.C.O. in charge of the British Free

Corps. At first he enjoyed the work, and many of the members of the B.F.C. liked him. There was probably a real geniality, an honest tenderness, between them. Cooper had come from the Eastern Front, the others had come from years of hunger and confinement; they found themselves clean and well-fed, and could exchange tales of woe in what was their native language, his father's tongue, in a good villa that was more than comfortable, that was cosy, among the woods, the sweet aromatic German woods.

Thomas Haller Cooper was beautifully built. He was very tall and slender, with a long supple waist and broad shoulders. He was very neat, with that neatness which means a religious state of mind, a cry to Heaven for approval. His forehead was very high, and his long face, narrowing from high cheekbones to a pointed chin, might fairly be described as coffin-shaped. His sleek seal-brown hair grew in a widow's peak deep down on his forehead, and receded sharply over his temples; he might have been wearing a close-fitting and peculiarly shaped fur cap. His dark eyebrows were very thick, and his mouth large and full, but hard. Many Germans look as he did; and such as do are usually Wendish in origin, descendants of a strayed Slav tribe that have lived in Germany for centuries, isolated from their own kind and interpenetrated with German blood, but remarkable for their special force. And he had the look of many young Germans who became Nazis, whether of his physical type or another: a look of the white-collar man who cannot climb up, because he has no special talent to make his own ladder and society will not let him use its existing ladders, which are reserved for other people. *Spiessbürger* is the German word for it.

It was one of the most remarkable fatuities of German propaganda that this young man was represented to the British prisoners of war as the son of Mr. Duff and Lady Diana Cooper. Enough prisoners of war must have listened to their wives reading aloud items from the gossip columns of the Sunday papers once a week over many years, and, even if they themselves had been studying the football news or "Amateur Gardening" at the time, would have gathered enough to know the only child of the most publicized character of our times was not of military age; and almost all of them would have known that that only child would not have looked or talked like Thomas Haller Cooper. His English was poor and inaccurate; he made such errors as to talk of making an "observance" when he meant an "observation." But his German was rich, accurate, and happy. He had been born and brought up in London, had been to school in London, had been a clerk in London, but his mother had built a Germany around him, he was a German who had never been out of his fatherland. In the material world he had tried to be English. He had a great love of the East and, though he had not a remarkably good record of achievement at school, he had studied Japanese and Chinese; and as he grew into his later teens had tried to find employment in branches of the government service which might take him to the Far East, but was rejected because his mother was a German. His other passion was for order; and he tried to join various police forces, here in England and in the Colonies, but for the same reason he was rejected there also.

This meant frustration for him; but considering what his mother had done to him, the authorities were not unwise. It cannot be put down in black and white how she wove the spell about him, or what the other enchantresses who work the same magic, brew in their cauldrons. The secret does not lie in the promise of conquest; though perhaps the lust for conquest is the price the Germans pay for possession of the sweet secret which, smeared on the eyes of children, makes them care all their lives long for no other sight. That secret is a lyricism which extends the kingdom of the nightingale, diffuses everywhere the perfume of the rose. The home where this man's mother lived was distinguished from all the other red-brick and stucco houses in a shabby suburban street by the wealth of flowering bulbs, jonquil packed beside narcissus, crocus beside grape hyacinth, which crammed the bow-windows of her ground-floor flat. They were not compact growths that florists sell; the uneven flower-spikes and sprawling leaves showed that she herself, the loving amateur, busied herself planting them in fibre and shut them in cupboards while the winter fell. When the spring came they made a truly German window. Loving this lovely Germany, her son joined the S.S., which bled and died that there should be camps where starved prisoners fell

on the bodies of their dead comrades and, if not too disgusted by
the lice, ate their kidneys and livers and the soft parts of their
thighs. This is a great mystery.

He travelled all over Germany with his charges. (It is one of
the curious features of the Nazi regime that it made the German
passion for travelling into a guiding principle of its administration. Prisoners of war, whether loyal or traitors, were moved round
and round and round the country long before the time when they
had to be hustled out of the way of the invading Allies. It is as if
in England we had moved the prisoners we held in the Isle of Man
to the West Highlands, to Wales, to the Isle of Wight, and so on.)
Always the billets were good, comfortable villas with gardens, set
among woods and heaths. The custody of these louts was not the
enterprise Thomas Haller Cooper had foreseen when he was
detailed to it. He kept his sense of superiority by withdrawing into
his favourite and unusual studies. In his room, instead of the
usual portrait of Adolf Hitler, there hung a fine Japanese print.
He had a solemn and sentimental love affair with a respectable
young girl called Gisela, to whom he expounded Oriental philosophy in immense long letters. He was really only a boy. In company he would murmur, as if in absence of mind, such phrases
as "Om Mani Padme Hum," and, on being overheard and questioned as to what they meant, would start and explain that such
phrases were always running through his mind, since he was, as
a matter of fact, a Buddhist. But his boyhood had not been a nice
one. Wishing to impress a member of the British Free Corps, he
boasted, quite untruthfully, that he had come to Germany because
he had, during a street-fight in the East End of London, killed a
Jew and had to get out of England in a hurry. This confession
was unfortunate. The name of his confidant was John Henry
Owen Brown.

But no amount of sitting about in the sun and mooning over
Oriental grammars and writing to Gisela and swapping lies could
reconcile him to the degradation of his charges. He tried to apply
a mild form of S.S. discipline to them, and they mocked at him
and staged a mutiny. That did not frighten Thomas Haller
Cooper. But when D-day came and went, and the gales blew and
did not blow away the invading Allies, and the Atlantic Wall was
as if it never had been, then he was frightened. He said to a mem-

ber of the British Free Corps, "I have been a bloody fool," and announced his intention to work thenceforward for "the other side." Again it was John Henry Owen Brown to whom he spoke. Thereafter this strong and proud young man had to cringe and smirk and flatter in the hope of survival, as it might have been thought that only old men would have to do, poor old men who are past their work and whose children have died before them. He visited prisoners of war and thrust kindnesses on the prisoners under the sceptical eyes of non-commissioned officers, terrible beings, worst when they were little creatures burned up by Indian suns till they had not left in them a scrap of blandness. These looked straight at him and, without speaking, said things about rats that left the sinking ships. But these missions were better than his duties with the non-wits of the British Free Corps, who daily grew more drunken, more desperate, more maudlin amorous in the arms of their whores, themselves daily more desperate. Often they cursed him and flouted his orders; and sometimes he let it pass, because he did not care, it was as if he had never been a willing instrument of Nazi power. But at other times he was prodded in the back by superior authority, which did not yet know whether it was definitely beaten, and which was not certain, if defeat was indeed certain, whether it was not going to die in its jack-boots; because, though it could pull them off and run away, pretending that it had never worn them, it had obeyed orders so long that it would not know where it should run. Everybody's brain was boiling.

Sometimes authority thought that, yes, it would pull its jack-boots off, and left Cooper to do what he would with the British Free Corps. Then he and his louts sat in a kind of vacuum, which slowly filled up with fear. But authority would change its mind and would buzz about Cooper's ears again, and he would disentangle his charges from their weeping whores and insist that they do a little drill, and see that they all kept up the pretence of an imminent dispatch to the Russian front. Sometimes events maddened authority into acts preposterous and tragic in their irony. On the night of February 13, 1945, the British bombed Dresden, in a legitimate attempt to end the war, which was nevertheless so costly that it discredited legitimacy and slaughtered thousands of refugees and turned to rubble one of the fairest cities bequeathed to our time by people possessed of virtues which we lack. The next day exasperated authority turned on the British Free Corps, which had just been brought there to improve German morale by straggling through the streets, alleged that they were in some way responsible, and clapped them all in prison, including that Herbert George who had been in trouble concerning the chicken, the pennies in the gas meter, the shirt and the scarf. At some point in this hubble-bubble, when authority was overcome by panic and felt that it must truckle to everybody, ear was given to the complaints of the British Free Corps against Cooper's attempts to discipline it, and he was sent away. He walked off with a straight back, determined to fight what was to come, down to the last ounce of his pride.

William Joyce now sat in his office, conducting his business with a quiet sacramental order. He had become wholly reconciled to his wife. D-day had been a crushing blow to him. All through his life he had been anxious, with the special anxiety of a very small man, not to make a fool of himself, and the first consequence of such wariness is to refrain from prophecies that may not come true. In his broadcasts he had mocked again and again at the idea of an Allied invasion of the Continent; and they had often been followed by songs, abominable and amusing lyrics coldly and lightly sung, which jeered at the Englishmen who were to lie dead under the Atlantic Wall. William Joyce was to afford, both in his broadcasts and in the programmes of which they formed part, proof that there are no half-measures in treachery; if a man does not love his country enough to concede its right to self-government he will end by not loving it at all, by hating it. Again and again Joyce had spoken with icy approval of murders wrought by the Germans on his fellow-countrymen; he did not feel he had to fear that this might make him unpopular if he returned to Britain, for he would return ringed with arms that would intimidate the British. Then the Atlantic Wall was broken; and it did not matter how much effort it had taken to break it, if it was unsubstantial, then it was unsubstantial as a dream. Henceforward, it was not to be Germans who were to kill Englishmen. There were perhaps to be more Germans killed by Englishmen than Englishmen killed by Germans, perhaps Germany itself was to be killed, perhaps William Joyce himself was to be killed, certainly William Joyce was to be killed. That possibility had always been clear in his mind. "Since I began these broadcasts, I have committed treason every day"; so his book had begun. As a revolutionary he must have known a sort of dry-mouthed staring peace as catastrophe flowed towards him from the east and the west during the first months of 1945. There had been much doing and the fruit of it was to be nothingness; there had been a fulness of life, there was to be an emptiness of death. To this end he had worked since youth, and he would have been disappointed by victory. But that he himself should die must have brought to him the torment that the prospect of death brings to us all. It is no use talking of the death-wish at that stage. We wish for death, but we have developed the faculty of imagination, we have built up the involved structure of our psychic lives, so that we can play out the drama of our life-work and our death-wish in fantasy, and give the death-wish its due of victory without ourselves going down to the tomb.

William Joyce sat in his office and distracted himself by exercises of the intellect. His last broadcasts were, in form, ably and carefully written political essays, much superior to anything he had put out over the air up to that time. In substance they were self-exculpatory. They warned England that she was being ruined by her participation in the war, and, destitute, would have to face a new and insatiable imperialist Russia; and rebuked her for having fought Germany instead of aiding her to fight against the Bolshevization of the world. This was nonsense. The week before Germany had brought England into the field against her by invading Poland she had signed a pact with Russia, and she remained in close friendship with her for the best part of two years; and no intelligent Englishman had wanted his country to go to war with Germany, because none was unaware that, if the price of defeat would be the reign of the Gestapo in England, the price of victory would be the disruption of Europe, and the destruction of its political and economic and intellectual harmony, which is the highest level man has yet attained. It was the horrible and unique achievement of Hitler to force the West to fight the most terrible of wars without the sustenance of faith in victory. So the tired man, night after night, stood in the Hamburg studio of the Rundfunk and warned his fellow-countrymen of a danger which they had always anticipated and which now no longer could be avoided. There came a night when he spoke as if he were either very tired, or drunk, or perhaps both. Then, on April 30, 1945, he made a broadcast in which, speaking slowly and with dignity and obstinacy, he admitted defeat. It ended with the sentences: "Britain's victories are barren; they leave her poor, and they leave her people hungry; they leave her bereft of the markets and the wealth that she possessed six years ago. But, above all, they leave her with an immensely greater problem than she had then. We are nearing the end of one phase in Europe's history, but the next will be no happier. It will be grimmer, harder, and perhaps bloodier. And now I ask you earnestly, can Britain survive? I am profoundly convinced that without German help she cannot." Saying these words, he plainly thought himself a statesman, but he had said nothing that could not be answered with a phrase from an old comedy, "Tu l'as voulu, Georges Dandin!" This was the last time that the insatiable hunger of his voice was to travel over the air. English soldiers came into his office a day later, found it not disordered but empty. He had gone out on his particular path to the end.

8

EACH man took a different path to the end. Little Mr. Banning got through the British lines and smugly reported at the British Embassy in Brussels, representing himself as having been engaged in anti-Nazi work in Berlin and having used his employment in the Concordia Bureau as a cover for doing kindnesses to victims of Nazi persecution. Not then, nor later at the Old Bailey, was he believed. He elected to go into the witness-box and give evidence in support of his plea. Since most of the traitors arrived in England destitute, they had to take advantage of the Poor Prisoners' Defence Act. A lawyer chosen under this act has not the control over his client that a lawyer has who is employed in the usual way, for he cannot tell such a client who disregards his advice to go to the devil and, elsewhere or there, find another lawyer. Hence many of the traitors made the mis-

take of giving evidence on their own behalf. Mr. Banning did
himself no good in the box; for one thing, like many witnesses,
he always cocked his head on one side when he was going to tell
a lie. But he did a great deal of good to another traitor, out on
bail, who attended his case. That traitor, at the preliminary
police-court proceedings, had put up the same standard defence
as Mr. Banning, the same story of having broadcast for the Nazis
in order to do under-cover anti-Nazi work; but, having watched
with a peculiar sick steadiness how Mr. Banning was run up and
down until he dropped under cross-examination, did not persist
in that defence and put in a plea of guilty. This was not the only
person in court who looked at Mr. Banning as at a reflection in
a mirror. He was like an actor playing Mr. Facing-Both-Ways
in a dramatization of *Pilgrim's Progress*. Not one of us in court
but had, of course, at some time or other done all he could to
keep an appointment at which he was to part from delight or
embrace the dreary, yet had not started soon enough for it, and
arrived at his journey's end exclaiming in horror because he was
too late for sacrifice. Not one of us but had performed for a
recondite virtue's sake some action which was both profitable and
open to some superficial moral objection: in other words, we had
done something which was immediately evil on the plea that it
was remotely good. Not one of us but had paid his proper due
of repentance for the lack of forthrightness on these occasions:
that is part of the game. What that game was, was illuminated
with a blinding light by this verbose and inconsequent little man.

This trial, which was painful, was also comic. That was chiefly
the fault of Miss Frances: of the American cabaret dancer whom
he had met at the American Church in Berlin and negotiated out
of Germany under a scheme for the exchange of civilian prisoners. The court looked on her with undisguised pleasure as she
advanced towards the witness-box. In fantasy it raised its tongue
to its palate and gave two sharp clicks. She was a lovely creature.
Her lips and cheeks were brighter than paint because of the
prodigiously healthy blood behind her thin and fine-grained skin;
her chestnut-gold hair had the strong untroubled lustre of an
animal's coat, the springing quality recalled what claims the flesh
can make—and they are many—to superiority over marble. But
she was also comic. For she was simple as puppies are. She was

grieved, as all of us were, at the sight of Mr. Banning in the dock, but it was as a puppy who sees its playmate locked in a kennel, and though a puppy surely suffers, the simplicity of the world it lives in compared with the complexity of the world in which we live makes even its suffering matter for smiles. She was comic, too, by reason of a strangeness in her dress, for she was one of those women who, perhaps because of some childish infatuation with an old photograph, hark back in their appearance to the ideals of a past generation. She had a lot of clothes on. So far as the sales-women had let her she had gone back to the days when Rubye de Reymer wore so wide a hat and so many yards of tucked and frilled chiffon that fifteen ospreys could alight upon her person. Miss Frances had not the ospreys, but their home was ready for them. The spirit of our age, however, cut off all this plenitude at the knee. There the skirt stopped, and it was seen that her lovely legs could have been snapped at the ankle by a cruel finger and thumb.

She would have been well advised, if she wanted to convince the Court, to stand on her head in the witness-box. The ordinary way up she was not a good witness. Her voice flowed past the Judge and jury giving them no more information than if it had been a rivulet of melting ice-cream. From the melodic lure of her voice it could be inferred that she was telling a romantic story of misfortune borne with courage, but the only time she could be heard, an old music-hall jest found itself functioning on the other side of the footlights. She was asked what she was doing in Germany that she needed Mr. Banning's help, and she replied plaintively, "Why, I was in trouble." This phrase in an English female mouth limits the range of her possible predicaments to one. The Court was suddenly sympathetic. But when she cooed on, softly as a distant dove, "Yes, for two years I was in trouble," it showed its relief too cheerfully. But all this did Mr. Banning no good. Her counsel, a handsome and at that moment intensely embarrassed young man, tried in vain to control his witness; but it was as if he were taking a puppy for a walk and had got the leash wound round his legs, and on the bench Mr. Justice Oliver put down his pen and held his reeling head between his hands. In his summing up he referred to Miss Frances, with an almost excessive detachment, in a tone suggesting that the law is a tomb and he was speaking out of it, as "a young lady to whom, I am sure, we would all be glad to be of service, if the occasion arose." Speaking less like a broken man, he went on to point out that Mr. Banning's obedience to what must be a universal inclination to be kind to Miss Frances was no evidence that he had indulged in his traitorous activities as a cover for anti-Nazi activities.

While the jury was considering its verdict she stood in the corridor with the two sad-faced friends of Mr. Banning who had put up bail for him to the amount of a thousand pounds and had loyally accompanied him to the court that morning, gentle elderly men who were probably friends of his family and had admired him since he was a boy for his great gifts. Her mouth, which was soft as a child's, was trembling; her voice, which was at once the voice of Desdemona and Minnie Mouse, ran up the scale as she complained, "Every time I tried to say something that terrible old man wouldn't let me." So she tried again when Mr. Banning's appeal came up. The Court of Appeal, held in a dusty library, is conducted on the most abstract terms possible, considering that the subject matter of the law is humanity. No witnesses are heard, only counsel, who spin the legal thread finer and finer till, in the opinion of the three judges, it breaks. But Miss Frances was there. She saw herself running along the railway tracks, waving a lamp to warn the oncoming express of the broken bridge ahead, or leaping over the ice-floes with her little brother in her arms, like the heroine of an early Griffith film; and indeed in her excess of scarfs she recalled Mary Pickford and Mae Marsh, though it was with skirtage they were so encumbered, and her skirtage was—and why not—brief. Glowing she rose and, throwing her head back and her classic bosom forward, cried out that she wished to speak for Mr. Banning. The Lord Chief Justice inquired whether she was a member of the English bar. A sillier question never was put. That thick varnish of beauty could have been preserved intact only by strict abstinence from study. But doubtless the Judge asked the question because dedication to certain sorts of wisdom implies a duty to ignore others. She replied that she was not. Lord Goddard announced that, that being so, the Court could not hear her. This was not an early Griffith film. So Mr. Banning went off to prison to serve his ten years' hard labour, an extremely severe sentence, indeed the most severe sentence passed on any of the persons charged under the Defence Regulations; and Miss Frances returned across the Atlantic, to make or break the American stage.

Probably Mr. Banning had been at his best in his companionship with this artless child, so sweetly soaked in the lucent sirops of her own beauty. Doubtless in some of those days of concentrated spring that Berlin knows, when the south wind at last brings warmth to a land long blown clean, purged clean by the other winds, he had stood beside her while she cried how cute a snowdrop was, and cooed over it like a mothering dove; doubtless he had sat by a fire in a big soft chair, forgetting the maniacal Dr. Hexler and the way the war news had gone, and explaining something about Plato, while she, although mending something, listened to every word, as she proved every now and then by telling him that he was making it all so wonderfully clear. It was for such friendships that the little man was made. But he had too liberal an allowance of the sin by which most of the traitors fell: which was pride. When one of the prosecuting counsel mentioned the title of his book, *Woe for My Comrades,* he said tartly, "It's a quotation from Sophocles," and tossed his head, as if to say, "You wouldn't know about that. It's poetry. And Greek. People like you don't care for that sort of thing, they only care for material success. Poetry and Greek, those were the things I and my wonderful German friends cared about. And today my sort of person is in the hands of your sort of person." But the prosecuting counsel was in fact a man of culture who knew much poetry and much Greek, and was treating him with civilized charity. Mr. Banning had rightly supposed that he himself knew more than many people about poetry and Greek, and he had based on this fact the fiction that his intellectual gifts were so prodigious and commanding that they entitled him to a position of power. The case of William Joyce was slightly different; for he possessed the structure though not the substance of such a prodigious and commanding intellect, and it was not possible for such an oddity to know what it lacked, having none of it. But most of the traitors not simply procured by their appetites had fallen into this preventable error of regarding their slight superiority to the average as an overwhelming superiority over all people of all places and all ages, which gave them the right to reject all traditional values and assume that every action and opinion of the community was wrong. Thomas Haller Cooper was correct in his observation that most of the youths he met as a suburban schoolboy or a City clerk were not, as he was, studying Oriental languages, and that they were abstaining from these studies because they were inferior to him in brains and imagination. But he forgot that in the world there are countless people who have had so much brains and so much imagination that they had become not merely students but masters of Oriental languages, and that he had not yet proved that he belonged to this class. Forgetting this, he had, in the event of the war, gone counter to the rules as laid down by the wisdom of states and had behaved as if he were already a German national when he was too young to go through the legal formalities of becoming one. But, indeed, he is no perfect example of pride, for his love of his German mother and of Germany would have forced him into that illegality in any case. The issue was confused.

Indeed, no trial was as confused as his. He was charged under the Treason Act and therefore had to be found innocent and let go free or found guilty and hanged; and the reason for this rigorous form of prosecution lay beyond doubt in the part he played as procurer of the British Free Corps. He was a member of the S.S.; they had found under his arm-pit the blue tattoo-mark of his blood group which was its secret and indelible sign. That enlistment he might not have been able to help. But to seduce prisoners of war, to tempt men weakened by captivity into giving up their birthright, that he could have helped, that he should have helped. What cruelty this was can be guessed from the hatred, too awkward and unexpansive to be feigned, with which the men in charge of the prisoner-of-war camps gave evidence against the traitors who tampered with their men. One such, a wizened little non-commissioned officer, brown and dry as a good potato crisp, snarled as he told of how Cooper came to his camp, and tried to see the boys separately, and how he had reminded him that that was forbidden under the terms of the Geneva Convention. As he described the big Foreign Office car in which Cooper used to travel he spoke with a winking contempt, as if he had been speaking of a kept woman or a man who lived on the earnings of a prostitute.

Indeed Thomas Haller Cooper was a pimp; but he was also naïve. It is said that at the preliminary police-court proceedings his jaw dropped when there came into the box, as one of the chief witnesses against him, an Englishman who had been working beside him in the British Free Corps on a seeming parity of treason, and he heard that the man had been a British agent. This was John Henry Owen Brown, to whom he had expressed consternation when D-day came and went and the Allied invasion stood its ground, and said that he meant to change sides; to whom he had made his boast of having had to leave London because he had killed a Jew. The boy was astonished. He and his S.S. friends had meant to be the ones that were hard, that were sly, that gave evidence for the prosecution. He was naïve when he went into the witness-box, as of course he insisted on doing. There he too told the same story as Mr. Banning of having worked for the Nazis only as a cover for underground work for the Allies, and, like Mr. Banning, he often cocked his head on one side while he told it; but he lied with a brassy fluency which announced to everybody who might otherwise have missed it the spuriousness of his story.

He was naïve, yet he was self-possessed. He was at ease in the court, and that was tragic. A court of law is the antithesis of a home, a place where people live, speaking easily and with only reasonable truthfulness, since they have not been sworn, and pleading guilty and not guilty at one and the same time, and passing sentences on each other and never carrying them out. But the difference did not appal the young man, for he had not lived in a home for years, for something like a quarter of his young life. He had been either in barracks or at the Russian front, or acting as jailor to the poor brats of the British Free Corps. He was so naïve he could not keep hidden the source of his self-possession in all its dreadfulness. When he left the witness-box and returned to the dock he tried to carry on the good impression which he quite falsely believed he had made by his evidence. So he threw out his chest and brought his feet down on the boards in a smacking strut. Not so has any Englishman, even the most highly drilled English soldier, ever walked. He could be seen for what he was. It had to be recognized that had there been a ring at the bell in the early hours of the morning, and one had opened the door and found this young man standing in the passage with a comrade or two just like himself, all in their jack-boots, one's heart would have missed some beats; and one would have had reason, for there would certainly have followed some hours in a cellar, or as like as not some years in Buchenwald or Belsen, or, not improbably, no years at all anywhere. Of course he was found guilty and sentenced to death. But the character that made his story of having worked for the Allies a plain imposture saved his life. "Do not dare to class me with the other bastards that have been standing in this dock," he said to a police officer. "I am half a German." This view was shared by authority, and for that reason he was reprieved.

The world can bear to shed blood. It has done that often. What it cannot bear is to see all its hopes drowned in that blood. In this war that has happened, and the war was the work of Germany. It is a mystery that a young man, seeking to be acquitted by a court full of people who had suffered in this war, should seek to win their favour by making himself a perfect example of the kind of German that shed the blood of the world and drowned its hopes. Of course it cannot have seemed to him that he was doing that. He was saying to himself, like a child, "I must please them, I must try to look a nice young man." To him all niceness was in Germany, a nice young man was a nice young German, which by German consensus of opinion was a Nazi. But it is still a mystery why to him, with a choice between England and Germany, all niceness seemed to lie in Germany. Again we must turn to that suburban street where the German woman's home can still be told at a glance because the windows are packed with the small heavy bulbs of that small massive flower the hyacinth, with the daffodils that encourage the weak spring sunshine with the strong summer sunshine of their rich yellow, with flowers that bloomed long before they were flowers, when they were still brown bulbs without a single sprout, in the mind of the woman who planted them in winter, who planted far more of them than her neighbours, and planted them more cleverly, because she cared more for them. That window is something to stand and stare at; if one could understand it one could understand our age. Germany has its flowers. It has its songs, in which there are its flowers, and the joy that flowers and songs bring. And the sadness that must be felt when such loved flowers grow in the home of a woman whose only son is serving a life sentence, that too is German. A tragic ending is as dear to a German as a flower or a song. Flowers die, songs stop, it is right that happiness should end. That is logical, but insane. Man is not a flower or a song, he must continue, though the continuation of life merely means that he must be far from floral, utterly unmusical. But the logical cannot be denied. If he is to be all flowers and music, he must die. Then, since tragic endings are so important, anything which promises to contribute to one, even a jack-booted young man whose face promises Buchenwald, has its prestige.

This confusion of loveliness and all that imperils it is no new vice, it has its roots deep in the soil of Germany, its prehensile growths take to themselves all those who have drawn their being from that soil. It took back Denis John the golden owl, the son of the North London baker whose parents had been born German and had become naturalized Britons. It determined the course of his path to the end, which was not what would have been predicted for the young prig who circulated in the safe and evasive London of the Peace Pledge Union with his pretentious friends. He and his companions had moved across Western Europe after their capture by the Germans in the Channel Islands, where they were evading military service, and had passed from camp to camp, everywhere defying authority although not without cost to themselves. They were silly, complicated, quarrelsome, courageous; not unlike the characters in the *Nibelungenlied*. They joined the British Free Corps chiefly in order to flout the old-fashioned prejudice of their fellow prisoners of war, and once in it, organized a revolt against the conditions, beating up some support from the confirmed rebels such as Ronald David and the misfits such as poor Herbert George. For that they were sent to a *Straflager*, a punishment camp, and there they learned what it could be like to be entirely unprotected, either by the police or by the recognized authorities of a prisoner-of-war camp. After seven weeks they petitioned the German authorities to let them go back to the British Free Corps on any terms, and were told that they might do so, but that if they ever gave any trouble it would be the end of all of them. This was in the autumn of 1944, when the authorities felt the chill of doom falling on them, and nagged and bullied the wretched little British Free Corps as a slum mother, fearing a visit from the rent collector, will scream at her children and drag them about.

In the early months of 1945, the British Free Corps, which had been on exhibition in Dresden, was sent to Berlin. "We had noth⸗ ing to do here," said Denis John afterwards, "and we all used to get around the town all day visiting hotels, cafés, etc." Very soon he fell in love with a girl called Lena; and this is perhaps the one real love affair amongst all those matings which were at once a prime motive and a consolation for the treachery of the men in the B.F.C. Lena had been a pupil at the school in Germany to which his German grandmother had brought him, and as school⸗ children they had been great friends. She had been in some trou⸗ ble during the war, for she had been brought back to Germany from Bulgaria, where she had been an army clerk, for anti-Nazi sentiments. Now she was working her passage back to favour in an office of the S.S. in Berlin and had a flat in the suburb of Duhlen⸗ dorf. The discipline in the British Free Corps was so slack that very soon Denis John was living in her flat and going to the bar⸗ racks only to draw his pay and his rations. As their passion grew they applied for permission to marry, but this was refused. It was a curious quirk of the Germans that though they often ordered German women to have intercourse with the traitors they never gave these people permission to marry, though why that particular egg seemed better to them raw than cooked is hard to see. But terror was driving duty out of German offices by then, and one could at least get a forged travel permit. With this the boy and girl went to Bremen, and there they went to a church and tried to persuade the pastor to marry them; and perhaps persuaded him to perform some ceremony. There was at any rate throbbing emotion; there was kneeling before an altar, while mystic author⸗ ity recited spells relating to the eternal, and the heart swelled and burst and melted into the circumambient cloud of solemn bliss.

Later it was learned that the authorities intended to send the British Free Corps to the Russian front as that swept from Polish to German soil, and at this news the British Free Corps took to its bed as one man. It is not surprising that the authorities took not much trouble to get it up again. The degree to which German life through despair had become frivolous can be judged from the curious hospital routine followed by Denis John. He had been taken in as a patient suffering from tonsillitis, but he spent only his nights in the hospital. Every morning, with nobody raising any objection, he used to rise and dress and go out to console Lena, who was with child. Their position was as preposterously dramatic as opera. He, a traitor, had to be got out of Germany before the British came; it is to be emphasized once again that all the traitors of normal mind from prisoner-of-war camps perfectly understood their position, for it had always been explained to them by the British officers before they left the camp. She, who had been adjudged too anti-Nazi to be safe company for the peoples of occupied Europe, could not get a permit to leave the country. The pregnant girl rushed about Berlin appealing to her friends with the various Ministries, who with the calm of delirium gave her what she wanted: an order transferring Denis John from the British Free Corps to the English propaganda department of the Milan radio, a forged travelling permit for herself.

This was in early April. The journey from Berlin to Milan took eleven days; dirty and tired and young, they stumbled out into the Italian spring which shone eternal among the confusion. At the German radio station a German officer shouted that he had been warned by Berlin that Lena's papers were forged, and that he meant to arrest her, but, turning aside to make provision for his own safety, let them both walk out of his room. Fortunately for them, the German system had not entirely broken down. One cell of this unit was still functioning. There was a cashier who in a reeling world retained the knowledge that everyone holding a travelling permit had the right to draw eight thousand lire, and so paid Denis John and Lena sixteen thousand lire. With this money they went out into streets perilous with the sniping and counter-sniping and grenade-throwing of partisans and Germans and Fascists, and found a hotel, and slept off their fatigue for two or three days. Then they crept out of the city along the road to Pavia, and stayed at a village called Bressane which looks from the flat lands, among the Judas-trees and the poplars, to the chestnut-covered slopes of the Ligurian Alps. There they stayed until the end of May, until the American troops came. Then they were put in a camp; and soon the boy was sent back to England and prison, the girl to Germany and the bearing of a child in hunger and among rubble. The type of such experience is the *"Liebes-tod"*: a great work, were it not for the feeling that the composer and his creations alike sucked suffering like a toffee in the mouth. It was doubtful from Denis John's statement if he would ever have fallen in love with Lena had there not been curving over the city where they met the breaking wave of a historic catastrophe. The North London baker who is Denis John's father, who stands in his neat lounge suit ready to serve his customers with the gingerbread made in the Continental fashion and the buns made in the English fashion, both as good as they can be in these times, his watchet-blue eyes heavy with sorrow, his skin shining like glazed china, as fair men's skins do when they are ill and tired, is perhaps more romantic than his son, because he tried to save his son from romanticism. The emigration of Germans to England and America was not wholly economic in its origin. It was in part a desire of the uncorrupted part of the people to save its seed from the *"Liebestod"* which sang itself in *Tristan und Isolde*, and was to be privately practised by Lena and Denis John and many another, and publicly consummated in the wide ruin from the Rhine to the Oder.

Denis John was sentenced to three years' hard labour. It was not a harsh sentence. For it must be remembered that while he was acting out his version of the *"Liebestod,"* many young men of his age had experienced the *Tod* without the *Liebes*. He had been dealt with by the civil courts because he was not a member of the British armed forces; and in that he was lucky. It is regrettable that any serious offences should be dealt with by court martial, other than those which have to be dealt with as quickly as possible by military or naval units operating in areas remote from civilization. The constitution of a court martial is in itself highly objectionable. Six officers who know nothing about the law and may not have the capacity to learn about it act as both judge and jury; and though they have a professional lawyer sitting with them, in the person of a Judge-Advocate, who directs them on questions of law, this does not correct the disadvantages of employing a panel of amateurs instead of a judge, and it drags out every case of any complexity to intolerable length and tedium, as every time a point of law is raised the court has to be cleared while the six judges ask and receive instruction. Just how unsatis-

factory such a court is can be grasped by imagining that one day
the judge should step down from the bench at the Old Bailey and
order the jury to take over his functions, appointing a stray K.C.
to explain the law to them as they went along, and clear the court
every time he made an explanation. The poor prisoner has not
only to endure this unnecessary prolongation of his trial, he is
faced with a dilemma concerning his defence. Either he has to employ an officer as his amateur counsel, or employ a professional
lawyer, who will be regarded by the judges with suspicion as a
tricky outsider who is trying to pull fast ones on them. When the
trial comes to an end he is subjected to an ordeal far greater than
is usually experienced in civil courts. The six judges deliberate,
just as a jury does, on his guilt. If they bring in the verdict of
guilty, they then take evidence as to his character and previous
convictions and retire again to consider the sentence, which is
usually, though not always, announced only when it has been confirmed by the Army Council, which may not happen for some
weeks. The anguish caused by this delay is increased by the lack
of any standard of sentences. Groups of amateurs dotted about the
country, functioning once or only a few times in their lives, cannot found or transmit a tradition of appropriate punishment;
and they sling out sentences which are likely to be, if they are
unimaginative, savage, and if they are imaginative, frivolous.

It is possible to appeal to the Army Council against these sentences, but such an appeal is held in secret, and the authority
does not disclose its reasons. The prisoner is also hardly dealt
with by the impossibility of ensuring a public trial by court
martial. Any member of the public can attend a court martial
which is not being held *in camera* for reasons of security; but
how any member of the public is to hear of a court martial is
not so plain. It can very easily happen that a man whose home
is in a remote part of England and whose trial takes place in
London will be tried without a single person being present except
the officers of the court. It also often happens that courts martial
take place in premises entirely unsuitable for the purpose, where
the correct legal procedure cannot be followed without deviation
and there is no proper accommodation for witnesses.

The prisoners of war who joined the British Free Corps and
the S.S. or who broadcast, who were tried by court martial, were

to illustrate the arbitrary character of this obsolete institution. Almost identical cases of a mild type were sent to prison for six months, two years, seven years, ten years, and fifteen years; almost identical cases of a depraved type were sent to prison for five years, ten years, fifteen years, and for life. Such a diversity of sentences must mean injustice and must bring the law into disrepute. One case was uniquely unfortunate. A boy named Henry Alfred Symonds joined the army in 1941 when he was fifteen years of age. It is not clear how, in those days of identity cards, he can have been accepted by the army authorities. Two years later he was captured in Italy, and was induced to join the British Free Corps. He was sentenced in 1946, at which time he was just twenty-one, to fifteen years' imprisonment. There was, moreover, an interesting antithesis between the policies of the civil and service courts. The civil courts obviously pursued a firm policy in their prosecution of treachery which was designed to make it perfectly plain to the public mind what that offence was and what traitors must expect. They brought to book the chief exemplars of the crime: William Joyce the broadcaster, John Amery the inventor of the British Free Corps, Walter Purdy the informer, and Cooper the volunteer in an enemy armed force, and got them sentenced to death. Then they prosecuted with an obvious anxiety not to gratify any desire for revenge, not to deprave the community by blood-baths and excessive use of the oubliette; and the cases gradually faded out, except for one or two who might have been forgotten and had plainly forced trial on themselves by their eccentricity. The armed forces, on the other hand, brought their prosecutions forward with extreme dilatoriness and an increasing animus, so that some of the earlier sentences were fatuously light and the later ones remarkably severe.

Alfred Vivian, the black-browed romantic who had been genuinely pro-German and had drunk the health of the Duke of Windsor in the mess of the British Free Corps, was one of the lucky ones, for he was a merchant seaman and was tried at the Old Bailey, and got seven years. Throughout the trial a handsome matron had been sitting in the court; but there were four other merchant seamen in the dock and it was not clear for whom she had come until, when this sentence was delivered, she raised her clenched fist and struck her knee with it, and rose, and left. Fuseli, painting Mrs. Siddons as Lady Macbeth, painted such a woman, such a gesture. People of this type need to construct round themselves dramas in which they play the leading part, and doubtless she had made her life in a riverside suburb into a very moving and uplifting drama, using her personal relationships as a fiery but solemn argument for love and decency. Seeing her anywhere, in the tube or in a fish queue, one would have halted to admire her look of proud, clean worth. It was a great misfortune that her son, forced by his inherited blood to build such a drama round himself, had not known where to look for a theme, so had fallen into this nonsense. When in the spring of 1945 he realized how disastrous this nonsense was likely to be for him, he acted in the same way as most of the British Free Corps. He rose from his hospital bed, stole or was given some civilian clothes, and, turning west to fly from the Russians, walked into the Allied lines, and was there well received as an escaped prisoner of war. The men who followed this course enjoyed a false sense of security that lasted for some time. Their stories were naturally accepted, those of them who had acquired a good working knowledge of the German language during their captivity were useful as interpreters to the advancing British and American troops. Since these would be the most intelligent, and all the most intelligent members of the British Free Corps suffered from a desire for power, they must have enjoyed being part of a victorious force. These men continued in this magical state of immunity for a matter of weeks or months. Till VE-day and for a long time after, the army had many other things to do than to chase unimportant traitors; and during this period of disorganization the men were sheltered by the rule of the British Free Corps and the British section of the Rundfunk that all traitors except the most important should work under assumed names. This did no more, and the Germans must have known it would do no more, than give them a short respite before arrest; although in one extraordinary case it gave a man total protection.

Late in 1944 a Captain X was withdrawn from an English prisoner-of-war camp in circumstances which led his fellow-prisoners, who had many reasons to think poorly of him, to believe he had become a traitor. At about the same time a Captain Y appeared in Berlin wearing the S.S. uniform. In March 1945 a few of the more helpless members of the British Free Corps were sent to join a Panzer division in the direction of the Russian lines under the now despairing Thomas Haller Cooper. There Captain Y appeared with an English batman and exhorted them to come with him and fight the Russians. The response was negative, and he and his batman drove off in a jeep. That is the last that is known of Captain Y. A short time after this, Captain X appeared in the British lines, sent back by the Russians; and told a convincing story of imprisonment in a concentration camp and escape. He won the complete confidence of the officers in the section of the British lines to which he was returned, and was given an excellent administrative post which might well have been permanent had it not been that certain people who were going through the papers of the S.S. had formed a strong suspicion that Captain X was also Captain Y. But nobody who knew Captain X had ever seen Captain Y. Certain of the traitors knew Captain Y very well; but they were not willing to be of any assistance. The few other members of the British Free Corps who had seen him were unable to identify him, and indeed were in such a state of panic and horror when they were listening to his ill-timed recruiting speech that they probably took little note of him. Throughout these inquiries Captain X stuck to his story of imprisonment and escape, which was impossible to disprove. So there the matter had to rest. If Captain X was Captain Y, then he was the luckiest man in the world, for if his identity had been proved he would certainly have been tried for high treason. He might well consider that his life had been given back to him by a miracle. When Captain X returned to England he almost immediately committed a series of pointless and unnecessary offences, and is now in prison.

The rest, who were not so lucky, sooner or later received the message they expected: that some officers of the Intelligence Corps wanted to see them. The one man who forced his arrest before its time was Ronald David, the Byronic wastrel who had been adopted by a spinster in New Zealand. He was in a sense one of the most debased members of the British Free Corps; he had liked the soft life, the whores and the drink. On him were found the photographs of thirteen German women, as well as mementoes of a steadier attachment. But he confessed his connection in the British Free Corps of his own accord, in order to gain permission to give evidence for the defence a the court martial of one of the "Big Six" of the Corps. The rest were led away; and statements were taken from them, usually by the Scotland Yard inspectors who had been lent to the War Office for such work. It is to be noted in passing that such men, whose intelligence and wisdom and soundness of heart are often astonishing, can at best earn about five hundred pounds a year. The statements varied from the suicidal and pretentious apologia of John Amery, which in some thousands of words showed that silliness can be as frightening as madness, to the artless inventions of Herbert George, the Disney dwarf who had fought with the International Brigade in Spain and deserted from it. He described how he had met a German girl called Hilda Henschel, and after speaking to her "found she was pro-English. I told her I wanted to escape and she said she would help me. I told her I had studied the theory of piloting a plane and eventually she told me she could find out where I could get hold of a plane, which she did. The plane was in an aerodrome about thirty kilometres away from Hildesheim. On the night we had a nasty raid and the airfield was damaged so I could not carry out my plans." He returned to England and rejoined his wife in perfect domestic bliss, although he had taken steps to divorce her when he was in the prisoner-of-war camp; and, determined to pick up all the threads, he became the life and soul of the Sheerness Communist Party. The poor little man had to leave this happy and busy life for two years' hard labour.

It would have seemed a pity to have bothered about this odd little soul; but such segregation was in his own interests. It was certainly a great relief to the licensed trade of Sheerness. On Saturday nights Herbert George would come into a bar and, after a drink or two, would be filled with a desire to entertain the company and would therefore relate his adventures, first in the International Brigade and then in the British Free Corps. This never worked out well. His imprisonment must also have been a relief to the officers of the Sheerness Communist Party, who are doubtless serious-minded men. This odd creature, and all the other odd creatures, then went into a world abhorrent to contemplate: a world of cold cells, of dirt, of mind-slaying monotony. "I never worry," said a legal official, "about men who are merely hanged. What worries me is that a man who has been in prison for ten years is no longer a man but an automaton, and that there are a certain number of men who must be sent to prison for ten years if certain crimes are to be suppressed." But penal reform is impossible without new prisons and more warders of a high type. Not for a generation will our bankrupt people be able to build new prisons; and the labour shortage means that it becomes more and more difficult to induce men to enter the exacting life of prison service if they are fit to do anything else. There is pain here, and it cannot be avoided. But the thought of Herbert George is reassuring, so certain is it that he will pass unscathed through his two years in a convict prison and will add this to his list of experiences and regard it as yet another source of distinction. All of the rest of them will come out as they went in, unchanged in their essential and dangerous quality. Because of their fundamental neuroses and the stimulus applied to these by their environment, they will be timber for the next international revolutionary movement.

9

WILLIAM JOYCE, of whom that cannot be said, left his Hamburg office and went out, in the company of his wife, to seek a safety which he did not by then believe could be found. First he slipped into his pocket a passport made out in the false name of Wilhelm Hansen: who was described as a teacher. He liked teaching, he was proud of his gifts as a teacher. It was dated November 3, 1944, but the date may have been as false as the name. Till the end he had refused to admit to himself that his Germany might be defeated, and it is unlikely that he would have taken such a precaution up to the last moment. Then it would be easy, for all over Germany people were sitting in government offices, forging papers, to deny their curious Christs at the third cockcrow. Joyce's wife had a separate passport. It had occurred to them that anything might happen: the worst might happen: they might have to part. So they started on their journey, and, like all the traitors who then closed the door behind them on the misery and futility which had grown thicker and thicker round them for the previous five years, they stepped out into the spring. But not for the Joyces any season of respite, for they could not, like their underlings, go into the British or American lines and tell a lying story and be given work, and be at ease for a little and hope for the best. Joyce, who at that time had only a vague suspicion that there was any doubt about his British nationality, knew that there was no hope for him at all if he fell into Allied hands.

So they took to the forest, the German forest: where the trees make so sweet a shade that the family can picnic, where the trees make so deep a shade that at their roots the dark traditions germinate and grow. The Joyces lived out there. By then the first birch leaves were small green flames against their silver bark, and the pines and the larches were manifesting their soberer sort of spring, and on the open heaths the tufts of young grass surprised against the darkling. The genius of the country took them to itself. They were obliged to enact their *"Liebestod."* Sometimes they spent a night in the towns or a village, more often they found their bed in barns and sheds at the wood's edge and heard the hoots of the owls, which mourn so softly, as ghosts might mourn for their own destinies; and by day they lay on the soft pine needles, while the sun shone on them between the tree-trunks as between the bars of a prison window, or, wanting to wash themselves or their clothes, knelt at the edges of lakes, and shuddered because the water was still too cold for the flesh, which has an inveterate preference for remaining warm. The love between them, which Joyce had so often mauled and manhandled, at this time established its value for ever. Now that everything else had failed them, it survived, not only intact, but intensified. Their joy in each other must have been transfused with agonizing self-reproach; for they might so easily have stayed in England. Both must have said, "No, it was not your fault, it was mine." Sometimes death must have seemed to be already standing beside them; sometimes they must have felt that everything would be all right, because it always had been. At all times they were horribly uncomfortable. The British troops were everywhere, and they

were under a real necessity to hide. William Joyce had always
been very exacting about his food. His mother had been a very
good cook; and a fellow-student of his at the Battersea Polytechnic,
questioned about him many years afterwards, could remember
almost nothing except that he had once taken him home to tea
at Allison Grove and the cakes and soda-bread had been wonderful. His wife had made it her pride never to ask him to sit down
to a cold meal. Now they ate at irregular intervals where they
could. They grew very thin and could not keep themselves clean
or neat. William Joyce developed a skin disease affecting the
scalp.

On May 28, 1945, they had been on the run for some weeks.
We were told at Joyce's trial of what that day brought to him. In
the evening he was walking in the forest when he came on two
British officers. Had he gone on his way they would probably
not have noticed him, for he was by then a very miserable figure,
and they were busy looking for loose wood to build a fire. But
he halted and watched them, and in the end he spoke to them.
Into the void which is a revolutionary's mind when a revolution
has been effected there rush old passions, faiths held and forgotten. He had been reared by his father to regard the British
army as the symbol of the power and the glory on earth; he had
hoped to be a British officer himself, he had boasted as a boy
that he had served under the orders of a British officer. Also they
were men of his own people, from whom he had been exiled for
five years and more. He told them where they could find more
wood; and he spoke in French. Nothing could have been better
calculated to draw their questioning attention to him. But William Joyce had always been proud of his French, which was
correct and fluent. Perhaps an ingenious part of his mind was
saying, "You are British officers. I had hoped to become a British
officer but I abandoned my hope. I was not a gentleman, I was
not the sort that is given a commission. But I can claim other
values. I have a good mind. Listen to my French, which I speak
better than most gentlemen." The two British officers stared at
him in interest; and he committed the act, which any man except
him could have committed with impunity but which was for him
suicide. He said in English, "There are a few more pieces here."

To every man in the world there is one person of whom he knows little: whom he would never recognize if he met him walking down the street, whose motives are a mystery to him. That is himself. It is possible that William Joyce did not know that he alone among men spoke with the blended voices of Tamerlane and Punchinello, and that whatever he said he also said, "I am William Joyce." The two officers, startled, conferred together. Then the junior of the two, Lieutenant Perry, asked Joyce in the idiom of his time, "You wouldn't happen to be William Joyce, would you?" Joyce put his hand in his pocket, meaning to take out his forged passport, and the Lieutenant, nervous as every member of an invading force must be, thought that he was feeling for a revolver, and drew his own and shot him in the leg. Joyce fell to the ground, groaning, "My name is Fritz Hansen." So little store had he set on the sole means left to him for escaping detection that he had not troubled to memorize the details of his forged passport, which was made out in the name of not Friedrich but Wilhelm Hansen, and that when the two officers searched him for arms they found not only his false passport but his real military passport, made out in the name of William Joyce. It is not possible to guess why he retained this. It could no longer have been of use to him in any conceivable circumstances.

One of the officers went away and made contact with authority; and eventually Joyce was taken to the military hospital at Lüne-berg. Mrs. Joyce had been arrested and taken to a prison camp, spent and dishevelled, saying in her habitual manner, which was jaunty and mechanically cynical, that she and her husband had expected this for a long time and that there was no use making a fuss about it. They were not to see each other again until after he had been sentenced to death. The news that Joyce was coming to the hospital arrived before him, and his stretcher was carried from the ambulance through a crowd of soldiers who were chi-yiking and crying out, "This is Jairmany calling." This must have been the first intimation to him that he was considered by the British public as a comic character, and there could be no more perplexing anticlimax. On May the 31st an Intelligence officer came and sat by his bed and interrogated him; and to the officer he dictated this statement:

I take this opportunity of making a preliminary statement concerning the motives which led me to come to Germany and to broadcast to Britain over the German radio service. I was actuated not by the desire for personal gain, material or otherwise, but solely by political conviction. I was brought up as an extreme Conservative with strong Imperialistic ideas, but very early in my career, namely, in 1923, became attracted to Fascism and subsequently to National Socialism. Between the years 1923 and 1939 I pursued vigorous political activities in England, at times as a Conservative but mainly as a Fascist or National Socialist. In the period immediately before this war began I was profoundly discontented with the policies pursued by British governments, first, because I felt that they would lead to the eventual disruption of the British Empire, and secondly, because I thought the existing economic system entirely inadequate to the needs of the times. I was very greatly impressed by constructive work which Hitler had done for Germany and was of the opinion that throughout Europe as also in Britain there must come a reform on the lines of National Socialist doctrine, although I did not suppose that every aspect of National Socialism as advocated in Germany would be accepted by the British people.

One of my dominant beliefs was that a war between Britain and Germany would be a tragedy, the effects of which Britain and the British Empire would not survive, and I considered that a grossly disproportionate influence was exerted on British policy by the Jews, who had their reasons for hating National Socialist Germany. When, in August 1939, the final crisis emerged I felt that the question of Danzig offered no just cause for a world war. As by reason of my opinions I was not conscientiously disposed to fight for Britain against Germany, I decided to leave the country since I did not wish to play the part of a conscientious objector, and since I supposed that in Germany I should have the opportunity to express and propagate views the expression of which would be forbidden in Britain during time of war. Realizing, however, that at this critical juncture I had declined to serve Britain, I drew the logical conclusion that I should have no moral right to return to that country of my own free will and that it would be best to apply for German citizenship and make my permanent home in Germany. Nevertheless, it remained my undeviating purpose to attempt as best I could to bring about a reconciliation or at least an understanding between the two countries. After Russia and the United States had entered the war such an agreement appeared to me no less desirable than before for, although it seemed probable that with these powerful allies Britain would succeed in defeating Germany, I considered that the price which would ultimately have to be paid for this help would be far higher than the price involved in a settlement with Germany.

This belief was strengthened from month to month as the power of Russia grew, and during the later stages of the war I became certain that Britain, even though capable of gaining a military triumph over the Germans, would in that event be confronted with a situation far more dangerous and complicated than that which existed in August 1939; and thus until the very last moment I clung to my hope of an Anglo-German understanding, although I could see that the prospects thereof were small. I know that I have been denounced as a traitor and I resent the accusation as I conceive myself to have been guilty of no underhand or deceitful act against Britain, although I am also able to understand the resentment that my broadcasts have in many quarters aroused. Whatever opinion may be formed at the present time with regard to my conduct, I submit that the final judgment cannot be properly passed until it is seen whether Britain can win the peace. Finally I should like to stress the fact that in coming to Germany and in working for the German radio system my wife was powerfully influenced by me. She protests to the contrary but I am sure that, if I had not taken this step, she would not have taken it either. This statement has been read over to me, and it is true.

(Signed) William Joyce.

This was a remarkable statement to be dictated by a man who had been brought into hospital three days before, not only wounded but suffering from malnutrition and exposure. But the mind that framed it was remarkable only in its structure. The substance was poor; and greatness depends on the substance of the mind, which is the mirror of all substances, and chooses between them, between good and evil, love and hate, the agreeable and the disagreeable. The situation of England was as he saw it. It was to her interest to form an alliance with Germany; for without a strong Germany the balance of Europe must be disturbed and world trade disorganized. But the substance of the mind, reflecting the substance of Germany, should have, if it were a true and bright mirror, reflected cruelty and murder and fatuity, a character with which the sane could conclude no alliance, however terrible the alternative, because it was itself the limit of terror. The substance of William Joyce's mind was not a true and bright mirror; he might know that A and B and C were linked by certain causal connexions, but he would never apprehend with any exactitude the nature of A or B or C. But at the time he dictated his statement he must have learned the

nature of Nazi Germany from his own painful experiences, working with the frenetic Hexler, learning what happened to those
that fell out with his masters. He must have known why Great
Britain had had to fight Germany, and been lying when he pretended that he did not. That pretence, however, was too late.
Our troops had been in Buchenwald and Belsen. It was certain
that whether Britain could "win the peace" or not, it had certainly been imperative that she should win the war. Nevertheless
it remains true that that statement was remarkable both as an
intellectual and a moral effort.

Sixteen days later he was flown to England. One of the soldiers
in the plane asked him for his autograph as they were crossing
the Channel, and he wrote him a scrawl—"This is the most
historic moment in my life, God bless dear old England"—which
reeked of that illiterate quality never dispelled by his University
education. He was taken to Brixton Prison, and there he did well.
When he first appeared at Bow Street after his arival he struck
spectators as a scrubby little creature of the sort that has never
known anything but scrubbiness. One of the reporters likened
him to a dusty London sparrow. But he soon improved and put
on weight and dignity, and an air which was not unlikeable and
which was new. In the past he had always shocked the people he
met, unless they were in the Fascist nexus, by the real or affected
brutality of his egotism. Now he shocked people as much by his
quiet pleasantness; by his humour, which was no longer boister-
ous and teasing, but gentle and remote and self-satirizing; by his
contentment.

Of all plants contentment is the last which would be expected
to grow within prison walls. But William Joyce had much reason
to feel that Brixton Prison was not such a bad place to be.
He was out of the alien forest, he was no longer enacting a
tragedy which was part of other men's tradition but not his. He
had food to eat, a roof over his head, and he was among his own
people again: among the unexcitable, matter-of-fact, controlled
English whom he had despised. If a warder now and then was
mean or surly, there was no Dr. Hexler here and this was no
concentration camp. But for the most part he found the prison
officials very kind and responsive to his efforts to give them as
little trouble as possible. It is to be remembered that William

Joyce had always liked the police, and his passion for discipline was so great that he may have found a sort of pleasure in conforming to prison routine. Into this cold grey snugness came his family; most often his beloved and loving young brother Quentin. From them, it is true, he must have learned that the revolt against his parents which he had carried on throughout his life had come to an end, because they had been vanquished in the world of fact, and, if they had not actually been killed by the forces whose cause he had espoused, had been tormented by them in their last hours. It is possible that he may have heard of his father's death not long after it happened, for Michael Joyce had died before America had come into the war, and the Joyces had relatives in the United States. But it must have been now that he heard for the first time of the death of his mother. That tiny and spirited being, though she had been persuaded to go into the country after her widowhood, had returned to London to be with her sons and daughter, and when she was stricken with a painful disease she was taken to St. Mary's Hospital, Paddington, where she lay dying during the summer of 1944, while the V-1's broke over the town. This news must have brought William Joyce a grief which though intense was warm and purging. Fantasy applies to our personal relationships a chill and commonplace formula which forces the members of our families to cast aside their individualities and play certain obvious and inferior parts, in order to throw what we hope is our obvious superiority into relief. Now that fantasy had to relinquish this material in William Joyce's mind, all its ends having been dreadfully attained, reality could reassert itself. Now in his cell there was room, as there had not been in the wide liberty of London, for his mysterious and loving father, his gay and loving mother.

In his cell there was also room for an intellectual exercise more complex, more absorbing, and more novel than any he had engaged in when he was free to study as he liked. When he entered Brixton Prison he believed he had no defence to the charge of high treason which had been brought against him. But his solicitors drew his attention to the passage in his statement in which he had alluded to his belief that his father had been a naturalized American citizen, and had forfeited his naturalization by failing "to re-register." If his father had been a naturalized American citizen when he was born, they told him, then he himself was an American citizen by birth, and nothing which had happened afterwards could affect that. Did he ever believe that safety lay in that resolution of his doubts regarding his status? It may be so. But it is said that, in conversation with a prison official, he described the defence which was to be put up for him and added, with a faint smile, "It will be amusing to see if they get away with it." Certainly his flesh would have derived something more than amusement if they had got away with it, but perhaps the gentle cynicism was honest enough. He had lived by his ambition. That part of his ambition which lived on his lips and in the forefront of his mind had been utterly frustrated. He was not going to be king. In all the world there was not one man, not the most pitiful blind beggar nor the most eroded leper, of whom it could be more certainly said that he would never, till the end of time, exercise the smallest grain of power. The other ambition, which lived in his heart and in the secret governing chamber of his mind, was as utterly fulfilled. The revolution had succeeded. He had seen Hamburg, and knew that more than a city had been destroyed; he had a nice historic sense and perhaps he recognized that a continent was dead; he had grown wise enough latterly to realize that a civilization had been murdered. Into his cell, each morning brought the white light that comes at dawn into a house where a corpse lies awaiting burial. If the dead were loved, then those who wake and see such light feel grief; if they were hated, their enemies wake to emptiness and bereavement, because the hunt is over. If the corpse were both loved and hated, then those that still live feel agonizing conflict; and if the corpse died not a natural death but had been helped on its way, then the immortal justice in their hearts tells them that they should pay for their guilt with their own lives. All these several pains torment the successful revolutionary. For him death is truly a release. Joyce's shrewdness knew enough to make him serene.

So he went to his trial, which was not like most earthly trials but was the pattern of such trials as must happen in the hereafter. For we shall be judged at the end unjustly, according to the relation of our activities to a context whereof we, being human and confined to a small part of time and space, knew almost nothing. Such judgment depends not on the blowing of a trump but on the existence of a mind that, being aware of the sum of experience and therefore able to estimate our worth in relation to it, shall judge us by taking cognizance of us, as it must since we are an integer in that sum. Indeed, such judgment is inherent in the existence of that sum of experience. If the upper air and the inner earth are peopled only by abstractions, it is still delivered. It is said that in few murder cases has it been wise for the accused person to give evidence on his own behalf; but here was a trial where a person under a capital charge could not conceivably give any evidence bearing on his guilt or innocence. He might, indeed, have embarrassed the prosecution to the point of impotence if he had given false evidence that he had not used his passport for the purpose of leaving England for Germany; and he must surely have known enough of the means employed for getting German spies in and out of England to have been able to spin a plausible tale. But he was not a perjurer. He had at least chosen to play out his drama in the real world. If sentence was to be passed on him, let it be based on the truth. But that condition was all he could contribute to his own trial. He could not speak of his own knowledge concerning his father's naturalization, or his status at birth, or the kind of allegiance he owed to the Crown, or the consequences flowing from possession of a passport. He might have been the poor soul in a theologian's dream waiting to hear if the divine caprice poured wine of grace into his cup and made it saved and unbreakable or left it empty and damned. But that is the dream of a finite mind. In the infinite mind there is reconciled justice and injustice. The moral sense of a man is clairvoyant: if he chooses to love rather than to hate he shall be right both in time and in eternity. William Joyce, knowing that he had struck against his own flesh, had written it down that every time he had broadcast he had committed treason. He took a short cut to the same conclusion reached by the lawyers who knew so much about him that he did not.

He was found guilty and he was taken to Wormwood Scrubbs: a prison standing on the western edge of London among flat and greasy fields where the sea-gulls gather in time of storm. It has a peculiar character, for it was built about seventy years ago in the full flush of the late Victorian enthusiasm for social reform, with the intention of reclaiming prisoners serving their first sentence by providing them with beautiful surroundings. Though, like so many Victorian buildings, it seems stuffy as stale seed-cake by reason of a marked prosaic error in the proportions and the drab colour of the materials employed, it is a work of great imaginative vigour, not irrelevant to its function. It is built round three places of worship, an Anglican chapel, a Roman Catholic chapel, and a synagogue, which wear about their Italianate façades certain clouds of solemnity; and the surrounding mass of administrative and cell blocks is broken by a number of campanili. Though the place suggests not only Ravenna and Pisa but a giant model of a lodging-house cruet, it nevertheless has the virtue of presenting extraordinary shapes that the inmates may well find appropriate to their own extraordinary destinies. A prison built with the simplicity of a hospital or a school might well seem heartless to convicts who know that they have lost their liberty by no event so natural as falling sick or growing up; but this alien and emotional ornament and these superfluous towers might be taken as implying knowledge on the part of authority itself that life could become completely strange, as it had been at the moment of their disaster, when a demon entered into them and they said "Yes" when they should have said "No." It was there he waited for the hearing of his appeals, in which he did not believe. There he changed to the man we saw at his later trials, who seemed no longer to trouble himself about his demon's unfortunate reply, but to ponder on an answer he must shortly make to another question.

His destiny was to be honest; to be wrong; to have his habitation "south the river." Wormwood Scrubbs lay on the scabbed edge of London, but nevertheless on the same side of the Thames as the imperial city, so his place was not there. The prison was seized by a spasm of madness and ejected him. The news that Joyce was within its walls spread amongst the other prisoners and they raged against his presence. Perhaps they were trying to upset the social verdict of worthlessness passed on them at the same time as their legal conviction; perhaps they were idiotically responding to the call of tradition, for throughout history treason has always been the crime most abhorred by the English, as parricide has been the crime most abhorred by the French; perhaps it was true of the criminal population, as it was of the rest of us at the end of the war, that the sanest were a little mad and the half-mad quite demented. Whatever their reasons, they howled against him with the simplicity of wolves. In his cell he heard the riot, lifted his eyes from the book he was reading and forced them back again, but finally laid the book aside and said hesitantly to the prison official who was sitting with him, "Those people are not calling out against me, are they?" He received an evasive answer, but was later to learn the truth, for one day as he was taking exercise some prisoners in cells overlooking the yard realized his identity, and, though they knew they would be punished for it, shouted curses at him and threw down on him what missiles they could find through the windows. It is said that some of the craziest convicts formed a plan to make a dash past the warders at a favourable moment, to seize William Joyce, and to murder him.

There was not the slightest danger that this plan could have been carried out, but this was not the atmosphere in which a man under sentence of death could be left to await the hearing of his appeal. So Joyce was taken away from Wormwood Scrubbs and sent to Wandsworth Jail, a shabby old prison, black as a coal-tip, set among the trodden commons and the discoloured villas, the railway viaducts and the long streets of little houses, which lie "south the river." His last days of his life in London were to be spent only a mile or two from the house in Longbeach Road where it had begun. Now his second wife, with whom he had lived only in his aspirant exile north of the Thames, was received into the district which was his real home. A man condemned to death has the right to see whom he chooses, and the authorities brought his wife over from Germany and lodged her in Holloway Prison, sending her over the river to visit him almost every day. They took great delight in each other's company; and on the morning of his hanging she retreated into a frenzy of grief which did not abate. It was necessary afterwards to send her back to Germany, for she had automatically become a German subject when her husband became a naturalized German. There it was necessary to keep her in a camp, for she was passionately pro-Nazi and could no more be let loose than any other Nazi propagandist. Nor, had she been allowed to return to England and her own family, could she have been left at liberty for her own sake. These two people had contrived their own ruin with a finality that not their worst enemy could have achieved by unremitting malice. Iago was a gentle child compared to their suicidal selves.

Thus the white light which came into Joyce's cell all these last mornings shone upon utter desolation. But he maintained his pinched serenity. That was the fruit of courage; and to say this is to say nothing, for courage of a sort which is not dimmed during months of waiting must have its source in something other than itself. It cannot be said that he was upheld by his faith in fascism, although he never recanted and his impudent hand scratched a swastika on the wall of the cell in the Old Bailey where he waited to be taken up to the dock. Of course he could not recant. It would have looked as if he were a coward trying to beg for his life, and he would have falsified the situation as much, and even more, by giving that impression, than he did by not admitting his disenchantment with Hitler's Germany. It is possible that the long book which he wrote while he was in prison, and which should certainly be published as soon as possible, as a matter of vital historical interest, attempts to explain why National Socialism would have worked if it had been handled by other personalities than the Nazis. That would be the way of retreat which would suggest itself to most minds. But in truth he had lost his faith. The old William Joyce, when he was asked by the Judge if he had anything to say before sentence was passed on him, would have thrown back his head and hawked out, "God save England and to hell with Russia," or some such slogan. This new William Joyce kept silent. If he was illuminated by a certain satisfaction it was not because he felt himself supported by fascism; but it was perhaps because he felt himself a Fascist. Men who are perfect specimens of a type feel pleasure in their representative perfection, even though the type itself is not happy. Byron was sleek at finding himself the archetype of the Romantic, although the essence of romanticism is suffering; and Tolstoy enjoyed being the archetype of the Anarchist, although anarchy is the most hopeless of faiths, being an aching discontent with time, which inexorably engenders order. A work of art gives satisfaction to the artist and the spectator because it analyses an experience and synthesizes its findings into a new form that makes people eager for fresh experience. It is natural enough that something of the same sort of satisfaction should be enjoyed by a human being whose character lies limned before the eye with the particularity of an anatomical drawing, so that it can be comprehended as never before, and judged.

10

THERE are several growths from the Fascist stem. Of these William Joyce could represent but one. He had nothing in common with the rank and file of fascism, which was drawn from the mindless, traditionless, possessionless urban populations that are the children of the machine. Those have wholly lost their sense of process. They have forgotten that whatever is not natural is artificial, and that artifice is the fruit of thought and effort and conflict with matter. To them a loaf of bread is something they can buy at a bakery; they do not think of the earth and the weather and the plough and the wheat and the harvest and the threshers and the mill. To them light and heat are what they summon by putting a match to a gas-jet or a finger to a switch; they do not think of coal and the pithead and the shaft and the dynamo. They therefore believe that all benefits can be obtained by quite small efforts, and they cannot understand why governments have not already given them full employment, preferably of a light character, high wages, cheap food, free recreations; and they therefore will work to put into power any men who say that they will be able to conjure up those goods by command. Such simplicity is infantile, and must be tainted by the first ugly brutishness of the infantile mind; so cruelty is inevitably an associate of the demand for dictatorship. Only in his love of street-fighting had William Joyce any tie with this kind of Fascist, whom he regarded cynically as the medium in which he had to work. His Irish peasant background had given him a sound enough understanding of process, and he thoroughly grasped the practice and the theory of the modern political

machine. It is certain from his broadcasts that he did not hold
the essential doctrine of the Fascist rank and file, which is that
government is easy. The kind of Fascist he represented was the
leader drawn from the small, uninfluential home, as distinct from
the leader drawn from the armed forces or from the aristocracy.

He was therefore representative of the newer type of Fascist
leader. Of the older types, the professional soldier who turns his
arms against his own kind and seizes political power is old as
man. The king, whom the foolish sneer at as a reactionary figure-
head, is this man tamed by law, forced by the Church, which was
the noble cunning of early Europe, to enter into a contractual
relationship with the people, to give them protection in return
for their allegiance. That brigadiers and admirals (particularly
when stone-deaf) should try to turn back the clock and have the
power of force returned to its early absolutism, is not unnatural.
Sir Oswald Mosley, too, is a type that reappears in age after age,
not to be abolished; such organisms, recognized in space, are
called "non-filterable viruses." The aristocrat who has a flaw in
him which is recognized by his own kind, but who will not accept
their verdict on him, and tries to rush over their dead bodies to
the place in the council chamber which they denied him, he is a
most familiar figure. From the earliest recorded time he, on our
island, has had again and again to be told to stop pushing; and
on the Continent, he has revisited again and again, choosing the
name of Wallenstein for one of his most positive reincarnations.
But the Fascist leader drawn from the small uninfluential home
is new as our own century.

He is the man who, whatever his origins had been, if he had
been born in favourable and not in unfavourable circumstances,
could not in any age, nor in any place, have been given a position
of power by the community, because of some innate flaw in his
character, such as made Mosley or Wallenstein inacceptable to
their equals. Till now he could pretend that the cause of this
failure lay not in himself but in his stars. He could maintain,
with a fair measure of truth, that it was impossible for him or
any other man without fortune, or useful connexions, to become
a national leader; and nobody could disprove his claim. He could
go to his grave, therefore, in the rounded contentment of a
genius who could have saved his country had he but been per-

mitted. But now this simple and profound order of satisfaction, which benefited millions, has been destroyed by the development of the democratic system. It is no longer true that any person of political talent can be debarred from exercising it by poor or mediocre origins. Joyce was born and bred in much easier circumstances than Ernest Bevin or Herbert Morrison or Ellen Wilkinson, and if he could not rise to the same heights the reason must be in his inferiority to them. He knew too that intellectually he was probably not inferior to them, for his academic attainments suggested that he had at least the foundations of a good mind. Therefore he was forced to search in other fields for the cause of his inacceptability, which he must have rcognized immediately it declared itself, possibly in the days when he tried to become an army officer, for he was as sensitive as he was coarse.

He was bound to suspect that it was a moral deficiency which rendered him unattractive. It might have been that he was in his secret heart not truly trustworthy, and that the world had spied it out; and that would be a horrible fear, since in his youth he certainly meant to be good, and if his intelligence recognized his latent capacity for cynicism and brutality it would be with stoicism rather than with exaltation. But he could rebut that suspicion simply by remembering the guarantee of high principle which he and his family, isolated in an enclave of history, believed themselves to possess as Irish supporters of the British ascendancy. Only the strongest moral fibre would have empowered them to thread their way among assassinations in service to the splendid symbol of the crown. Beyond all doubt William Joyce was not prevented from winning political eminence by external circumstances, nor by intellectual inferiority, nor by moral baseness. There was but one other possible impediment. It must be that he was rejected because he did not please. But that is what none of us can bear: to realize that we do not please, that we are not liked, that we are not loved.

Rather than make that admission William Joyce would tear out by the roots the process by which, throughout the ages, the leaders of the state have been accorded their leadership. For the making of a king is twofold. He is consecrated by the Church, and he is chosen by the people. That is, he promises to follow the law that is the reflection of heavenly order in the mirror of man's mind; and he is liked by the people, he is loved by the people, they lift up their spears and shout when they see him crowned, their hearts are warm within them when they see him given the compliment of power, they have no fear that he will misuse it. This relationship is not essentially altered between the electors and the elected in a modern democracy. There is the same promise to discover and execute the law, the same reliance for dynamic force on the heat of liking. But since William Joyce was not liked, he would drive out the element of liking from the governmental situation. He asserted that power should not be won by love but should be seized by force. If the masses would not like him and choose him as their leader, then he would find a few men who liked him and they would help him to seize power. But that prescription would not answer, for if the mass did not like him it was probable that the few also would find something in him unpalatable: and indeed the private history of Fascist parties depicts a confusion of unpalatable men whose gorges rise at one another and who look angrily to see if the others' gorges do not rise at themselves. It is for this reason that fascism develops its international character. The leaders must look outside their country for supporters to aid them against their enemies and their friends, who are perhaps also their enemies, inside their own country; so these will have an invasion up their sleeves, to trump all aces. Mussolini, the first Fascist ruler of our times, cultivated the friendship of Fascist-minded men in the Balkans. Hitler cultivated the friendship of Mussolini; Franco cultivated the friendship of Hitler and Mussolini. Treason is inherent in fascism, and in that William Joyce was a traitor he was more respectable than those half-Fascists who would not take the last fence and spent the war in Brixton Jail. What he had chosen to be, he was.

But there remains a mystery in William Joyce and all those others who are Fascist leaders because they are debarred from high positions in the state by reason of intellectual inferiority or moral baseness or failure to please. Why is it so important to them that they should stand on the political platform, hold office, give commands with their own voices and be personally feared? A man who is not acceptable as a national leader is given by our system the opportunity to exercise as much political power as is necessary for his self-respect and the protection of his rights. He can vote in Parliamentary and local elections; and he can serve his country as a private Member of Parliament or a member of a local authority or as a member of a special committee. Why should William Joyce and his kind howl after impossible eminence when in the common run they had no occasion for humiliation? There are other means of establishing exceptional value. If Joyce was not loved by the mass he was loved well by some near to him, and to some was a good lover; to his brother Quentin and to his second wife he was light and warmth. He was also a good teacher; happily he transmitted the tradition of knowledge, happily he saw it happily received. That surely should have been enough for him: to be a good brother, to be a good husband, to be a good teacher. Many are given less. Yet he hungered for the mere audience, for the wordless cheering, the executive power which, if it be not refined to nothing by restraint, is less than nothing.

Perhaps right was on his side. Perhaps it is not enough to be a good brother or to be a good husband, or to be a good teacher. For human relationships are always qualified by questioning. A brother, and a wife, and pupils, have their own selves to maintain, so they must sometimes defend themselves and keep back their secrets; they will sometimes pass over to the attack and seek out the secrets of the brother, the husband, and the teacher; and often time changes them, so that there is not acceptance, only this questioning. It would be better for a man to have a relationship with a person who knew all about him and therefore had no need to question him, who recognized that he was unique and precious and therefore withheld no confidence from him, who could not be changed by time though by his steadfastness he might change time and make it kind and stable. Those who believe in God enjoy such a relationship. It would be impertinent to speculate about Joyce's relationship with God, about which we know nothing relevant save that he left the Church in which he was born and that he inscribed himself on the Nazi records as "a believer." But it can be taken that his mind had been trained over the trellis erected round him by society, and that that trellis was cut in a non-Christian or even anti-Christian pattern. Whether he enjoyed his relationship with God or not, he must often have believed that it did not exist.

But even those who take the greatest pleasure in ridding themselves of faith in God find that the heart then loses its occupation, for want of a friend who shall never tease nor misprize nor go away. Such friendship cannot be given by a personal friend, since these faults are the signs of personality taking care of itself; and those who desire it and have discarded the idea of a superpersonal God must look for it in those fields of life furthest removed from ordinary personal relationships. The most obvious of these is politics. There a leader can excite love in followers who know nothing of him save his public appearances, and who, even if they achieve the closest oratorical union with him, would be deterred by a sense of impertinence from questioning him about his private affairs. That love is unqualified; for no party can cause its enemies to rejoice by admitting that its leader has any faults, and what parties profess they soon sincerely feel, especially in crowded halls. That love swears itself undying, too; for no party can afford to let itself be overheard contemplating the exchange of its leader for another.

Therefore the man who would have been happy in the practice of religion during the ages of faith has in these modern times a need for participation in politics which is strong as the need for food, for shelter, for sex. It feeds his soul, it keeps it from the wind, it drives out that terrible companion loneliness. Such a man is well met with the man who during the ages of faith would have known ecstasy in bending the knee to a cardinal and saved his pennies in the vain hope that before he died they might pay for a pilgrimage to Rome, who in the meantime would have bought the most swindling pardon from the most drunken travelling friar and killed his fattest capon for him, who would have grown simpleton-simple at the very name of a saint, who would have held out his dying hands in expectation that a divine hand would seize them and lead a way into Paradise. Such men, strayed into our age, find cardinal and pardon-selling friar and saint and God in the political leader, who wears authority and directs a hierarchy, who promises them his devotion, assures them that he can conceive no higher end than serving them, and prophesies that he shall never tire of it. No wonder that these two kinds of men, the leaders and the followers, are not content with voting but must make a physical entrance into the political world, to see, to touch, to hear, to cheer; for there they bring to earth, thus making certain of him, the God for whom their ancestors had always hungered but whom they had never induced to come closer than the speculative distance of the sky.

It is, of course, an unsatisfying relationship, this cross-hallucination of two people each of whom believes that the other is God. Neither has a shadow of right on his side. So, presently, they change sides, and each pretends that he himself is God. The leader looks on his followers as his creatures, and, not being God, omits to give them free will and the right to work out their own salvation. The followers curl their lips at the leader, who is presumptuous enough, being human, to exercise his control over all-knowing divinity. Then the leader forms round him a hard core of followers, specially loyal to him by reason of infatuation or bribery, to impress and in the end to terrorize those more critical. Then the followers close in on this leader to divest him of his oppressive authority, and to direct these conspiracies throw up new leaders, who, in time, are resented, protect themselves with their own gangs, and are attacked, and either maintain their power by bloodshed or are deposed by bloodshed. These clumsy wrestlers roll together on the floor of civilization, crying out complicated declarations of their identity which are couched in the forms of dissent even when they agree, for when one gasps, "You are God," the other answers in a repressive roar, as if his claim had been disputed, "No, I am God." This disorder, though accompanied by cries, gasps, cheers, and shouts, nevertheless seems to accomplish itself in silence, as if it were happening behind glass; for none of the persons involved ever speak of the real motives which impel them to their agony, but continually refer, in accents of assumed passion, to motives which do indeed preoccupy some people, but not them. The chief of these is the desire to end poverty. But William Joyce had never in his life known what it was to be hungry or cold or workless, and he did not belong to the altruistic type which torments itself over the plight of others; and indeed there was probably no callousness in this, for surely had he himself been destitute he would have been too completely absorbed by his rages and his books ever to notice it. His was another hunger, another chill, another kind of unemployment. But the only people in the generation before him who attacked the governing class had been poor or altruist, and since their attack had been successful, their vocabulary held a tang of victory.

So William Joyce and his kind borrowed their phrases, and spoke of economics when they thought of religion, thus becoming the third wing of a certain triptych. In the third and fourth centuries of this era Europe and North Africa and Nearer Asia were racked by the economic problems caused by the impending dissolution of the Western Roman Empire. The study of economics was then barely begun; there was as yet no language in which the people could analyse their insecurity and design their security. But during the preceding centuries the earth had been visited by Christ, and several men of genius had been impressed by his personality and excited by its bearings on the discoveries made by the ancient philosophers. Hence the science of theology was developed to a stage where quite simple minds could grasp the outlines with which it firmly delineated universal experiences, and the inarticulate learned from it to use confidently phrases more expressive than they could have invented. Therefore those suffering economic distress complained of it in theological terms. They cried out to society that its structure was wrong, in terms that, taken literally, meant that the orthodox Christian faith was mistaken; they rushed from the derelict estates where they must starve, to towns where they lived as leanly, into the desert where they could eat well on brigandage, and said that they did it because they had had a peculiar revelation concerning the Trinity. Now, in our day, those suffering from religious distress complain of it in economic terms. Between the two wings of the triptych shone the rich panel of European civilization.

It is undignified to be the victim of an historical predicament. It is a confession that one has been worsted, not by a conspiracy of enemies nor by the hostility of nature, but by one's environment: by the medium in which one's genius, had one possessed such a thing, should have expressed itself. As harsh is it for an actor to admit that he cannot speak on a stage, for an artist to admit that he cannot put paint on canvas. So the victims of historical predicaments are tempted to pretend that they sacrificed themselves for an eternal principle which their contemporaries had forgotten, instead of owning that one of time's gables was in the way of their window and barred their view of eternity, so that possibly they had been wrong in relation to the sum of things, and were at any rate obviously not really right. But William Joyce pretended nothing at his trials. His faint smile said simply, "I am what I am." He did not defend the faith which he had held, for he had doubted it; he did not attack it, for he had believed in it. It is possible that in these last days fascism had passed out of the field of his close attention; that what absorbed him was the satisfaction which he felt at being, for the first time in his life, taken seriously. It was at last conceded that what he was and what he did were matters of supreme importance. The police-car brought him up from the black Wandsworth Jail through the streets, never grand, thronged by the people, never great, of South London; it slid across Waterloo Bridge to the fretted neo-Gothic outlines, alluding to Christianity, associated with power, symbolizing tradition, of the Houses of Parliament, where the Victoria Tower raised up against the winter skies Big Ben, the portrait of time, wrought large, to be seen by those on both sides of the river, who are alike subject to its discipline. He had thought that because he was not yet accepted on the imperial side of the Thames nothing that he did was of great moment, but now it had appeared that he had been involved by his birth in a war between the forces in the community which desired to live and those which desired to die, in a war between the forces in himself which desired to live and those which desired to die. Time was the battlefield set apart for the waging of such wars, and in time he had no other value than attached to his bearing in that battle. If he had borne himself well he would be saved, but if he had been an evil soldier he would be damned.

Surely he felt pride and relief at understanding how he stood, for it had been his fear that, bearing no great name and never having been allowed to earn one, he and his doings were not priced in any catalogue. It was an end to mediocrity. It was the beginning of such distinction as would ideally be conferred on him in a society which believed that a man's soul was immortal

and precious to the higher powers. Thus made serene (for all
who saw him would concede his serenity), he waited his time.
It cannot have been easy waiting, for events made mouths at him,
as they always do at people who have been spatch-cocked by
history. In all trials of importance there are strange coincidences,
oddities in name, overlappings of time. William Joyce would not
have been human if he had not hoped for his life when it was
appointed that the result of his appeal to the House of Lords
should be given out on December the 18th; and it was on December the 18th that he had been tried at Lewes Assizes on a charge
of riotous assembly, and had been acquitted. Confined in his cell
he knew moments of hope, succeeded by moments of despair
when that hope failed; and these were succeeded by moments of
another hope when it appeared that all previous estimates of the
imbroglio were false, and that even if justice executed its harshest
imperatives it would have another outcome, cutting across its
length and breadth and depth in a direction not till then predicted, which would be glorious; though what was inglorious
would not be forgotten.

Such alternatives of hope and despair, such visions of hope and
despair relating to eventualities not of this earth, are known to
all of us, confined as in a cell in the flesh. On the floor of the
courts where William Joyce was tried there was tested an issue
of how far the letter is divorced from the spirit; it was debated
whether a man can live all his life among a tribe and eat their
salt and in the hour of their danger sharpen the sword intended
by their enemies for their breasts, and then go free because of
something written in an old book which said that this man was
not truly of that tribe. But in the upper air above these courts
it was argued whether the God with whom man can have a perfect relationship is the dream of disappointed sons imaging a
Father who shall be better than all fathers, or is more real than
reality. This other trial was not concluded, not being confined to
time or space. For it is expansive as the life of clouds, which
overpass the horizons binding any human habitation; it began
with some remote birth and will not now end till the last death.
It is this uncertainty which gives life its sickening and exquisite
tension. Under that tension the fragile body of William Joyce
quivered as he sat in his several docks; for though his speech

was a blunt instrument his substance was not dense, it offered no gross resistance to the wave of this pulse. Now his silence had the terrible petitioning quality we had heard in his voice in the past. Though he was calm, his wonder at time as it streamed away from him could be felt. There was visible through his flesh the thin shaking flame on which, by the direction of other thin shaking flames, a white hood was presently to fall as an extinguisher.

I I

IN THE person of William Joyce there was condemned by the community the extrovert who seeks to find in politics what in other ages he found in religion, and usually makes his search on the field of fascism, with its marches, its shouting, its bright colours, its blows, its violence. Six months after he was hanged there followed him into the dock Dr. Allan Nunn May, Lecturer on Physics in the University of London, the personification of the introvert who makes the same transference but is better pleased by the secrecy and drabness of communism: which is fascism with a geographical and glandular difference. He was a scientist, and therefore as representative of his breed of fascism as Joyce had been of his. For the new Fascists, who stepped forward after the war to carry on the old business under a different label, were in England under scientific domination. It had been the claim of the violent men who formed the Nazi-Fascist movement that they should be entrusted with power because they were endowed with a greater amount of physical strength and vitality than the mass of the population: an amount which would enable them to seize that power if it were denied them. It was now the claim of the scientists who formed so influential a part of the Communist-Fascist movement that they were endowed with a greater amount of special technical knowledge than the mass of the population: an amount which would enable them to seize that power if they were denied it. There is a similarity between the claims of the Nazi-Fascists and the Communist-Fascists, and no less similarity between the methods of putting them forward. The claims depend on an unsound assumption that the man who possesses a special gift will possess also a universal wisdom which will enable him to impose an order on the state superior to that contrived by the consultative system known as democracy: which will enable him, in fact, to know other people's business better than they do themselves.

If this assumption seems less patently absurd when it is applied to a scientist, the reason is simply the dizzy novelty of science. The study of physics or chemistry is no more likely than the study of harmony or counterpoint to develop social omniscience in the student; nor have these or any other branches of science made any contributions to the technique of government which would give them any right to intervene as experts. It frequently happens that the B.B.C. asks certain Communist scientists to speak about the age we are in, and they are always remarkable for the vanity with which they claim that the advance of science at last made it possible for man to contemplate a planned and abundant economy for the world. But modern science has in fact done almost nothing to give man the precognizance necessary for planning, and still less to guarantee any kind of useful abundance. It cannot foretell or control the foundation of all economy, which is weather. It has not yet found a way of providing cheap houses, or a cheap and convenient source of light and heat and energy, or a cheap and reliable food supply. The groundless boasts were, like the equally groundless boasts of the Nazi-Fascists, covers for a threat. Mussolini and Hitler and Mosley, when they said that they and their followers could govern because of their physical strength and ruthlessness, meant that they and their followers had enough physical strength and ruthlessness to beat and shoot anyone who refused to be governed by them. The Communist scientists, when they said that they and their associates could govern because of their technical knowledge, meant that they and their associates play a sufficient part in the development of modern processes used in modern war and industry to be able to blackmail society if it would not accept their dictation. The one demand is as absurd as was the other. Obviously any fragile doctor or research worker had as much right as any brawny Fascist to have his say in the conduct of the community; and obviously any teacher, or any factory hand, or any housewife, is as necessary to the state as a scientist and has as much right to self-government.

There was a significance in the manner of speech adopted by the Communist-Fascists. The Nazi-Fascists shouted as if their lungs and more were in superb condition. When heard over the air their voices suggested tall, stout, virile bodies, under perfect control, which were either richly invested with sex or lacked it because it had been displaced by some still fiercer dæmon. These Communist-Fascists spoke thinly and with a hesitancy that seemed to be assumed, that was exaggerated at times to a stutter, as if to make it plain that they renounced the body as unimportant and based all their claims on pre-eminence of intellect. What more than this they do when they do this was shown when Dr. Allan Nunn May stood in the dock at the Old Bailey. Nature itself had done much to commit him to the Fascist-Communist choice; for he was poorly built but had a great head, bulging at the back like the head of a fœtus, in a conformation often found in men of exceptional talent. He was very bald for a man of thirty-four. Though he resembled William Joyce in the meanness of his physique, he had made a very different use of it. For Joyce had made himself a little knuckleduster of a man by hard exercise, but this man plainly had never remarked that he had muscles. Certain virtues flower from respect for the body, so he had them not. All the Nazi-Fascist traitors, even down to little Herbert George, acquitted themselves better in the dock than Dr. Allan Nunn May. They held up their heads and bullied their words to march out untrembling from their mouths. They invoked courage; and the effort of making natural cowardice give way to this guest distracted their minds from their plight and in that time revealed to them, which they had not expected, that man can score a victory over fate other than its reversal. Dr. Allan Nunn May made a finer revelation. In his appearance there were indications of an extreme fineness of intellect, unfoldings of a lacework of perceptions, of associations, of interpretations, which made the Nazi-Fascists seem like hogs rooting among the simple unimproved beech-mast of the world. No matter how he stooped and wavered, out of his head proceeded mental patterns intricate and brilliant as the etchings of frost on a winter pane. Surely the others, the Nazi-Fascists, were not fully human. Neither was he.

But the skin of Dr. Allan Nunn May was glazed with sweat; he could scarcely force the plea "Not guilty" past his chattering teeth; and his body assumed without shame the very shape of fear.

In all other things as well, the trials of William Joyce and Dr. Allan Nunn May were the black and the white. When the Nazi-Fascist stood in the dock the court was full of his simple and forthright and ungifted followers, open in their grief. When the Communist-Fascist followed him into the same dock his complicated and secretive and able associates were elsewhere, aiming to feel nothing because only the Party, the substanceless structure of the movement, was of importance. It had been the singularity of Joyce's case that it depended entirely on evidence regarding matters of fact and law, which he could have neither confirmed nor disproved, since he was unaware of them till the time of his trial. His destiny had depended on outward events. But there was no evidence at all against Dr. Allan Nunn May except his own statement. He had been interviewed by one of the most remarkable personalities at Scotland Yard: a quiet man to whom people confess. He applies no pressure to them, and it appears to be simply the sense of his integrity that makes them anxious to tear out the adjusted page of the ledger and add up the figures again. Dr. Allan Nunn May's destiny had depended on his interior life.

There was as complete an antithesis between their handling of their destinies. At every point of William Joyce's life he had shown brisk competence. At every point of the episode which brought Dr. Allan Nunn May to the dock, and was apparently the only remarkable episode in his existence outside his scientific studies, he behaved like an idiot. No person of greater intellectual eminence has ever been charged in the English courts with a grave crime: no criminal has ever admitted to having behaved with greater folly. He had voluntarily entered the service of the British government during the war, as the senior member of the nuclear physics division in the unit devoted to research on the atomic bomb, and signed an undertaking binding himself not to give any information concerning his activities to any unauthorized person, and acknowledged that he would become subject to proceedings under the Official Secrets Act if he broke that undertaking. Later, he said, he came to the conclusion that his researches were contributing to a situation dangerous to mankind unless they were made available to all scientists, of whatever nation. This was of course not a completely honest account of the situation. It omits the important factor that he had long been a member of the Communist Party, and as such would feel obliged to act on all instructions originating from Moscow, and would have had to hand over to any person named in these instructions any material they wanted, no matter what his opinions about the transaction might be. Nor does his attitude towards the atomic bomb explain why, as he himself confesses, he gave information concerning electronic shells, or gave the Soviet Intelligence Service advice on whether to utilize the services of a young Englishman named Norman Veal, an employee of the Scientific Research Council, as a spy. It is difficult to understand why these scruples had not occurred to him when the post was first offered to him, as he knew the nature and aims of the work he had to do. In any case his duty was plain. He could not disclose the results of his researches because he had signed an undertaking not to do so. No society, whether capitalist, socialist, or communist, can survive for ten minutes if it abandons the principle that a contract is sacred. But he could have resigned from the post, which would have caused serious inconvenience to the authorities, and explained his reasons to his fellow-scientists and to the general public. He did nothing of the sort. When in Canada, working at the Atomic Energy Project, he handed notes of his researches and samples of the metals he was using in his experiments—in spite of his pretence that he wanted to share his knowledge with all the scientists of the world—to a man who was simply a Russian agent, and who gave him no guarantee that he was going to communicate the secret to scientists of other nations, and was so far from being a scientist that they were unable to converse on the subject of the atomic bomb at all.

The only flicker of personal feeling in Dr. Allan Nunn May's statement arose from his annoyance at the idiotic questions this agent had asked him. There was obviously a possible pitfall in these proceedings. Before the war Nazi-Fascist agents frequently pretended to be acting for Russia; and there remain with us General Franco and Colonel Perón who are not passive figures on the international scene. It was made plain during the trial that Dr. Allan Nunn May was the last person to detect such an imposture, since he was lacking in all natural shrewdness; and it is unlikely that he had the particular knowledge which would have enabled him to test the agent's credentials by questioning him. He becomes an enigma at this point; for, though it is difficult to conceive what he was if not a disinterested scholar and Communist-Fascist, he accepted from this agent a bribe of seven hundred Canadian dollars, which is the equivalent of a hundred and sixty pounds. The bribe is said to have been "seven hundred dollars and a bottle of whisky"; but this is to make it more bizarre than it was. It seems that the phrase should run "seven hundred dollars in a bottle of whisky." This sum is small enough payment for an act which might have brought its perpetrator to the gallows; but it is much too large to be put down as a reimbursement for out-of-pocket expenses. Then, after having taken the irrevocable steps of having acted as a spy for Russia and having taken money for his services, he went into reverse, and on his return to England failed to keep an appointment with a Russian agent outside the British Museum. It is hardly necessary to say that he thereby put himself into the way of certain unpleasantnesses. It was logical enough that when the English police approached him after this he should have made a statement admitting his guilt. But it was not logical that he should have withheld from them the identity of the Russian agent. He later robbed that reticence of its only possible excuse by disclosing that the agent was Russian. The only Nazi-Fascist traitor whose conduct was comparable in fatuity to this Doctor of Science was Walter Purdy, whose education had begun and ended in an East End elementary school and who was looked on as an eccentric by all his fellows. There could be no more conspicuous demonstration of the unwisdom of deducing from the specialist achievements of any individual, group, or class, that they could be properly entrusted to take over the general task of government from persons of lesser achievements.

To the very end, to the moment when the sentences were delivered, the contrast between the two trials was maintained in its acuteness. The guilt of William Joyce was a light matter compared to the guilt of Dr. Allan Nunn May. It is impossible that what Joyce did could now harm anyone; he tried to do evil

and failed. But the samples of minerals Dr. Allan Nunn May gave
the Russian agent, uranium 235 enriched and uranium 233, threw
such light on elements in the form that the British and American
conception of the atomic bomb had taken that they were immediately flown to Russia; and if ever Russia drops an atom bomb
on Great Britain or America, the blame for the death and the
blindness and the sores it scatters will rest largely on this fatuous
and gifted man. Far more than William Joyce did he deserve to
be hanged, yet he was condemned to ten years' penal servitude;
and whereas nobody in court except Joyce's followers was greatly
moved when the sentence of death was passed on him, the
spectators were plainly appalled when the Judge passed sentence
on Dr. Allan Nunn May, though none of them was his follower.
The Attorney-General, Sir Hartley Shawcross, showed that he
was sick at heart under the necessity of making the speech for
the prosecution and waited for the sentence with an apprehension
rarely shown even by a defending counsel. It was the light about
the man's head which made the thought of his imprisonment
intolerable: the changing and complicated intellectual patterns
proceeding from his brow and spelling out a meaning which men
required. All present knew that the power to make such divina-
tions is intertwined with a special liability to feel pain and panic:
for him imprisonment would be such a hell as death would not
be to William Joyce. Dr. Allan Nunn May was precious to us as
William Joyce was not, because he was something which man
must be and is not yet, save here and there, and with great
difficulty. William Joyce had courage; but though it is a terrible
thing not to have courage, to be courageous carries a man out of
that terror but not a step further, unless he has other qualities to
transport him. Millions of men have been brave, but have been
nothing more; and the brute creation is also brave. Dr. Allan
Nunn May had that which differentiates man from the brutes:
he had not only that intellect, but that kind of degree of intellectual power, which can break down the smooth surface of appearance and uncover the reality which is now hidden from us,
which can give man knowledge so new to him that he can become
a new man. But in the dock he proved that the new man will be
no better than the old if he succumbs to certain temptations,
which for him will be specially strong. A man with so dynamic a

mind will be specially conscious of the vacuum left by the disap-
pearance of God; his legitimate pride in his special gifts will be
great enough to swell easily into a pretence that he is God. History
has shown again and again that as soon as a man believes that
he is a god he behaves far worse than the average human being.
There follow impious conspiracies against the wills of others,
though through each and all of them the purposes of hidden
reality might declare themselves. Conspirators grow confused
and therefore use methods they once would not have used; and
grow frightened and therefore are cruel as the frightened are;
and are outmanœuvred by other conspirators and therefore are
shabby and outmoded and futile. The man of the past and the
man of the future, William Joyce and Allan Nunn May, were
on a perfect parity in the dock. Men who in any age do not
respect life, reverse time and step back over the threshold of life,
into the chaos which is always waiting.

I 2

THESE traitors were not a peculiar product of this war
between Great Britain and Germany. They were in a business which has been carried on since the beginning of history.
Faint cries from the past tell us how the Illyrians were ashamed
when their blood worked for Rome, how Central Europe blushed
over renegades who joined the yellow barbarian hordes; and the
Republic of Venice entered on its books how it competed on
the Mediterranean coasts with the great corrupter Islam, who for
centuries made aliens like William Joyce beys and pashas and
emirs, and gave scholars like Allan Nunn May honourable places
as tutors, and picked the British Free Corps from among the
galley-slaves. The men who stood in the dock in the Old Bailey
were enduring their two-hundredth incarnation or so, allowing
three generations to a century and putting the first complicated
civilization in the fourth millennium before Christ.

Their business is not always treachery, in the sense of aiding
the enemies of their own country. They were traitors incidentally.
They were gangsters essentially. The gang spirit is friendship

which does not consume its fires on warming the inner circle where friends live, but turns them outward, to burn with flame all the rest of the world. Some gangs, in the past and in the present, have been satisfied to be bandits. Others have liked government: Rome itself in its middle age was often the private possession of gangsters. When such men seize power they are as detached from and hostile to the local population as any foreign administrator could be. Hence it is no great step for them to accept aid from any imperialist power or any international system which wishes to buy suzerainty over the territorial unit they are trying to control. The force which impels men to engage in these transactions is not simply to be defined as desire for power. To become a successful gangster a man must have a degree of ability which would have given him a reasonable amount of power in any society. The power which gangsters desire is that which enables them to stop the people round them from living the life which they would themselves wish to live; that is to say, to destroy the society of which they are a part, not by replacing it with another created at the pace of organic growth, but by killing society.

This situation never exists in quite a simple form. The Nazi Party claimed the right to govern first Germany and then all Europe on the plea that its theories alone would solve all economic and political and social problems. The Nuremberg Trials showed that the dynamic force which gave the Nazi Party the power to govern was the sadist ambition of a number of gangsters. But actually some of these men honestly believed in the Nazi theories, and certainly attempts were made over a long period of years by these men and their equally convinced followers to carry them into practice. The significant element in this case, which is present wherever the gangster seizes power, is the rise in the rate of deaths by violence. Whenever a minority imposes its will by force, it does not stop killing when it has broken the resistance against it, even if it revives resistance by its continued killing. There is here a delight in death; which is a question of taste on the profoundest levels of being. In every type of society this delight may manifest itself, and it is hard to imagine that it can ever be eliminated by any change in material circumstances. It is advisable for countless reasons that all men should everywhere enjoy abundance. But it is well to realize that everywhere there are some men to whom the fruits of abundance will taste bitter, because they dislike all life.

Those who are imperialist or fascist or communist, or who hold any other faith which moves to its goal by the subjection of peoples, must needs raise William Joyce from the grave and enfranchise Allan Nunn May from prison and the sense of guilt. These are the instruments by which nations are enslaved. It is for men to decide whether it is pleasant to use such instruments. But what the use of such instruments involves cannot be judged only by what was seen of William Joyce and Allan Nunn May. These men both were fortunate in their misfortune, for they were given by their destinies the chance to wrestle with reality, to argue with the universe, to defend the revelations which they believed had been made to their spirits; and that is man's glory. But treason also takes to itself the madmen and the children, and for them there is no glory.

II

THE INSANE ROOT

I

THE FIRST people to come into Room No. I of The Central Criminal Court, where John Amery was to be tried for high treason, were two American officers, who sat and stared about them for some moments before any came to join them, drab figures in a court sallow with November. They were the soberer sort of soldier, their faces lined and greyish with the prolonged overwork that led up to and away from D-day. There arrived next the Director of Public Prosecutions, Sir Theobald Mathew, a long-headed, tall, slender Irishman with jutting eyebrows. He watched his clerk set down an enormous file at the counsel's table and turned away, moving as if he had reason to feel something like pleasure: better put it down as unusually acute interest. Then the regular personnel of the court filtered in. First came the chief prosecuting counsel, the Attorney-General, Sir Hartley Shawcross, just home from the trial of the war criminals at Nuremberg. The fall of those desperate men to their last place in the pit can also be looked at from another point of view: a creditably conducted incident in a sunnily successful career. There is nothing callous or even smug about him, he has indeed the gentlest and most charitable of tempers; but he is fortunate, visibly fortunate. Had Pippa passed him she would have added him to her list of proofs that all's right with the world. He was followed by the counsel for the defence: Gerald Osborne Slade, who was counsel for Joyce, who pecks at his cases like a sparrow, as tireless and as careful of the smallest grain; and his assistant, John Foster, he who spent the first years of the war at the British Embassy in Washington, dark and high-coloured and genially menacing, like a Renaissance bravo.

The three long tables in front of the judge's bench were soon filled up with lawyers and those two strongly contrasted types

who had to be present at all the trials—the men with iron faces
who belong to the special police, and the Military Intelligence
officers, who are usually of notably mild appearance, having
been detached from the ordinary army service because of their
clerkly gifts. Indeed the court looked very much as it was during
the trial of William Joyce except for the spectators. When Joyce
was being tried, the court became a background for him and his
followers, who, though they were scattered in twos or threes,
achieved by their emotions an effect of unity, so that the remembered scene has the quality of a chapter in a legend of martyrdom. The people who had come to see John Amery tried were
drawn by an interest in the treason laws, or by a recollection of
his broadcasts, or by curiosity about the black sheep of a deeply
respected family; but there were no apostles, for there was no
leader. The eyes turned towards the dock that day were certain
to be dry. The trial of John Amery was the end of a long story
desiccating to the heart.

It began years ago in the Augustan age, among children of
promise. Some time in the 'eighties, the impudent red-haired son
of the brilliant politician Lord Randolph Churchill was sent to
the famous public school Harrow. Exploring the possibilities of
the establishment, he came on the swimming bath and found a
very small boy standing, fully dressed, at its edge. He fell to the
obvious temptation, but he realized, as the victim turned about
in the water and struck out for the side, that it was one of the
lions of Harrow, Leopold Amery, who, though small in stature,
was older than his assailant and of awesome accomplishment both
as a scholar and an athlete. Obviously the situation was awkward.
The young Winston's first attempt to put matters right was not
inspired. "I am very sorry," he said. "I mistook you for a fourth-
form boy. You are so small." But his guardian dæmon came to
save him in the end. "My father," he added, "who is a great
man, is also small." This was the beginning of a lifelong, bicker-
ing, and unbreakable friendship.

Leopold Amery never grew much in inches. In any gathering
he can be easily picked out, the small and stocky protagonist
with the fighting look that little men often have, but not tetchy:
on the contrary, happy with the happiness enjoyed by those whose
bodies are in good shape. All his life he has kept up his skiing

and sailing, and his mountaineering to the extent of climbing
the Matterhorn just once again, for old times' sake, when he was
sixty-five; and he, who was born in 1873, is still notably neat-
footed and buoyant of tread. In mind he grew as he did not in
body. He worked well at Oxford, took a first in Greats, the combined course in classics and philosophy which attracts the best
minds, and was elected a Fellow of All Souls' College. This is a
curious institution which, unlike other colleges, does not undertake the teaching of undergraduates, but tries to bridge the gulf
eternally existing between thinkers and men of action by housing
together some of the one and some of the other. Thus, graduates
who are engaged in scholarly pursuits, whether in literature or
history or law, mingle with graduates who are engaged
in public affairs. Only the first-rate get these fellowships, and
Amery, if not a first-rate intellectual, was a first-rate man.

During the past fifty years, Amery has spun a triple thread of
the law, journalism, and politics, and there are few knots in it.
He filled various administrative posts during the South African
War and the two world wars and in the intervening times of peace,
in Parliament and out of it. Sometimes he found himself in the
same cabinet as Winston, and then there were tremendous fall-
ings out and makings up. His particular interest has been the
economic development of the Empire, which he has regarded as
the instrument for extending the rule of law over the earth. For
that reason the left sees him as a jingo. But nobody, left or right,
has ever seen him as anything but an honest man; the worst that
his enemies have ever discovered about him is that he holds (or
held) shares in a company manufacturing a purgative which is
perhaps not so physically redemptive as its makers claim. As poli-
ticians go this is not a grave fault; and people like him for the
perpetual intrusion of his schoolboy toughness. In 1927, because
he was Secretary of State for Dominion Affairs, the Canadian
government by way of compliment christened an eleven-thousand-
foot peak Mount Amery, and thought no more about it.
They were enchanted when, two years later, he came over and
put blood into this paper courtesy by making the first
ascent of the peak, being then fifty-six years old. But there is
more in Leopold Amery than the public servant and the athlete.
These might be the virtues that spring from insularity and run in

grooves. But Leopold Amery has a taste for the whole world. He has travelled everywhere, and not only officially, but in shirt sleeves with a rucksack, finding a quick way into foreign lives by his remarkable linguistic gifts, enormously enjoying any festival he may come across, a wedding or a christening or a harvest supper. Whatever is pleasant and of good repute, he has sought it.

Fairly late in life, going out of his thirties, Leopold Amery married a beautiful young woman. She was the sister of Hamar Greenwood, a Canadian who came over to England and, becoming involved with Lloyd George, entered politics and reached cabinet rank. He was remarkable only for his unpopularity. Twenty-five years ago he was Secretary for Ireland and was held responsible for some of the ungodlier passages in the severance of England and Ireland. It was he who let loose the Black and Tans, the English troops recruited and trained in a spirit alien from the modern tradition of the British army which envenomed the last year of the union. But in that unpopularity his sister had no share. It is conceded by all that Mrs. Amery is as good and kind as a woman may be, and that if she had a fault it lay in her idolization of her two sons. It is said that she made the lives of their pastors and masters burdensome with her urgent effort to ensure that they should be happy and respected and long-lived. The younger son was Julian Amery, who, if one may go by such signs as are visible in the twenties, rewarded her obsession. Authority gave him important work in this war and it is said he performed it well. He is certainly delightful in appearance and manner. The other was John Amery, who at the time of his trial had lived thirty-three years and had been in trouble for most of them.

John Amery was not insane, he was not evil, but his character was like the kind of automobile that will not hold the road. As a child, he would be taken by his parents to a hotel at some holiday resort and would be discovered in a corner of the gardens or in the lounge, after dinner, amusing the guests with some mimicry or musical fooling. But the entertaining monologue would become a dribble of nonsense, the dance would go on too long, and there would break in a hint of frenzy. The child would turn from a pet to a pest, and sooner or later there would be trouble, trouble of an odd unpredictable kind which could not

be guarded against, which was not cruel or cowardly but slapped
the normal human process in the face. What is one to do with a
boy of fifteen who from school issues prospectuses for a film-
producing company and collects money from investors, not with
the intention of embezzling it but inevitably with that effect?
What is one to do with him when he is so really or apparently
delicate that it is not possible to subject him to the discipline of
work? One can but say hopefully that he will not always be fifteen. This is, however, not necessarily true. There are some who
are always fifteen. John Amery continued, into his twenties and
thirties, to like glossy, costly automobiles as an adolescent likes
them, and as an adolescent he liked glossy, costly women, disre-
garding the plainest whorishness. And in such automobiles and
with such women he delighted to visit those grandiose hotels
which delight the immature and revolt the mature as the very
antithesis of home.

But on these adolescent appetites was superimposed a wholly
individual gift for complication. He was convicted seventy-four
times for automobile offences which for the most part were not
just breaches of regulations but quite unforseen embroideries
on the commonplace process of travelling from point to point
aided by a combustion engine. He fell in very public and generous love with a well-known prostitute, whose identity could not
be disguised because she had for most evenings during many years
stood in the most conspicuous spot in Piccadilly. He stripped
concubinage of the simplicity which is its undoubted advantage;
marriage, always so much more complicated, he made into a
game like snakes-and-ladders, with his family and himself playing
against each other. He fell in love with a lady older than himself,
and when his family had employed the most recondite legal
means to prevent their union, circumvented them by marrying
her in an Orthodox church in Athens, a place not covered by
their strategy. As for those hotels, credit was to him what orches-
tral tone is to a conductor. In business, an obsession with films
led him to some honourable though brief connexions with the
industry, but also to participation, perhaps innocent, in a firm
which bribed clerks in the offices of reputable motion picture
companies to tell them when any directors were thinking of engaging young and unknown actors and actresses. The heads of

the firm would then rush out and engage these actors and actresses to work in imaginary films on long contracts with low
salaries, and then sublet them to the reputable motion picture
companies at a large profit. He also stranded an entire motion
picture outfit in Africa in extraordinary circumstances. Nobody
could imagine how he had got the credit to take them out there;
but there they were, in quite the wrong continent.

When John Amery was only twenty-four his loyal but exhausted family had to let him become bankrupt. He failed for
five thousand pounds, with assets nil. That was in the autumn
of 1936. The following summer he evoked a yelp of protest, oddly
passionate for official proceedings, from the receiver in charge
of his estate, though such men are usually inured to the financial
optimism which soars like a lark from the heart of the imbecile.
Amery had asked for a discharge from bankruptcy, so that he
could add another and crazier story to the crazy edifice of credit
which he had built on the site where, given his nurture, a more
noble structure might have been raised. Did there always have
to be equivocation added to fatuity, and risk joined to incon-
sequence? The answer, through the years, in various sorts of
court, was that there seemed indeed to be some such necessity.
Nothing in John Amery's life was simple, nothing was of good
repute. After his bankruptcy he left England, his family giving
him an allowance. Let this exile not be counted as unkindness on
their part. Under English law it is an offence for a bankrupt to
obtain goods on credit without disclosing his situation, and he
could not possibly have fulfilled this obligation. The new, immensely long, and shark-nosed automobile would have been too
tempting; another hotel might have been opened in London. He
would have had to go to jail.

Once abroad, John Amery was absorbed into a bath of purity
which was washing clean many a poor tarnished body. At that
time the Spanish Civil War obviously offered a theatre for left-
wing gallants, and so generously did they play their roles that the
labour movement in every country in Europe is the poorer for
the young men who died there. But the war also offered an
asylum to certain persons who, if of no definite political faith,
knew that they were failures, refused to recognize that they had
failed from inability to achieve the average standard, and pre-

ferred to think that they were natural leaders who had been
trodden down by the inferiors. These found new hope in Franco's
fascism. It is true that there was some genuine pro-Franco feeling
in all countries, but it is also true that there was at this time a
great deal of money flowing out of Spain. Never before did corruption so slime the British press. There was honest and intelligent Roman Catholic support of Franco. Letters to the newspapers constantly appeared stating, and of course truly, that nuns
should not be raped, and many of them were written by old
journalists of the baser sort, who, to take the pence and write
the piece, had had to push back the garbage can behind which
they had been sleeping for the last ten years. There were other
more demanding and more lucrative tasks laid before the enter-
prising. There was gun-running. Many right-wing ne'er-do-wells
were drawn to Franco by greed, love of adventure, and the hope
of being accorded a value which, till then, all societies had denied
them. John Amery was irresistibly attracted by the hope of at-
taining this triple gratification which had always been denied
him by his loving but so conventional family, with their excessive
lamentations over trifling automobile accidents that might have
happened to anyone, and over hotel bills which could have easily
been settled if hide-bound officials had been able to see that there
was no reason, just because one had promoted six companies,
that one should not promote a seventh.

John Amery was not an unsuccessful aide to Franco. It is
claimed that he held a commission in his army and was in the
fighting-line. In any case, he had a fairly continuous career as a
gun-runner and as a liaison officer with the French Cagoulards;
and in these capacities received a *laissez-passer* which gave him
as much right to come and go as a Franco Spaniard. But he had
no place of honour in Franco's Spain. In any state that cared for
survival, his type would be rejected.

When the Second World War broke out, John Amery was
living on the borders of Spain, at San Sebastián. He crossed over
to France, possibly under orders, and lived with a Cagoulard
group, knowing or at least meeting the French Fascist leaders
Jacques Doriot and Marcel Déat. Among the Cagoulards were a
certain number of enthusiastic and shapely young women. With
one of them, Jeannine Barde, John Amery contracted a perma-

nent relationship. Sometimes he said he had married her. Mark now the peculiarly flimsy silliness which does not know enough to come in out of the rain, which, indeed, stays outside while it is raining and, when it stops, goes inside just as the ceiling is falling. John Amery remained inactive throughout 1940 and 1941, when there was a very good chance that Germany might win the war. He was called into activity by the Germans when they wanted some person who would catch European attention to conduct an anti-Russian campaign at a time when they were making peace overtures to the Russians; but it is unlikely that the idea of using him would have come into the Germans' heads had not Amery himself, instead of quietly drinking himself to death in a Savoy village, repeatedly volunteered for service with the Germans. So in 1942, when it was becoming obvious that the Allies had at least a chance of winning, he began to broadcast from Berlin. In 1943, when the Allies' position was improving daily, he went into a camp of British internees at St. Denis, near Paris, and attempted to raise an anti-Bolshevik Free Corps to fight with the Germans against the Russians. This is the classic type of treachery which every educated person knows at once for the base and fatal act it is, for Sir Roger Casement committed it during the last war and was hanged for it. In 1944, when it was practically certain that the Axis was defeated, the poor young idiot travelled all over Europe, visiting Norway, France, Yugoslavia, and Belgium, and talking to large audiences which inevitably contained many members of the resistance movements. It is not true that he was caught up in the machine and could not break loose. If he had been a little more drunken the Germans would have let him go back into obscurity. They found him almost impossible to handle as it was, and conceived a lasting hatred for him which was to find expression after the end of the war. But, like a child who tries to obey an angry nanny, Amery tried to keep sober, and kept sober enough to carry on this job long enough to leave no possible loophole for his safety.

Again and again throughout John Amery's life his family must have said to themselves, "He can't be doing that, but, my God, he is!" They must have said it to themselves with unimaginable agony when they heard him speak on the radio; for in this supreme folly was disclosed his private sweetness that forbade them ever to free themselves of their love for him. His voice was young and eager and honest and good-natured, and he sounded like a crusader when he talked anti-Semitic nonsense and declared that London was in a state of shame because the Lord Mayor was a Jew (and so he was; and a very decent body too). There could be seen the city of his desire, rising in the radiance of unspotted honour, its purity a fitting casket for his own, for he was one of those who are reborn every day no matter what the night has brought. It is a curious example of the fatuity of German propaganda that these broadcasts should have been widely announced as by the elder son of the Secretary of State for India; the public felt a wave of sympathy for the Amery family, and an increased disgust at the Nazis.

At the end of the war John Amery was captured by the partisans in Italy; and when he was questioned by a British Military Intelligence Officer he asked for a typewriter and proceeded to type a statement some thousands of words long, which was brilliantly composed, put the noose around his neck, and gave the history of two different people. One of these was a wise young man of lofty principles who sought to reconcile England and Germany in order that together they might fight the rising tide of communism, and to that end travelled about Europe, a weary Titan urging common sense on statesmen who for some reason would not heed the voice of sanity; the other was a crazy harlequin enmeshed in unfortunate adventure. "After a few days in Paris and travelling under the names of Mr. and Mrs. Browne, I arrived in Berlin early in October 1942," he wrote. For a time this inveterately companionate "I," who was always travelling under the names of Mr. and Mrs. Somebody, was to be alone. "On April 7-8," he wrote, "my beloved friend and political revolutionary, Jeannine Barde, died." The poor creature's death was said not to be natural. By some accounts she killed herself, life being rendered unendurable by the sour flavour of treachery, the air raids, the humiliations of life dragged out in dependence on the Nazis who knew that these two had no alternative employers. By other accounts she died because of a blow received at a wild party. The circumstances of her death, whatever they were, increased the Germans' distaste for Amery; and their feeling for etiquette was further outraged by his failure to attend her funeral, though as like as not it was through unbridled grief that he absented himself. But to the wandering wit sorrow is no prison. In no time he was on his feet again. "In the end of September," he wrote, "I returned to Paris. Once more much political talk, and on October 4 I remarried at the German Consulate. Politically, the situation remained almost unchanged." And at the end of the statement comes Harlequin's supreme antic. This man awaiting a capital charge writes: "Moreover, the colonel commanding the Piazza di Milano, who brought me from Sarono to Milan, undertook at the time to have returned my property that was seized by the partisans when they arrested me. Of this nothing has so far been seen. It consists of one suitcase (important documents and personal effects), one overcoat, one fur coat, and two silver foxes, a 20-litre petrol tin, full, one Lancia Aprilia motorcar No. 78410 MICDI."

When John Amery was brought to England, it was widely believed that he was not going to die. His case was postponed several times in order that evidence might be collected for his defence, which rested on a claim that he had become a naturalized Spanish citizen, and it was known that his brother Julian had gone to Spain to collect evidence in proof of that claim. It seemed quite certain, when the court assembled, that the search had been successful, for nearly a whole side of one of the three tables in front of the bench was taken up by a number of trim and plump and florid young men who were said to be Spanish lawyers. Before them there appeared presently that famous figure of the courts, Mr. Salcedo the interpreter, a Spanish Jew, lean and brown and white-haired and antique in courtesy, who passed around the table shaking hands with his compatriots, not perfunctorily but as if they would presently be engaged in a considerable enterprise together. Julian Amery, his young face sleepy with the extreme of strained reserve, his slender body lounging in a dogged attempt at ease, was talking to the defence counsel, and it was said that he was to be the principal witness for the defence. This could hardly be, unless his search for evidence of his brother's naturalization had been successful. There had been distress among the kindly officials of the court because Mrs. Amery had applied for a seat. It might be that they had no reason for perturbation; she might joyfully witness her son's acquittal.

But if there was a wealth of Spanish lawyers, there were lacking some of the court's most usual features There was no judge,
there was no jury, there was no prisoner. The Lord Mayor and
two aldermen, in their fine black gowns and jewelled chains,
took their places on the bench, but the chair under the sword
of justice was empty. In the jury box, leaflets of instruction lay
yellow on the dark wood at each juror's place, but there was none
to pick them up. The kitchen chairs in the dock were naked in
their discomfort. (Surely that is the last ungraciousness of society,
that it should make its failures learn their doom sitting on a hard
wooden chair.) Half-past ten had passed, though that was the
hour at which the trial should have begun, and one could set
one's watch by the law courts. Half an hour passed, and still there
was no judge, no jury, no prisoner.

Just after eleven a messenger came to the lawyers' table and
spoke to John Amery's counsel. The dock is a shallow square box
without a lid, with glass walls rising on all sides except the side
which faces the judge. A staircase runs down from the dock to
the cells where the prisoners are kept from the time of their arrival in the prison van at the court till they are brought up for
trial. From the gallery of the court, one can look down into the
staircase, which is lined with those obscene creations, white sani-
tary tiles. There was seen a sight rare in the courts: the counsel
going through a door in the glass walls of the dock and down the
stairway to the cells. They looked like ravens in their black
gowns, stooping as they gathered up their skirts. While they were
gone, people in the court, particularly the lawyers, began to laugh
a great deal as they talked among themselves. This had nothing
to do with anything they were thinking or feeling about the trial
of Amery. It was a collective nervous reaction, like the storm of
coughing that sometimes sweeps through a theatre when a play
is going badly. After twenty-five minutes, Amery's counsel returned. There was talk with Sir Hartley Shawcross, from whose
look of gentle, reflective well-being nothing could be learned,
and with the Director of Public Prosecutions, who nodded as if
something had happened which he had foreseen. There was a
flurry of messengers. The trial began.

The Judge entered in shrivelled and eccentric majesty. It was
Mr. Justice Humphries, a very old man whose age was crisp as

a fine winter night, with a fierce wit on his tongue and a fiercer wit on his face, where there is often written what he will not let himself say lest necessary institutions fall. He had a son whom he named Christmas, who grew up to be president of the Buddhist Society and the Ballet Guild. To such a fantastical world, resembling Peacock's novels, does Mr. Justice Humphries belong. He made a little, stiff, old man's bow to the court and sat down, small in the depth of his red-and-purple robes, to try the poor shadow who had been brought into the dock. It had been said that John Amery was deeply diseased with tuberculosis. There was no truth in it. The prison doctors, who are nowadays able men, pronounced him free of this or any other disease. But it was with his body as with his mind. He was, judged by any accepted standard, not mad, but he was not sane. He was free from disease but it would have been absurd to call him healthy. His skin was yellow and grooved round the small bones of his face by long exhaustion and fear and the immediate strain of the moment, which was evidently frightful to him. His face was the muzzle of a little monkey; and it could be seen that in youth there must have been here much animal vitality and charm, as well as an animal secretiveness that would make him incomprehensible. He wore an overcoat that was the colour of the bloom on grapes, and a black-and-lime scarf of the heavy and subtly coloured sort that used to be sold at the expensive shops on the Croisette at Cannes. The weight of these good clothes was too much for the worn trifle of his body. He leaned on the ledge of the dock, his small, bare hands very white and limp. By his appearance he made, as prisoners so often do, the ultimate appeal against human justice. It is not fair that some vessels should be made for honour and some for dishonour. The lawyers in front of him seemed guilty of a kind of theft in having so much prospering vitality while this creature had none. The two American officers who had been the first in the court seemed grasping in having secured those lines on their faces which spoke of fatiguing service of an honoured sort.

Again the kitchen chair in the dock seemed monstrous, and it could hardly be imagined that John Amery would be able to sit through the trial upright on this bleak piece of carpentry. But such anxiety was immediately proved unnecessary. They read out the indictments against him, charging him with having made treasonable broadcasts and speeches and having attempted to seduce British subjects from their allegiance, and asked him whether he pleaded guilty or not guilty. It had been supposed that he would answer "Not guilty." Then the jurors would have been called in and sworn, and the counsel would have addressed the Court, and the routine would have rolled on for perhaps as long as four days. But when the question was put to him he answered, "I plead guilty to all counts," and the trial lasted eight minutes. A murmur ran through the court which was horrified, which was expostulatory, which was tinged with self-pity, for this was suicide. If he pleaded guilty he must be sentenced to death. There is no alternative sentence for treason. It is not in the power of any judge to substitute imprisonment, and there is no appeal. There is only the possibility that the Home Secretary may advise the Crown to reprieve the condemned man; and this happens only in certain circumstances, not to be found by any eye in the case of John Amery. In effect, the young man was saying, "I insist on being hanged by the neck in three weeks' time," and the strength of his desire to die was forcing his weak voice through his shuddering lips and ignoring his pain, which was great, for he was blasted by what he did. He was like an insect that falls on a hot stove and is withered, and what he did felt like an act of cruelty to the whole court. It rejected the life that was in all of us. It could be perceived that the legal tradition whereby a man under a capital charge must be urged by every possible means to plead not guilty is no meddling excess of humanitarianism but is an expression of the fundamental belief of living things in life. It relates to that saying of Charles Dickens which so profoundly impressed Tolstoy, that whatever power gave us life, and for whatever purpose, he was sure it was given to us on the understanding that we defend it to the last breath. It is true, of course, that there are conditions in which a man can die without betraying his life, because his death will give it the spiritual value without which material existence is worthless, but these conditions do not usually arise in the criminal courts, which practise on the plane of simplification.

The old Judge leaned forward and said to the clerk of the court, "Before that is recorded . . ." and broke off. Then he said to Mr. Slade, "I never accept a plea of guilty on a capital charge without assuring myself that the accused thoroughly understands what he is doing and what the immediate result must be, and that he is in accord with his legal advisers in the course he has taken." Mr. Slade stood up and answered, no longer like a bird but speaking with obvious careful fidelity to a prepared model, "I can assure you of that, my lord. I have explained the position to my client and I am satisfied that he understands it." This passage had the quietness of the worst sort of nightmare. It was as if he had said, "Yes, this man chooses to be walled up, and all proper arrangements have been made to get suitable bricks." The old Judge's eyebrows and the corners of his mouth made a queer pattern. Yes, life has to be defended to the last ditch, but what a damned thing it is! He said, "Right. Let it be recorded." Then the clerk of the court asked John Amery if he had anything to say. The young man answered, weakly and politely, "No, thank you." The attendant placed the square of black cloth on the Judge's head, but the Judge did not deliver the death sentence. Instead he leaned forward and asked, "You do not want to say anything?" Still in the same well-bred and dying voice, the young man said, "No, thank you, sir." It was quite clear that he was morally satisfied and that he was congratulating himself on having at last, at the end of his muddled and frustrated existence, achieved an act crystalline in its clarity, an act which fulfils the conditions in which a man can choose to die without betraying life. Yet none of the many people who were watching him with the intensest interest had the faintest idea what that act was, with perhaps the exception of the lawyers, who were bound by professional etiquette to keep silent.

It was immediately spread about that John Amery had suddenly insisted on pleading guilty for the sake of his family, to spare them the prolonged humiliation of his trial. That would have provided a simple explanation had it not been for the Spanish lawyers. They must have attended to give testimony in support of John Amery's story that he had been naturalized as a Spanish citizen; and their testimony must have been previously examined by Amery's counsel and judged to be conclusive. Had it been so, then he would have been acquitted, and by that his family would have been spared much of the pain and humilia-

tion inherent in his case. And if John Amery's motive for pleading guilty was really concern for his family, it was odd that his
counsel did not mention it when the Judge questioned him about
the plea, thus softening what was an oddly stark statement. There
was also the suggestion that he pleaded guilty simply because he
wanted to die as quickly as possible, without enduring the slow
torture of the trial, but the impression given by his flinching
flesh was that he wanted very much to live, and there was that
in his air which suggested that by his conduct he was serving
more than himself. It is, of course, possible that his counsel did
not know his motive. That animal secretiveness may have made
him put forward nothing to them but some babbling nonsense
such as used to break his teachers' hearts, or he may have been
cut off from their comprehension and their kindness by his old
gift for complication. His inhabiting devil may have long ago set
forces working which had produced an event so monstrous that
it was almost as hard to grasp as it would have been to foresee,
so monstrous that even he would have recognized it as intractable and surrendered to despair. In any case, his end was as his
beginning. What should have been light was dark. There never
was a more turbid martyrdom.

Perhaps there was a clue to the nature of that monstrous event
that day in court. It could be seen by those who looked about
them during that period of waiting that the Spanish lawyers did
not all belong to one party. They seemed to be split into two
groups. Perhaps one group had come to put forward papers in
support of John Amery's claim to be a naturalized Spaniard, and
the other to prove that those papers were forged. How that situation might have arisen was indicated some months later to a
traveller in Spain who found himself at a dinner with a member
of the Franco government. This traveller remembered that Julian
Amery had gone out to Spain with letters from the British authorities asking the Spanish authorities to give all facilities for
searching the records for proofs of his brother's claim, and that
shortly afterwards a British law officer, bearing credentials from
the same fount of authority as Julian Amery, had also gone out
to Spain, apparently on some errand of investigation. It occurred
to the traveller that perhaps the Spanish politician might have
met one of these visitors, and he mentioned their names. "Now,

tell me," said the Spaniard, "just what happened in that case. What made the British government change their minds about John Amery?" "Change their minds?" echoed the traveller. "Yes," said the Spaniard petulantly. "First they wanted not to hang him, and then the next thing we knew they wanted to hang him."

It must be remembered that John Amery probably believed that he was a Spanish subject. Once he heard of the defence that William Joyce was raising, his feather wits would easily convert the *laissez-passer* he had received from Franco when he was a gun-runner into a certificate of naturalization. His brother must have gone to Spain to look for the evidence of that naturalization in the belief that it existed, and unprepared for complaisance. It would not have crossed his mind that any Spanish official would misinterpret the request of the British authorities that he should be given facilities for such a search, since such a request would have been made on behalf of any reputable person in a like position. In good faith he must have brought back the evidence of his brother's Spanish citizenship, in good faith his parents and their legal advisers must have accepted it, and John Amery, in his mental twilight, would not have been surprised that his myth had become a fact. But by then Amery's private papers had fallen into the hands of British Intelligence Officers. It was unlikely that a Spanish official, however willing to oblige, would invent a date on which an imaginary ceremony of naturalization was performed which would fit into the accounts of his life contained in these papers. It was inevitable that the deception should bemuse the Amery family, inevitable that it should be uncovered by the prosecution. It is not possible to think how life must have appeared to the Amery family at the moment of the disclosure. A persecuting destiny had for long inhabited their older son's body, inextricably confused with what they loved. They had conquered it, for it had never made them fail their son. Now it must have seemed to them to have broken loose and ranged the earth, acting at a great distance, acting through men so stupid that they were dangerous even when they meant to please—that they could not recognize what pleases the civilized; acting through the supposed neutrality of inanimate objects, through volumes in the shelves of a registry office, which could have been judged eternally innocuous through dedication to uninteresting fact. The Amery family stood together under the shadow of this astonishing doom; but were not together, for John went from them. He escaped into another fantasy. Now he saw himself as a martyr in the Fascist cause, and swaggered as he had done when he drove the high-powered automobile he had not paid for at ninety miles an hour on the wrong side of the road to the hotel where he would not be able to meet the bill. That was the source of his faintly consequential air in the dock, his air of knowing something.

The Judge spoke some words to him before passing sentence, expressing hatred of his crime. Many people thought the Judge heartless, forgetting that a very old man might well feel himself on an equality with a prisoner under sentence of death, and might even think that the prisoner would find a precise evaluation of his position more interesting than tenderness from a stranger. Also the Judge seemed baffled, like the rest of us, and there was a certain ineptness in his enlargement on a passage in the depositions which described how John Amery had visited the camp at St. Denis to enlist internees for his renegade British Free Corps and had been warned by some of the men that he was committing high treason but had taken no notice. It was not a point worth making, so far as Amery was concerned, for by that time his magic circle was sealed, and he must have thought that he was giving the internees an opportunity to join the winning side. Yet, if what the Judge said had little application to Amery, he seemed to say it because his mind had been shocked into flight underground to some place near the sources of our general destiny. The Judge said slowly, with accusation and querulous wonder in his voice, "They called you traitor and you heard them." It was as if he spoke to all men, marvelling at their knowledge of good and evil and their preference for evil, and looking at his own heart from far away that he might see the cause.

2

THE ghost of William Joyce certainly haunts the Old Bailey, for there he knew what must have been, to that gallant exhibitionist and obstinate confessor of his faith, in a profound sense the happiest days of his life; and during the treachery trials which followed his, he was surely the most contented of ghosts. Not then were the courts crowded; not then was it difficult to find a table in the neighbouring restaurants; not then did people wait in the streets outside. Such things happened only when he and Amery were up for trial, and he could fairly claim that Amery had family behind him and that he himself was the only traitor to cause such a stir by his own personality. Greatness went from the treason dock with Joyce; and no other case was a work of art, a posed picture, like the trial of John Amery. But the other traitors were nevertheless strange and disturbing figures, and their trials were full of dream-like incongruities, evoking laughter even while they dismayed by recalling something which it would be preferable to forget and which cannot be completely remembered. For people do not become traitors unless they are unable to fit into the society into which they were born, and the cause of that incapacity in their case is a disturbing society which catches those around them off their guard and therefore provokes them in their turn to strange behaviour. Hence their lives become a chain of fantastic events. And the trials were certainly a debauch for the connoisseur of the law. Machinery set up in the past was acting on the material provided by a present so novel that it was almost as mysterious as the future; and the results were never more astonishing than in the case of Norman Baillie-Stewart. He was one of the oddest of these odd fish, though very dull, and in his sentence the legal wheel turned full circle and, making an innovation, arrived at the archaic.

He might be considered the most tragic of the traitors, for he started with great natural advantages. He, the officer whom British officers would most wish to blot off their rolls and out of human memory, looked like the ideal Guardee of Ouida's dreams. When he came into the dock the noble sculpture of his head and the dignity of his tall body were astonishing. But his handsome face was so sullen that he might have been dead. It was impossible to imagine that he would ever laugh or weep again. He looked the more inhuman because he was wearing one of those thick and shiny German raincoats which are dead black with white highlights. The addiction of the Nazis to these garments is an extravagant present to the psychologists. These people who wanted to drench the earth in blood cannot stir from home without protection from the rain; so, as like as not, Freud is right and aggression is the other side of fear. Baillie-Stewart's gloomy aspect could not simply be put down as natural in one standing in the dock, for he had a very good reason for feeling relief. He was not going to be hanged, and in any other age that would have been his fate. But of course the life that had been given back to him was not going to be worth living. It is the essence of treachery that those who commit it would still be severely punished if the law forgot its duty to provide deterrents to crime and did not lay a finger on them.

Baillie-Stewart's initial advantages were not only physical. In 1927, when he was eighteen, he passed tenth out of the Royal Military College at Sandhurst, which is the English West Point. During his subsequent career in the Seaforth Highlanders he attracted the attention of his superior officers by his general competence and a marked mechanical gift. But there was something very strange going on in his head, of a sort that can be grasped by consideration of his name. For he was born Norman Baillie-Stewart Wright, but in his early twenties took the name of Baillie-Stewart by deed poll, as the legal act of adopting another surname is called. He explained this step later by saying that it was his mother's maiden name, and that as her brother had died it had been thought advisable that he should carry on the name. This was quite simply not true. His mother had been a Miss Baillie. No family called Baillie-Stewart exists. He probably took the step from snobbery of a very naïve sort, for a double-barrelled name, in England as in most Continental countries, usually betokens a certain degree of social elevation. It was the custom for a gentleman who married an heiress to add her name to his, and this custom has for some time been discontinued in England, though it is still practised in France and Germany; so a double-barrelled name in England usually means that the family is or has been rich and is of some antiquity.

It would be interesting to know how the Wright family reacted to this curious event. Probably suspicions were aroused which might have been confirmed, if families were reasonable, in 1932, when he was charged with having communicated information about certain military matters to the German government. The arrest caused a sensation, because it was the first of its kind in living memory, and because he awaited trial in the Tower of London and was therefore known to the newspapers under the good romantic title of "The Officer in the Tower." It was hoped by some of the public that he would prove to be the moving spirit of a Phillips Oppenheim conspiracy against England, and by others that he would be vindicated as the victim of an error. But the trial took quite a different course. It turned Baillie-Stewart into a comic character of a peculiarly indecorous kind. He was to England in the early 'thirties what "Daddy" Browning had been to New York in the middle 'twenties.

His offence was the minimum which could have brought him into the sphere covered by the Official Secrets Act. The information he gave to the Germans was minuscule and no more than they could have derived from a careful study of the photographs in English periodicals. It is said that he had shortly before met a young German woman resident in England, in whose company he had learned to appreciate the art of love and to disapprove of the Treaty of Versailles; and here is the first sign of the difference between Baillie-Stewart and the other major traitors. He is the only one of them who might have been diverted from the road to jail by a competent psychiatrist. In Joyce there was a false deployment of the forces which fight for human victory. In the case of Amery there was a disturbance in the normal stresses of life which pull against one another and produce a tolerable destiny: a man who was too mad for psychiatric treatment but not mad enough to be certified happened to be born at a time when two important European powers were experimenting with rule by the insane. But if Baillie-Stewart had been sent to a sound analyst it is probable that he would never have found himself in the dock. He apparently had a sexual fixation on German women; and as he was sexually active, this meant that he had a fixa-

tion on Germany. He was never interested in fascism. It was first
and last Germany, whether under the Weimar Republic or under
the Nazis, which obsessed him, though it is doubtful if this obsession turned easily to espionage. But young German women
who lived in foreign countries and had love affairs with officers
were frequently not disinterested. It is said that Baillie-Stewart's
young woman soon threatened to withdraw her favour from him
if he did not give her some information to send home to Germany, and the worthlessness of the notes he sent to Germany
suggest that he was acting under some such persuasion and not
by his own free will. When it became known that he had handed
over this information, and he was questioned by his superior
officers, they would probably have accepted his plea that this information was too worthless for it to matter whether he handed
it over or not, and allowed him to resign quietly from the service,
had it not been for one damaging fact. He had received some
money from Germany: ninety pounds. It was his attempt to account for the receipt of this money, and the effect it had had on
the officers who interrogated him, which appealed to the ribald
side of the British public.

Norman Baillie-Stewart, né Wright, alleged that this payment
related to an incident which had occurred when he visited Germany in 1931, as he in fact had done on a holiday when he was
waiting transfer from one regiment, where he had found himself
unpopular, to another. During his travels he had gone to see a
gentleman called Herr Obst, who had introduced him to a young
lady called Marie Louise. He was at that time, as it appeared in
the trial, engaged in the pursuit of a German film star, but Marie
Louise became enamoured of him and asked him to correspond
with her under the pseudonym of Alphonse Poiret. It was never
clear why a pseudonym should have been necessary. There were
suggestions that Marie Louise's friends and relatives might have
objected to such a correspondent, but it was never explained why
they would have objected less to a correspondent named Alphonse Poiret than to one named Norman Baillie-Stewart. In the
course of the correspondence which followed, the story continued,
she had sent him ninety pounds, out of gratitude. Pressed by the
colonel who was examining him as to the reason for this gratitude, he stammered out that it related to a tender scene which

had reached the extremity of heterosexual tenderness. The colonel suggested that it would be useful if he could recall at what hotel in Germany he and the young lady had stayed. Baillie-Stewart confided that this was not possible, for the tender scene had taken place in a park. This is in line with an ancient tradition; but all the same it seemed an odd venue for a young lady so strictly brought up that her correspondence was supervised. But what park? He did not know. But there was a lake in it. The tender scene had happened beside a lake.

This story is an index to the peculiar quality of Baillie-Stewart's mind. He is a stranger to humanity; he does not share the common reactions of humanity. This means he cannot lic; he cannot imagine the normal patterns of behaviour. It had come to his knowledge, since he himself was a handsome young man, that sometimes handsome young men are paid for their embraces by infatuated ladies. It had come to his knowledge that people who feel the desire to embrace often yield to that desire in very odd places. But he could not make a credible story based on these quite sound observations. Tears ran down people's cheeks as they read the reports of the case, so madly ludicrous was Baillie-Stewart's story. They laughed even more loudly at the naïve evidence of the colonel to whom this singular evidence had first been told. Asked at the court martial what effect it had had on him, he replied, "When he told me the remarkable story of getting ninety pounds for one act of intimacy in a public park, I was so astonished that I asked for an explanation." It was unfortunate that other remarks made during the trial also suggested that Baillie-Stewart's real offence was that he had disregarded a recognized ceiling-price. The Judge-Advocate in charge of the trial once asked him, "Do you consider that the ninety pounds which you received was in respect of services rendered to her over a fortnight and eighteen hours?"

The trial was brought nearer reality by the improbable appearance, as a witness, of the English Benny Goodman, Mr. Victor Silvester, famous as the leader of the Correct Tempo Band. The prosecution had laid some emphasis on the inability of Baillie-Stewart to provide any but the vaguest particulars about Marie Louise. She was fair and about twenty-two, and that was all he was able to say. He did not even know where she lived. The prosecution took this blankness as proof that Marie Louise did not exist and that Baillie-Stewart had had dealings with German officials and had received the money from them. But Mr. Victor Silvester gave evidence which brought the image of a real woman into the courtroom. He said that when he and his wife were fulfilling an engagement in Berlin shortly after Baillie-Stewart's visit to Germany, they had been approached at a hotel tea-dance by a young woman, fair and about twenty-two, who gave her name as Marie Louise. During their conversation, which touched only trivial things, they asked her if, as she had a French name, she was French, and she laughed and replied that, on the contrary, she was very German. From Mr. Silvester's report there emerged a picture of a real person, and what is more, of a real person who was in high good humour and had found a particular amusement in searching out English company at that particular moment.

After the trial was over Mr. Silvester sent to the War Office a letter which had been posted to him from Berlin, written in Tarzan English and signed Elsa Schutz. Schutz means shield, protection. "Dear Mr. Silvester," it said, "I write for my friend Fräulein Marie Louise to ask you not to make the inquiries for her any more. She has done all she can, but the conditions are so, she cannot do what she would like. If she comes to England, it must be that she is taken for a bad woman. . . ." It is impossible not to hear the faint sound of a distant giggle. Here it must be remarked that Mr. Silvester is the most respectable of men, whose integrity cannot be doubted. It is psychologically significant that he chose the title "Correct Tempo" for his band.

Baillie-Stewart was found guilty and was sentenced to five years' penal servitude. He had made himself loathed by the authorities during his trial. They found him surly and ungracious, and believed him to have assured his father that he was innocent, with the result that the unhappy Mr. Wright spent much more money than he could afford in trying to confirm the story. Baillie-Stewart made himself as deeply detested by the staff of Maidstone Jail, where he served his sentence. The higher officers were vexed beyond endurance by his perpetual complaints, and his sneering bad manners made it difficult to guarantee his fair treatment by the warders. Nobody was sorry when he was released in

January 1937, and he must have emerged in a state of joyous hope, for he had become more and more pro-German while he was in prison, and during his sentence the Weimar Republic had given place to the Nazi Reich. It should have been a case of "I run, I run, I am gathered to thy heart"; but there came a curious impediment to the embrace.

An English convict does not usually serve the full term of imprisonment to which he was sentenced. He earns a remission of so many days according to his good-conduct marks, which may amount to as much as a third of his sentence. This remission amounted tò very little in Baillie-Stewart's case: only two months. Till that period was up he was, according to routine, released only on a licence which required him to report to the police at regular intervals and forbade him to leave Great Britain until the date on which his sentence expired. Baillie-Stewart could have gone abroad in March 1937. But he did not leave England until August, and then he went not to Germany but to Austria. This was not the result of any preference; for he made the most vigorous efforts to become a naturalized subject, not of Austria, but of Germany. These efforts, strangely enough, met with a curious lack of encouragement. In Vienna he was taken under the wing of a Nazi agent, an English or English-speaking woman who had assumed the name of Edith Shackleton, a celebrated London journalist, and falsely claimed to be the sister of Sir Ernest Shackleton, the explorer. She introduced him into Nazi circles and he was notable for his enthusiasm for Hitler. In 1938 the Austrian police accused him of pro-Nazi activities. All the same, his naturalization papers did not come through. Long after the normal period of completion had elapsed he was still petitioning the German authorities to admit him to citizenship. This might seem evidence that there is one real International: that, diverse as the human mass may be, and severed by natural and artificial barriers, there is one body which, scattered over the whole earth and serving beneath the myriad banners of the sovereignties, acts in real unity. It might be that Baillie-Stewart's papers were held up because a civil servant had lost them: that while innumerable officials in Washington, London, and Paris were losing the papers of people who wanted to get away from Germany, their counterparts in Berlin were doing the like for this refugee who was feeling the other way. But that was not the explanation.

The existence of another reason for the delay was proved on the outbreak of the war. The Nazis allowed him to enter Germany and took him into their employment, but with the most noticeable coldness. He was given none of the opportunities to work against his country which one would have thought the Germans would have offered to a trained English soldier who might, dropped by parachute, have been a most dangerous saboteur. He was put into broadcasting, and the Propaganda Office and the Foreign Office played their usual game of battledore and shuttlecock with him. He finally got his naturalization papers; but he was kept in one small room or another, sometimes under orders from William Joyce, whom he detested, writing broadcasts which were often revised and sometimes scrapped. He was not even allowed to recruit for the British Free Corps, though the value of an authentic officer of attractive appearance would obviously have been very great. Unless he had been actually interned, his reception could not have been chillier. And on Christmas Eve in 1941, an intoxicated employee of Goebbels gave away the reason. He was talking to an American resident in Berlin, saying that some time during the evening he had to look in for a moment on a party given by the traitor broadcasters, and he went over their individual characters and cursed them one by one. "As for Baillie-Stewart," he said, "he is a spy the English have planted on us, and we know it."

That remark rings true when the incidents of the trial are recalled. The story told by Baillie-Stewart must have been valid to some extent. It cannot be doubted that on his German holiday he did meet a man and a woman who called themselves Herr Obst and Fräulein Marie Louise. For the interrogating Colonel gave evidence that Baillie-Stewart seemed genuinely surprised when he learned that *Obst* is German for "fruit," that Marie Louise is the name of a variety of pear, and that *poiret* means "little pear." It is almost beyond belief that he invented the story and hit by chance on names that fell into the orchard category; or that he should have invented the story and chosen such an implausible batch of names. But the colonel does not seem to have pointed out to him, and may not have known, that the slang meaning of *poire* is "a credulous fool, a dupe." The merriment of the Fräulein Marie Louise encountered by Mr. Victor Silvester comes back to mind, and the hardly disguised facetiousness of the letter from Elsa Schutz. It appears certain, in the light of the official's remark, that a gang of German counter-espionage agents had met Norman Baillie-Stewart and had been just too clever in their estimate of him. His story of wanting to be a spy had struck them as odd; and they did not realize that its oddity was due to the fact that he was a very odd man. They sent him the ninety pounds to encourage him to come closer to them. Perhaps they were startled when Baillie-Stewart was arrested. But then the peculiar evidence given by Baillie-Stewart must have aroused their suspicions that his was a bogus trial. Why should a sane man make such a poor job of defending himself? Then, too, that suspicion was bound to be nourished by some of the evidence which was brought against him. In the train that took Baillie-Stewart into Germany when he was going to see Herr Obst, there had been a very attractive young woman to whom he had introduced himself. In the course of conversation with this stranger he explained that he was going abroad "to do the most difficult thing he had ever done in his life," and had rambled on with such hints at an exciting mystery, stopping so nearly on the hither side of explicitness, that as soon as she read of the case in the papers she wrote to relate her experience to the prosecution. The Germans might well have said to themselves that the man was not born who would behave like that when he was going abroad to act as a spy, whether he was moved by a genuine desire to commit treachery or whether he was only going to pretend to be a traitor. It must have seemed to them false evidence, brought as part of sham proceedings. This suspicion would be strengthened by the circumstance that the young woman had been allowed to appear before the court under the title of Miss D. It would become ineradicable when the Germans found out that he had changed his name. Why would a man who was born Wright call himself Baillie-Stewart on the ground that that was his mother's name when it was not? There was, of course, no reason at all, except perhaps some remote misadventure, such as the failure of the two halves of his brain to synchronize or an excess of protein in his blood. But the Germans had, put into their hands, the tempting hypothesis that Baillie-Stewart, having committed himself to an enterprise bound to bring shame on him, had changed his name to spare his family.

Therefore the German War Office smiled sardonically when Baillie-Stewart sought entrance to Germany after his release in 1937. There began then for this young man an existence which reproduced in reality the fancies of the most unhappy type of lunatic. The man at the corner table was really watching him. His letters were being opened. His friends were his enemies. The bogus Miss Shackleton, after the charming evening, went home and wrote it all down in a little book. If it had not been for Baillie-Stewart's neurosis he would have recognized these things and returned to England. But his love of Germany and German women persisted. The life of fantasy, they say, proliferates in prison. After a dream has seduced a man into the dock it accompanies him to his cell with the confidence of a victor, it possesses him without fear of the competitive seductions of reality. Insofar as his dream turned him from England, it saved him pain. His father had suffered acutely in body and mind during his son's trial, and had died while he was in Maidstone. Insofar as his dream turned him towards German women, there went with him everywhere a fair woman who was said to be the same who had induced him to be a spy, though whether it was Marie Louise or his earlier love was not known. He struck those who met him as not gay, in spite of this companion. He was evidently one of those who make gloomy rendezvous with their sexual necessities and return unrefreshed, though determined not to abandon the routine. Moreover, it is indeed possible not to recognize certain experiences, yet to be aware of them and to be emotionally affected by them. It is very difficult indeed to believe that he did not notice for what it was, the German refusal to use his services, since he had not been a fool when he was in the army; though it may not have struck him, so conscious was he of his integrity as a traitor, that by putting him in the British radio office they were keeping him in a box and could lift the lid at any moment they pleased to see what he was doing. But it must have galled him, with his social ambition, to work under the control of William Joyce, who was indubitably not a gentleman; and he must have shared the resentment that all the traitor broadcasters felt against the Nazi bully that supervised them. But in the statement he made after he was arrested by the Allies there is no indication whatsoever that his obsessional love for Germany had diminished.

When Germany collapsed, Baillie-Stewart escaped from Berlin and was found some months afterwards wandering about the Austrian mountains in a Tyrolian costume very ill-suited to his height, with forged identity papers. Like most of the traitors, he was hungry when he was taken, and, though he was fed, had to be roughly lodged until he was sent to England, as conquered Central Europe was in no tidy state. He was charged, on his first appearances at the police court, with high treason. A convicted spy who after serving his sentence had gone abroad and re-entered the service of the foreign power for which he had betrayed his country could not hope for anything else. In the course of these preliminary proceedings he made a remark oddly incongruous with his virile appearance. When he was requesting the magistrate for time to prepare his defence he said, "I learn that my mother has died during my absence, and I have no one to turn to." The atmosphere of these treachery trials was extremely matter-of-fact, and an appeal to sentiment was rarely heard; the accused knew that that was not a profitable line to take. Moreover, "I have no one to turn to" is a phrase with a definite character of its own to the English ear. It would be natural only on the lips of a fragile and elderly woman or a deserted wife. His statement also exhibited a peculiar defection from masculinity. He gave his affection for a German woman as the cause of his treachery. It is interesting to contrast that admission with the allusions made by Joyce and Amery in their statements. Joyce mentioned his wife with classic protectiveness. Amery praised his companions as fellow-Fascists. Both men would certainly have felt that they were making themselves ridiculous if they had ascribed their political opinions to the influence of a sexual infatuation. What is more, if their political opinions had been due to any such cause, they would have had the sense not to mention it in an English court of law, which would find it far from endearing.

The sum of the confusions within this dour creature was a habit of feeling passionate emotions which were not reciprocated. He loved Germany and Germany did not love him. He hated

England; and when he had betrayed England it had laughed at
him for a week, sent him to prison for a moderate term of years,
and then forgotten him, and on being reminded of his existence
and told that he had betrayed it again, still could not bring itself
to be bothered about him. When he came up for trial at the
Central Criminal Court the charge against him had been reduced
to an offence against Defence Regulations 2A; and the prosecuting counsel and the defending counsel and the Judge wearily
agreed that it really seemed absurd for the English courts to concern themselves with an Englishman who had acted with perfect
legality in his desire to abandon his British nationality, and who
had started taking out his German naturalization papers so long
ago that, had it not been for the sluggishness of Berlin officials,
he would have become a German citizen at a time when the
countries were at peace and such an action was no offence against
the English laws. In fact, England yawned in Baillie-Stewart's
face and said, "Have it your own way." The humiliation of his
position was emphasized at the trial by the personality of the
Judge, Mr. Justice Oliver, a large, handsome man who had probably never done anything not very sensible in his whole life, and
whose sense was so sound that he had missed very few of the good
things of life. In the dock Baillie-Stewart was piteous and inconvenient, but more inconvenient than piteous, like a dray horse
that has fallen in the street. When a dray horse falls there always
appears an efficient person who inquires where ropes can be got.
Mr. Justice Oliver was that person. Contemplating the closed
door of Baillie-Stewart's face, he reflected that if this man wanted
to be a German the best thing was to let him have his wish. So
he asked Baillie-Stewart's lawyer to find out whether his client
would give his promise to go back to Germany and never to return to Great Britain; and he asked the prosecuting counsel to
make inquiries as to whether the Allied Control Commission
would find it convenient to receive Baillie-Stewart in Germany.
So the court adjourned.

The next morning Baillie-Stewart was very gloomy when he
entered the dock. This was partly a matter of the interior life.
There were running round the court, among people who did not
know his reputation as a convict, rumours of his peculiar surli-
ness and ungraciousness to those who were doing their best for

him. But also he had received bad news. The ropes found by Mr. Justice Oliver had not put the dray horse on its legs again. Baillie-Stewart had been offered, as a great concession, the prospect of returning to the rubble and ashes which was all that was left of the country to which he had given all he had and which had grinned at him with the misplaced acuteness of an idiot. He had accepted this offer, making in exchange the promise that he would never return to the place where he was born, where he might find the irrational affection, springing from ties of the blood, which was all his repellent quality could be sure of attracting. But that grim contract was too favourable to be permitted as part of his destiny. The Allied Control Commission had been forced to object to it. Since it was bound to penalize people who had actively collaborated with the Nazis, it would only have to take in charge this extreme collaborator the minute he arrived back in Germany. It was not said in court where in Germany he had been domiciled. But had it been necessary to return him to the Russian zone, his story might have been short. It is possible that this decision of the Allied Control Commission gave him back his unhappy life a second time.

The Judge could do nothing else than send him to prison. This queer creature could not be allowed to go free. It would have made the punishment of others for like offences seem unfair; and assuredly he would have found some new way of getting into trouble. Quite a few of the traitors were arrested only because they drew attention to themselves, not from any loyalty to Nazi principles but from a desire to push their personalities into the limelight. So Mr. Justice Oliver had to pass sentence on Baillie-Stewart, who faced him like a dead man standing upright, a dead man who had died alone, with nobody to shut his eyes. He told him that he was perhaps the worst citizen that England had ever produced, which was not a very apt or precise description. He had obviously done far less harm in his life than John Amery, and was less politically dangerous than William Joyce. It would have been more accurate to say that he was the most alarming citizen that we had ever produced. For it is man's terror that the magic which created the universe out of nothingness may one day start working backwards: the rabbit will recede into the empty top-hat, the lent watch will never return, when the screen is taken away there will be no magician, and as the audience rushes forward to seek him they too will abruptly be nothing. That this might indeed befall us was threatened by the singularly perfect negativism of this man, who had cancelled everything in its life by its opposite, who had felt the extreme of patriotism for a country which was not his own, who had gone about the business of spying as noisily as a postman, who was now to be a prisoner on terms antithetical to any previous condition of captivity. For the Judge sentenced him to five years' imprisonment, with a recommendation to the Prison Commission that he should be released and sent back to Germany as soon as the state of the country permitted it. His jailers would watch as eagerly as he would for the first moment when it was thought possible to release him; and that moment could not come until the country that was to receive him had been wholly purged of every element that would not want to reject him. It was as if there had at last been translated into terms of existence one of those negative mathematical quantities which till now have seemed to mean nothing, merely to indicate that the symbolic system on which they are based has outrun its business of representation.

3

NEITHER John Amery nor Norman Baillie-Stewart was certifiably insane. They never saw things that were not there. They never committed actions which gave the community an instantaneous shock. Their suicidal policies were long-term, and they could successfully apply logic to their experience on a small scale. The actions by which they offended normal standards could so well have been committed by men who were not mad but bad; and Amery has been matched in incoherence and Baillie-Stewart in sullenness by countless people who conduct their lives in the most reasonable way. Nevertheless, the minds of both these men were not so adjusted as to bring them happiness or favour their survival. They were what are called psychotics: they fell into the darker of the two categories into which the maladjusted are divided. Neurotics, who cause less distress to themselves and their neighbours than those in the other category, are at war with their own natures. Their right hands are in conflict with their left. Psychotics, and it is those who commit purposeless crimes and prefer death to life, are at war with their environment. Right and left hands strike against the womb that carries them.

This has its bearing on power politics. The psychotic will very readily take sides against his own country. He is as if decreed by Heaven to be a prop for any neighbouring power which desires to swallow his fatherland. He hates the people round him, he hates his fellow-countrymen, because he hates the real world, which he knows through the testimony of his senses. His power of fantasy enables him to build any country which is the declared enemy of his fatherland into an ideal and beloved world; and it will perform that miracle whether the enemy be Great Britain, America, Germany, or Russia. The bloodstream of any international movement which seeks to destroy the independence of the smaller nations must be fed by a vein of madness.

III

THE CHILDREN

THERE were also the children among the traitors, the ones who thought like children, and felt like children, and were treacherous as children are, without malice, only because someone was giving away sweetmeats or because the whole gang was chasing the dog.

Most of these were children with men's bodies; but some were children in body as well as mind. Of these the most notable was Kenneth Edward, for history manœuvred him into positions where he was forced to record his own simplicity. In normal circumstances he would never have taken up his pen except to fill in a coupon for a football pool or make a date with a girl. But in war he was compelled to write certain brief notes which convey the terror felt by a child when the grown-up who has seemed so kind goes away and does not come back, the shame felt by a child whose innocent hedonism becomes aware of adult values, the relief felt by a child at the sight of a confident hero: emotions that have very rarely been set down in childhood.

When the Second World War started, Kenneth Edward was a moderately naughty little boy of thirteen living in a Cornish town with his father, who was a policeman employed in a naval dockyard. When he left school he worked for three or four months as a kitchen boy in a Cornish hotel, which must have found that he exaggerated rather than relieved their labour difficulties. He did not get on with his father, and he went to sea at the beginning of 1940, as deck-boy in an ammunition ship. In May he transferred to a steamer called the *Cymbeline,* and in September, when he was not yet fifteen, he was aboard the ship when she was sunk by a German raider. For six weeks he was kept a prisoner on the raider, and then he and two of his shipmates were landed in France and put in an internment camp. In

November they were taken out and he was separated from them, and was sent to another camp, and to another, and then to another. He was not sure where these camps were, or how long he stayed in them. Eventually he was put in a camp near Besançon, where there were some Englishwomen among the internees. One of these women was released and allowed to go to her home in Paris, and she got permission to take the boy with her. Even during his trial, when years of anxiety had made his face puffy and glum, it could be seen that he must have been a charming boy, pretty and jolly and impudent. For some time he was mothered by this woman, but as he grew nearer military age this situation was naturally not tolerated by the Germans. He describes what happened in these words:

Then I was sent to a camp near Drancy near Paris, in which I found myself alone with a lot of Jews I stayed in this camp with them for three months and then I was transferred to St Denis with all the Jews on August 29th, 1942. On June 9th I escaped from St Denis and I could not get away from Paris So I gave myself up on the 10th of July 1943 when I returned to Camp I had a dogs life from the Jews because they believed I gave one of there number away seeing he had escaped and was hiding unbeknown to myself quiet near to where I was an he was caught three days after. I stayed in camp then in a hut to myself because even my best Friend would not speak to me until it was found out that I never gave him away. Soon after a man Came to our Camp and he Called himself John Amery he called some men to a hut in the Camp and spoke to them about a Legion of St George that had been formed in Germany. Then he put some big Poster in the Camp, which said that a said Legion had been formed and the strength of this Legion was a little 1800 men P.O.W. and those R.A.F. planes that had come from England to fight Bolshevics which I can truly say I did not understand what it meant untill a few months ago, he said it was our duty to come and fight for England and Europe. So I spoke to the Camp Captain Gillis a German who said it was good and that most of my friends had vol. but he could not tell me their names, so I thought if he said it was good it must be so. I told him I would join too.

This letter explains why it was right to hang John Amery, if it be right to hang anybody: why he must be ranked as a criminal. This boy Kenneth Edward was by now not quite eighteen and had undergone two and a half years of imprisonment, varied by life in Paris under the occupation. A fortnight after his interview with Gillis he was taken to a private house where he met a German called Plack, of the Foreign Office, and John Amery, who was introduced to him as the Foreign Secretary of England. They took a great deal of trouble to persuade this illiterate child with no military training to enlist in the Legion, and this was not folly. A gay and good-looking boy, in high spirits because he had regained his liberty, and bubbling over with talk of the fine time the Germans were giving him, might have been a very successful recruiting-agent in English prisoner-of-war camps. To John Amery, who all his life had cultivated the cruder pleasures and knew nothing of the puritanism of the hero, Kenneth Edward must have seemed a much more potent instrument than he was; and Plack was helping to put on a performance for the outside world. England had to be persuaded that Germany was more hostile to Russia than ever before, so long as the peace proposals were being discussed. In order to get hold of the boy John Amery told many lies which he must have known to be lies. He said that several of the boy's friends in the camp had joined, but he would not give their names, on the pretext that he had been asked not to disclose them. In fact, none had joined. He also declared that three British submarines had been brought in to St. Nazaire, and three British planes had been grounded, one in Holland, one in Belgium, and one in Germany, all by crews anxious to enlist in the Legion. It is not possible that he could have believed this.

Kenneth Edward did not immediately yield to this persuasion. So he was taken back to the camp and told that he had a week or ten days to make up his mind. It was at this point that his naughtiness passed to a degree of culpability which deserved and later received punishment. For the camp was seething with denunciations of Amery. Nearly all the internees had recognized his speech as the raving of a crazy traitor, and a number of them had remembered his criminal record. There were other boys there as young and as unfortunate as Kenneth Edward, who kept their heads and their courage. But it must be remembered that Kenneth Edward had had his differences with the camp when he was under suspicion of betraying the escaped Jewish prisoner to the Germans. It was probably resentment against this injustice which made him succumb after a few interviews with the Camp Commandant. So about three weeks after he saw Amery he was handed over to an English member of the Legion named Tunmer, who took him to Paris. There they lived in a house managed by French collaborationists in the bleak and surrealist district on the outer edge of Auteuil, where gaunt buildings tower over a landscape made unnatural by the attack of the fortifications on its contours, in the Boulevard Exelmans, not far from the solid yet fantastic viaduct of the Pont-du-Jour. Tunmer took Kenneth Edward to see the sights of Paris and gave him some money to spend on amusements, and promised him he would soon be having as nice a time in Berlin and that the war would soon be over, for Britain and Germany were drawing together. There was doubtless a real tenderness and pity in the older man's dealing with the boy. For after eight days of this holiday-making two men in civilian clothes came to the house and took Tunmer away. He was a British agent.

Kenneth Edward did not know what to do; and later that same day John Amery paid him a visit to see how he was getting on. When the bewildered boy told him what had happened he showed signs of surprise, and, in the plea that it did not seem safe for him to stay in the house when such things were going on, he rang up the Gestapo. Whether he took this step in good faith or not, the consequences were alarming. Three Gestapo men came and interrogated Kenneth Edward about Tunmer, and threw him into jail for about a week. Amery, with his long experience of Franco Spain and collaborationist France and the radio traitors' circle in Berlin, must have known perfectly well into what an unending night of terror he was leading the boy when he recruited him. At the end of the week's imprisonment Kenneth Edward was taken under guard to Berlin, where he was met at the station by Amery, his Cagoularde wife who had succeeded Jeannine Barde, and Herr Plack. They greeted him affectionately and took him back to Amery's rooms in the Kaiserhof, a luxurious hotel looking out on a great square. It was not in the same class as the Adlon or the Esplanade, for the Germans would not have given Amery their first-class accommodation, but it was in the same line of vulgar splendour as the Eden. Kenneth

Edward was dazzled by it, and greatly impressed by John Amery's good looks; and he enjoyed playing with Amery's dog. Amery gave him three hundred marks and kept him with him for some hours, lying about the growing strength of the Legion and preaching a crusade against Russia. Finally he took him over to the German Foreign Office, which was not far away, and introduced him to a Dr. Hesse, who inquired with what must have been inhuman irony as to his readiness to fight the Bolsheviks and gave him the three propaganda books *England Faces Europe, Root of the War,* and *Fire Over England,* which were supposed to be written by Amery and probably were in part. It is unlikely that with his lack of stability he should have written all of them. Kenneth Edward was then taken by Plack to a boarding-house and settled in a comfortable room.

But he did not see Amery for a month. Plack kept him supplied with money and cigarettes, and he drifted about Berlin with nothing to do. Then Amery summoned him to the suite at the Kaiserhof, and introduced him to Thomas Haller Cooper and a group of German officers who had been engaged for some time past in spotting likely traitors in the prison camps, and had brought along their chief catch, a corporal of the British Free Corps, a man of Lithuanian origin who had been educated at an English public school and had volunteered for the British army in New Zealand. "Drinks," Kenneth Edward reported in one of his statements, "were supplied by Amery." The British Free Corps was launched onto the sea of alcohol on which it was to sail until its shipwreck. At the end of the evening Amery said to the boy, "You will soon be with your unit now, and will start training soon with the Corporal." But no call came for him, and it was the last time he was ever to see the man who, pitiful himself, had been so pitiless towards him. By now it was September. In the next three months Kenneth Edward was to live in a peculiar limbo. Berlin was constantly raided. Plack ceased to take any interest in him, and he was so poorly fed that he nursed the Red Cross parcels he had had in camp. He was unable to write to his family or receive letters from them. As he spoke very little German he was repeatedly put under arrest; he thought it happened on as many as twenty-three occasions. Again and again he wrote to Amery asking him what he was to do, but received no answer. The last time he was arrested his captors put him in a cell and beat him with a blackjack in revenge for the damage the R.A.F. were doing. In desperation he went to the Foreign Office and reminded the authorities of the interview he had had when he first came to Berlin; and on the 1st of January, 1944, he was sent to a house on the outskirts of Berlin where there were a handful of men who had volunteered to join the British Free Corps and were now under the command of Thomas Haller Cooper.

Kenneth Edward was not very kindly received. The German authorities issued an enlistment form which required the recruits, with touching trust in their good faith, to state whether they were of Jewish blood and had any criminal record. He was not asked to sign this, because, he thought, "I wasn't very trusted and had been brought in by Amery." That there was some feeling against him was indicated by his position as the one and only private in the British Free Corps. All other volunteers, without a single exception, were made officers. The explanation he gave was probably correct. The Germans had by this time found that John Amery was more than they could stomach. Nevertheless, they used Kenneth Edward by sending him on recruiting tours through the camps. But they had fallen into the pit which is dug for all corruptors of youth: the procurer who stocks his brothel with virgins does no such thing. The happy and pretty boy they had enlisted to speak fair things to melancholy prisoners was no longer happy or pretty, and his words had had little power to lift the heart since he had seen Tunmer spirited out into the interminable curve of the Boulevard Exelmans and exorcised into nothingness by two quiet conjurors in civilian clothes; and since he had first known Amery so well that he could sit in his grand room and drink his liquor and play with his dog, and then found that he did not know him at all, so that in hunger and during raids and under blows from a blackjack it was useless to hope for his help.

He made no recruits; and, on finding himself in the month of May 1944 in the course of a tour at the merchant seamen's camp near Bremen, he heard something of the Security Officer who was in charge: Captain Notman. This man was as all men would

wish to be: comely, strong, courageous, never perjured, much
beloved. Learning his repute, Kenneth Edward wrote him a
letter in which he threw himself on his mercy.

But it's not been for the last month that I have realized I am a
traitor to England and by what I am doing I am causing my Mother
the greatest agony she has ever felt so I implore you not for my sake but
for my Parents' sake to help me to get out of the mess I am in. I'll
face anything if I can get out, but if it is possible to see Brigadier-Major
Interne I think he will see that I don't get down the mines Because
I am scared for my health and I would (I have realized) like to come
to Milag with Real Englishman, I thank you Sir.

When Captain Notman got this letter he came out of his
office and talked to the boy, whose presence in his camp on
these tours he had till then ignored. He formed a good opinion
of him, and wanted to take him to the Kommandantur to make
his statement before the Kommandant of the camp and trust to
this man's humane feelings. But another Englishman in a position of authority advised Kenneth Edward not to go; and it is
possible that this was the wiser counsel, for Captain Notman was
not aware how John Amery's prestige had fallen in Berlin and
how the Germans were savaging the traitors. As an alternative
Captain Notman advised Kenneth Edward to stay in the British
Free Corps, and, since Switzerland was the neutral power named
by Great Britain to protect the interests of its prisoners of war,
to go to the Swiss Embassy in Berlin and put his case before the
officials there.

This Kenneth Edward did, a month or so later, and a Swiss
official promised that he would find out what could be done for
him and then write to him. But of course the boy never heard
from him. Prisoners of war who lose their status through treachery are not a class which it is possible to protect by international
action, since it would be impossible to make the threat of repris-
als against a similar group which is the only weapon which guar-
antees the protection of prisoners of war. In his misery he made
another attempt to get in touch with Amery:

                                                    Dresden. 4.11.44
Dear Sir.
    I write you a few lines and hope that you may receive them. Well Mr
Amery it is a long time since I saw or heard from you last and I some-

times wonder how you are getting on. I hope you are in good health the same as this leaves me. I saw in the French papers that you were wounded on your way to Lyons, but I am glad to know that you have recovered. I am still in the British Free Corps we expect to go to the front in two week's time, but I don't think there is anything in it. We are doing Pioneer Training for the past six weeks and I like it very much I speak a great lot of German so I can tell a few were to get off. How is your wife and dog? I hope they are still in good health. Have you heard from Mr and Mrs Plack. How are they? would tell them I should like to be remembered to them and I would like to have a line from them some time, I cannot write to them because I have not there present address, also would you be so kind as to give Mr Adami my best regards. I must close now because it is time for me to go on Garde duty. All the Boys sends there Best Regards so goodbye for the time.

Yours truly.

Kenneth Edward

The forced cheerfulness of this letter contrasts strongly with the honest misery of the letter he had written six months before to Captain Notman. His motive in writing it was probably the hope of getting in touch with Plack, who had once helped Kenneth Edward when he was in desperate straits, as he was again. In November 1944 the British Free Corps was drinking and whoring and quarrelling to keep its fear away, and the Germans were raving at it to keep their fear away. It cannot have been pleasant to be its solitary private at that moment. He was inevitably one of the unhappy residue of the Corps which was hustled to the Eastern front and forced toward the fighting line under the leadership of Thomas Haller Cooper, who, himself just released from arrest by the Germans for the sole reason that his power to hold anything was vanishing, was going on fulfilling the orders they had given him; partly because his German blood found contentment and swelling music in death among flames, partly because he was a young man in his twenties and he was at a loss to know what else to do. He dragged Kenneth Edward into the battle somewhere near Shoneberg. "The minstrel boy to the war has gone," never less gloriously, never with less comradeship to sustain him, never with much more than mere fear to distress him. In the two statements he made before the Court he gives contradictory accounts of what he did when the Russian wave broke over him. In one he said that he got hold of a civilian suit and changed into it, in the other he said that he kept on his British Free Corps uniform and did not rip the flashes off it as most of his comrades did. Whether this contradiction arose from a confusion of memory or from careless lying, it shows a puzzled sense that there was a right way and a wrong way of behaving in these circumstances and a desire to escape further shame, even if it were only in the world of the imagination. This profound embarrassment was the last trouble to visit him in his exile. The collapse of the German army was so complete that he passed without difficulty to the Russian lines and there surrendered, and he was presently handed over to the Americans, who sent him back to England by air.

He did not seek employment at home, but took work in London. In July 1945, Military Intelligence had collected enough information in Germany to be very sure of what he had been doing during his captivity, and he was sent for and interrogated. He made one statement, and should have returned the next day to make another; but instead sent a letter saying that he had been told that he was under no obligation to make any statement, that he refused to make another until he had consulted his father, the police sergeant, and that he had gone back to Cornwall, where the authorities could always put their hands on him if they wanted him. In November 1945 he was again interrogated, since yet more evidence had come in, and in the following February he was tried, with Denis John and Alfred Vivian and Ronald David, and the eccentric Herbert George, all of them being merchant seamen. The reason for his prosecution must have been the part he had played in the recruiting campaign, for certainly the policy of the Crown in bringing these charges of treachery was to assert the sacredness of the prisoner of war and guard him from molestation in any future war. If it be objected that he was young, it should be remembered that among the prisoners of war whom he had through weakness attempted to seduce were boys younger than himself but of sturdier soul. He was given nine months' imprisonment, which was the lightest sentence passed on any traitor. As he left the dock he gave the V sign to some members of his family who were sitting in court and looked plumply stoical. Without doubt he would be able to support another nine months added to his four years of continuous hardship; he was physically robust. Without doubt he would forget the terror and the loneliness and the beatings and the bullyings; he was not sensitive. There had been done to him, however, an injury which struck not at the body nor at the nerves but at a deeper part. Captain Notman was the kind of person whom he respected; and he had committed himself to a way of living which the Captain held in contempt, which he was unable to abandon even after the Captain was aware of him.

2

THE hotel at Portsmouth had once been famous for its claret and its port; many an admiral had enriched the purple patina of his complexion in its panelled dining-room. Now the taxi driver could hardly find it. "Nobody comes here now," he grumbled, "they all go up to the new hotel in the town." That, indeed, had been the intention of the female journalist whom he had brought from the station; but every room in that had been booked weeks ago. Very few hotels were still standing in the town. "People don't like coming down here to the docks now," he went on grumbling as he crawled along, poking his head out each time he passed one of the few houses that stood up like towers among the rubble on the harbour's lip. "I don't like coming down here now myself." Within, though the war had been over for nine months, the windows were still boarded up. At this spot as rigorous a blackout had been imposed as anywhere in the world, and there was no labour available to take apart its firmness. The female journalist, arrived in her bedroom, found that there were no towels. She had forgotten that this was possible, and indeed it might not have been so; though nearly every hotel in England was short of linen and asked the clients who booked ahead for lengthy visits to bring their own, they usually did something for transients, if it were only to give them a quarter of a worn-out bath-towel. But it was too late to bother anyone about that, so she dried herself on cotton-wool.

In the morning she rang for the maid and asked for some sort

of a rag but was refused. The maid was a slow and pleasant creature, for this part of the world is getting on to the west; and the
further west one goes, the slower and pleasanter people become,
until one runs into Cornwall and the dark, sceptical Celts.
Mournfully she said, "The mistress won't give out any linen, not
an old dish-cloth, and I can't ask her for it. Her nerves are so
terrible bad. She was here all through the blitz, and her son was
in Japanese hands as a prisoner of war, and has come home very
ill. He is yellow, quite yellow. It is as if the Japanese had wanted
to make him like themselves. But about the towels, I'll tell you
how most people that don't bring their own make do: they take
the part of the sheet that's folded under the mattress and dry
themselves with that. It's quite safe, you can leave it hanging
when you go to bed, then the damp won't mount through the
mattress and you won't get rheumatics."

The female journalist was anxious not to make difficulties,
but she pointed out that this prescription would hardly help her
when she wanted to have a bath. "But how long are you going
to stay?" asked the maid. She was plainly going to argue that in
two or three days the issue need not arise. "I don't know," said
the female journalist. "Just as long as the court martial of Stoker
Rose goes on." "Oh," she said, her calm face clouding, "are you
here for that? It is a most terrible thing. The only naval man to
be charged with treason, and him a Portsmouth man. But I don't
believe a word of it. They are trying him for telling the Germans
all about radar equipment, but what would a stoker know about
radar equipment?" She was behind the times, not only our own
times but our fathers' times, about the elementary matter of
bathing, but she could speak sensibly about radar, for she could
speak of naval matters just as such a woman brought up at Sara-
toga Springs might speak of racing. She had moved all her life
among people who were masters and slaves of a certain technique, and they had made her wiser than herself.

The morning brought no light because of the boarded windows; and as the powdered-egg omelette was eaten in the panelled room where the admirals had drunk their port a rat ran
across the floor, a horrified waiter running after it and striking
at it with a napkin. It was not that the place was dirty. It had
been remarkable for its dogged cleanliness. But a house near by

was being torn down, and its rat tenants were looking for new homes. Outside was a Portsmouth made oddly idyllic by destruction. In this district round the harbour the houses had been so close-pressed that neither streets nor houses made any individual impressions. Now quite a quarter of the houses had gone, and most of those which remained disclosed the comely character of homes built for simple but prosperous people two hundred to a hundred years ago. Where fire or blast had torn down an outer wall, rooms shone with the clear pastel colours to which weather turns even the vilest wall-paper, and were marked with vertical lines of fireplaces where the dead had warmed themselves when they were quick. Where the houses had gone entirely there now grew wholesome country grass, not merely the purple willow-herb which alone will grow on the poor soil of London's bombed sites. It was as if a mad village green were wandering through the town.

The court martial was held at the Royal Naval Barracks, which are built round a vast asphalt square with sides of three or four hundred yards. The wind which sweeps over it is salt. One remembers what is easy to forget in this town where the harbours and quays are as private to the state as the Kremlin: that one is by the sea. In one corner of the square some hundreds of bluejackets were marching and counter-marching in a mass that looked as threatening as a thundercloud, though today men with arms no greater than they can carry are, relatively speaking, innocent as lambs. Beyond the square, red barracks, a clock tower, and a chapel—dreary buildings set up by convict labour in the nineteenth century, with gaps filled up with black huts where bombs had struck to the very ground—drew the background and established the confines of a huge enclosed and un-fanciful community. On the nearer side of the square were tall red blocks of barracks, a labyrinth of them, here and there scalped or hollowed by bombs, with lines of two-storied huts set in the alleys between them, to house the departments left homeless by the damage. In and out of this chipped solidity there tripped the sailors, dark as priests in their long full coats and long full trousers and close round caps, gay as children, nimble as ballerinas, and as grim as they were gay and nimble, by reason of the courage and discipline that stiffened their faces. Their gaiety was odd, considering that the bomb damage inflicted acute discomfort on nearly all of them. At night many of them were sleeping in hammocks under tarpaulin roofs that leaked under downfalls of any persistence, and others who could not support that discomfort were spending their own money to lodge in overcrowded rooms in the town; and all day they were working and playing in quarters so scant that everyone had someone's elbow in his ribs.

The air chattered. Loud-speakers were perpetually roaring that one bearing this name and that number should report somewhere immediately. At every corner the men who were obeying these calls were running full tilt towards each other, swinging clear with a grin at the very last moment, and skipping on their way. At the end of the labyrinth of alleys between the tall barracks, near a boundary wall, was a squat little house ordinarily used as a school for certain courses. Here they were to try Stoker Rose. "But," said the rating who was guiding the journalists from the gate, "we don't reckon he's guilty. A stoker wouldn't know nothing about the radar on his ship. Nor about the defences of Portsmouth Harbour, and they say he told the Germans about them too." Stoker Rose, he added with pride, was to be defended as well as he could be, not just by an officer, as usually happens in courts martial, but by two professional lawyers, a King's Counsel and a junior: that is to say, a senior lawyer who has been recognized by the authorities as a legal practitioner of ability and performance, and an assistant. Their fees had been subscribed by naval stokers who wanted to clear the good name of their comrade and their kind.

To make a courtroom, folding doors had been opened between two schoolrooms. In the larger one, on rising tiers, sat the spectators, who were all naval personnel, male and female. The women all looked charming, because the officers of the Wrens (who are English Waves) wear black tricorne felt hats which make all but inoperable cases charming in a high-bred eighteenth-century way, and the non-commissioned ranks are soubrettes in sailor caps. The men, officers and ratings alike, had the beauty given by health, the dignity given either by the possession of character or the long-continued imitation of character, and that not monotonous uniformity given by submission to a common discipline. Sickliness and weakness which one would have taken as part of the pattern in any ordinary crowd here seemed remarkable; so too would any sign of the uncertainties of thought. In what had been the smaller room seven captains, glorious in gold braid and wearing their swords, sat at a long table covered with red baize, their backs to the only wall in which there were windows. These were the Court. The one in the centre was the President of the Court. Facing them across the table sat the Deputy Judge-Advocate, a naval officer trained in the law whose duty it is to instruct the Court in the legal problems presented by the case, though he cannot advise them on matters of fact, nor on the verdict, nor on the sentence. At a small table covered with green baize, right in front of the Court, almost touching the press table, sat the Prosecuting Officer, who was in full naval uniform and wore a sword, but who was in private life a lawyer. He was a heavily built man who moved with a slowness that was aggressive, a criticism of all who were more speedy. At another table covered with green baize, set against the opposite wall to the Court, sat the two officers who were the Accused's Friends— which is the technical term used for the officers acting as amateur lawyers for the accused person in a court martial—and the two professional lawyers who had been employed by the stokers to defend their comrade. These two lawyers were the only people on the floor of the court who were not wearing the uniform of the King's navy. They had, of course, in their white wigs and their black robes, some sort of repartee to the blue serge and gold braid, but they had no equivalent of the sword. They were always slightly at a disadvantage. Actually the King's Counsel had fought in the last war, and his junior had seen active service with the navy in this war and had been gravely wounded, but all the same the naval men and the lawyers looked at each other across the gulf which always opens when a professional fighter faces a civilian. The service man, pinned down to specialist studies and a limited discipline, feels inferior to the civilian with his greater range and flexibility, and libels the civilian by pretending that he uses all his advantages to develop craftiness. The civilian feels inferior to the service man because the other is usually physically fitter and is dedicated to the primitive virtue of courage, which often atrophies in the civil life of peace, so libels him as a thick-

skulled martinet. It might have been thought that the war, with
its immense conversion of civilians into service men, would have
ended that conflict. But it reasserts itself today as if the Powers
had just fought Waterloo.

There was only the flimsiest of docks: practically a symbolic
dock, a hip-high screen of varnished wood, such as children might
make to use in a charade. Behind it stood Stoker Rose; and behind him was standing the petty officer who was the Master-at-
Arms of the court, holding a sword pointed upwards. The Deputy Judge-Advocate, who was an elderly captain, frank in kindliness as proved men of action can dare to be, gave them the signal
to sit down at the first possible moment. Stoker Rose sank down
in his seat in an attitude of collapse which was surprising. He
and Dr. Allan Nunn May were the only traitors who did not pull
themselves together in the dock and try at an appearance of
courage; but he was the better of the two, and he was perhaps
compelled to make a poor show by his physique. His head lolled
on the long stalk of his neck, and when he was standing his body
had that vertical sag which is one of the least admirable attributes
of the lily. In face he resembled an idealized version of the Duke
of Windsor. His hair was pale gold in the light and mouse-
coloured in the shadow; under his blue eyes there were pouches;
and his lips were full. At the moment his colour was earthen. It
was obvious from his demeanour that he had little physical courage. One at least of the spectators was in a like case. But the two
were the whole minority. Physical courage was an element in the
climate of the barracks.

It appeared from the statements of the prosecution that this
young man, who was now twenty-three, had been a stoker on a
motor torpedo boat, known as an M.T.B., on a night in March
1943, exactly three years and ten days before the court martial,
when it was sunk off the Dutch coast. He was picked out of the
water after some hours by the Germans, who took him to Wil-
helmshaven, where he remained while a tremendous R.A.F. air
raid flattened the town about him, and then to the celebrated
prisoner-of-war camp near Bremen known as Marlag-Milag Nord.
There in the pleasant month of May he was approached by an
American sailor named Williams, who had formed a plan to
escape in company with another American sailor named Schaper.

Williams asked Rose if he would switch identities with him. This was a common device to confuse the authorities during an escape. It meant that the police searched the countryside for someone looking like the man who had failed to answer the roll-call, not like the man who had actually escaped. After this request had been endorsed by Williams' commanding officer, Rose consented. As soon as Williams and Schaper had gone he was arrested by the camp officers and grilled for some hours. In the end this lad, who till he joined the Royal Navy had driven a coal-cart in Portsmouth, was forced to admit that he was not a native of Boston, Massachusetts. All this grilling was a sham, a device not to extract information but to excite fear. Rose's tormentors had known from the first who he was. For as soon as Williams and Schaper had got clear of the camp they had been arrested, for the simple reason that Schaper was not an American sailor but a German Intelligence Officer who had learned his English in America. Schaper then saw that Williams was put in a concentration camp, and transferred his attentions to Rose, for some reason not immediately comprehensible, as he was of no special value to Intelligence. His attentions were formidable and repellent. From evidence given in other cases it is known that he was a fair man six foot two inches in height and broad for that. His teeth were very badly stained; and he suffered so much from varicose veins that his vast limbs were always swathed in elastic bandages. He had curious pleasures: he seems to have enjoyed having sexual intercourse with women in the presence of other men.

It was on the ensuing events that the three charges against Rose were based. He was charged first with traitorously holding correspondence with the enemy between, roughly speaking, the time of his first intimidation and the end of the war; secondly, with traitorously giving intelligence to the enemy, during the first two months of his intimidation, concerning the fitting of radar equipment on British ships and aircraft; and, thirdly, with traitorously giving intelligence to the enemy concerning naval and harbour facilities at Portsmouth.

The first two witnesses for the prosecution turned out to be, to all intents and purposes, witnesses for the defence. The first was the captain of the M.T.B. on which Rose had been captured, who was eager to admit that Rose had had no opportunity to observe the nature of the radar equipment on his vessel, and that by some oversight Rose had never been instructed, as all soldiers and sailors should have been during the war, that if he should be captured he must tell the Germans nothing but his name, number, and rank. The second was a radar expert who defined the kind of radar equipment that was installed on a M.T.B., and added that a stoker would know nothing about it.

There then passed into the witness-box in slow succession two Canadians named Edwin Barnard Martin and John Gordon Galaher and an Englishman named John Welch, who had led lives during the war that were singular not in themselves but in the peculiar renown they attained without knowing it. They were among the half-dozen men who were living in a hut outside the P.O.W. camps at Lamsdorff in Silesia to which Rose was brought to meet Schaper after he had connived at Williams' escape. Martin and Galaher had been captured in 1942 at the raid on Dieppe. Welch had been captured in 1940 outside Dunkirk. It had been already proven against Martin and Galaher, who had already been tried and convicted when they gave evidence against Rose, and it was alleged against Welch, who was at that time awaiting trial, that they had been engaged in the least attractive of the activities open to traitors: when a new batch of prisoners came into a camp they mixed with them and pumped them for information which they then reported to the German Intelligence Officers. In return they got the same rations as the German soldiers, which were twenty-five per cent more than those given to the prisoners of war, and slightly more comfortable quarters; they were given enough money to buy liquor, and a number of German women were detailed to supply their sexual needs; they were allowed to wear civilian clothes and go to the pictures and walk in the woods and, sometimes, visit the nearest big town; and for some of them, such as Martin and Galaher, there was reward in the work itself.

Edward Barnard Martin, of Riverside, Ontario, must have been a pretty baby, and later the small boy for whom old ladies spread biscuits thick with jelly. His like can be seen at the barbecue and on the steamboat, a girl swooning love-silly in his arms, himself trim and upright and ready to make a getaway. His eyes were clear blue under eyebrows that arched like circumflex accents, and his tiny mouth parted under the shadow of a moustache. His nails were badly bitten. He had been sentenced to twenty-five years' imprisonment by a Canadian court martial. An allusion to this by one of the lawyers appalled the spectators, for though in Great Britain we sentence people to imprisonment for life, this actually means twenty years, and that is often remitted by years; but Martin himself was cool and brisk. Doubtless his hobby can be pursued in jail. Some fellow-prisoner or warden will one day, probably as a result of doing him a kindly act, come down suddenly when he thought he was going up. And at this moment Martin was happy because he was having a day out of prison which he was spending in an attempt to condemn to prison, and perhaps to death, a young man with whom he had lived in comradeship for two years.

He described how Rose had arrived at the informers' hut in a state of misery which could be imagined from the boy's present aspect in the dock. His head was drooping towards one shoulder, and he was staring out of the window at certain treetops which showed above the barrack-walls. His lids were bluish-silver, as if smeared with the eyeshadow which women used in the 'twenties. Occasionally the blood rushed backwards and forwards through his body so that his face was white, then scarlet, then white. This was in Shakespeare. "Death is a fearful thing," he said, like Claudio. "And shamed life a hateful," had answered the traditions of the service. And, like Claudio, he had persisted, "Ay, but to die, and go we know not where . . ." To settle this argument in Claudio's favour, Schaper had one night made him drunk with spirits and had in the morning produced a paper covered with compromising statements bearing his signature. He had pointed out to the boy that his switch of identities with Williams had one dangerous consequence for him: if he disappeared now there would be no necessity for the German authorities to account for him.

It was then, according to Martin, that Rose began to give information, which he himself claimed was always false. But Martin said that he had given information first about the radar equipment on the M.T.B., of which his captain had proved that he knew nothing. He also insisted that Rose had given information about Portsmouth, where Rose's parents were still living. To prove this, Martin alleged that he had one day gone into Schaper's office and had passed the leisure hour examining the files, in which he had found a folder of eight pages concerning the harbour and naval facilities of Portsmouth, signed by Rose. There was charm in the conception of a German Intelligence Officer who left his files open for inspection by his alien and highly unreliable employees, and was of such an amiable disposition that his employees would risk being found ransacking his office. Martin could not say how Rose had signed himself, nor undertake to recognize his signature.

He told another story which was as poor as evidence, yet was probably true. One day during August 1943 the traitors had turned on the radio in their hut and had heard the B.B.C. announcing a raid on Portsmouth, and one of them had said to Rose, "I suppose this is some of your work. I hope you are proud of yourself." He had not denied this accusation, and had blushed. This news was in fact never given out by the B.B.C., yet the incident may have occurred. It was probably given out on the broadcast in English by the German radio. In the picture of the traitors' life which was built up by the testimony in this and other cases it was apparent that they spent much of their long idle days in almost meaningless chatter about treachery, just as prostitutes fill their leisure with babble about sex; and, like prostitutes, they were always being shocked by each others' impudicity, which, they alleged, passed the bounds of legitimate trade. Probably Schaper, as the Madam of the establishment, asked Rose questions about Portsmouth, though he must have known nothing a stoker knew would be likely to supplement the excellent maps drawn up on the basis of our English maps, their espionage, and aerial reconnaissance. Doubtless Rose sighed nonsensical answers. Doubtless the other traitors taunted him with the supposed effects of his alleged treachery, though they must have known that Portsmouth had been bombed again and again before his capture.

John Gordon Galaher, of Windsor, Ontario, followed him into the box, and, because prison was a horror to his goatish disposition and he had been there for six months, stood like a dead man not so efficiently raised as Lazarus. When he was asked a question his mouth worked under the stubble of his moustache and then hung open. Usually his hands were clasped behind him; sometimes he brought them forward and rubbed them together. They were curiously marked, as if by untidy stigmata. Staring upwards at nothing, he repeated names of men with whom he had lived for years as if they were words in an unknown language whispered to him from a great distance. Perhaps the doctor gave him an injection that evening, or he had something better than prison food; for the next morning he was not so purely and simply a corpse, his earthly attributes could be perceived. From his dark ginger hair his receding forehead sloped to a long nose, a stalactite of a nose under which his hungry mouth continually twitched. His eyes, which were dull grey flecked with hazel, winked about him in libellous apprehension, imputing to his surroundings a malignity of which they could hardly ever be capable. In the middle of his forehead were three short deep lines, expressive of the same denigrating fear. His career had been inevitable. A man who saw the world as he did, vile in cunning, would have no resource but to outmatch it by vile cunning.

The story he told was the same in substance as Martin's, and differed only because he was a simpler man. Martin might have been an automobile mechanic or a clerk. Galaher had been a barber, and the establishment which employed him probably went in less for elegance than for utilitarian control of the hair's disposition to grow. Martin had given a miniature performance; all his life he had been careful to do as little as he could and keep his brittleness intact.

The goat in Galaher's loins made him skip high, whatever pipe was played, and he gave a bravura performance in a role of repellent baseness and heartrending *naïveté*. He saw the court as comprised of persons who, like all persons gathered together in public, proposed to believe in virtue. Or did they really believe in virtue? Perhaps so. He could believe in virtue too if he bade himself. Then let them all be virtuous together. At his own court martial he had been described as "the ears and the eyes of the Germans." He had been the informer to end all informers. With his wide grin and his wide hands that could fall so brotherly about a fellow-comrade's shoulders, he plucked out secrets from the most honest hearts, through the most disciplined lips. Even before the war he had been able to persuade; often and often he

had induced the gang in the bowling alley to believe what was
not true concerning his prowess with women and his defiance of
the boss. Well, now he was back in peacetime again, and he was
ready to set about persuading this gang at the Portsmouth court
martial that his activities among the prisoners of war were so
benevolent that a just comparison could be found not among the
heroes but the heroines of war, in such figures as Florence Nightingale or Edith Cavell. He described how, when he and the other
traitors searched the prisoners for private possessions and took
them away, they were careful to set aside maps and compasses and
cigarettes and smuggle them back to their owners, and how he and
his friends took pains to get them their rations. "There were a
hundred and one little things we could do for the prisoners," he
declared priggishly. He declared that the German houses he and
the traitors visited in the towns near the camp, which were in fact
mostly brothels and beer-houses, were the homes of anti-Nazi
civilians. But in this orgy of self-justification he spared time to
say a good word for Rose when he could. He repeated Martin's
improbable stories of Rose's giving information to the Germans
about radar and Portsmouth, but he described how the boy had
gone more than once to see certain German officers and, weeping,
had begged them to release him from this servitude and send him
back to an ordinary prisoner-of-war camp, but had been told
that this could never be allowed because "he knew too much."
Though Galaher certainly lied in saying he aided these attempts,
his account of them was probably exact in all other respects, for
it tallied with other stories told in similar cases. Only active resistance to orders which would have led Rose to Buchenwald or
death would have freed him from his association with the traitors.
We were back to Claudio and Isabella. "Death is a fearful thing."
"And shamed life a hateful."

Galaher's simplicity gave him sometimes a sort of childishness.
"What did you do with your time?" he was asked, when he was
speaking of the life he and his friends had led in huts outside
various barracks. He answered, "We played cards. We read books.
We went walks in the woods. And sometimes," he said, with sudden gusto, "we went swimmin'." One saw his hairy and sweating
body raising a diamond spray of water in the sunlight, one heard
the harsh and meaningless cries with which he would have ban-

ished tranquillity in order to proclaim his pleasure. The traitors were often disconcerting in their appreciative references to the simpler delights. It is as if, called upon to enact the austerer chapters of *Pilgrim's Progress,* they had insisted on living the lives of Huckleberry Finn and Tom Sawyer. But Galaher's sensuousness, which was apparently immense, had its graver consequences. He was himself not content with his servitude, as he found Schaper a brutal master, and once agreed to make an attempt to escape in company with Rose. They collected maps, compasses, and food, and made a plan to dodge the guards; but at the appointed hour Galaher was missing. He had overstayed one of those leaves in civilian clothes to which the traitors were entitled, and twenty-two guards were sent out in search of him while he lay lost to time in the unfortunate bosom of a prostitute.

Now that things had gone ill with him, his simplicity had not matured into wisdom, it had acquired no dignity; it had merely become grotesque like a gargoyle. He was asked why he had come to give evidence against Rose, and it was suggested that he had hoped thereby to re-establish his reputation and increase his chance of winning his appeal against his sentence, which was, incredibly enough to our ears, even longer than Martin's. "You are serving a life sentence, are you not?" asked Mr. Curtis Bennett. "And by Canadian law that really does mean imprisonment for life, does it not?" "Yes," said Galaher, staring at a nothingness which was within a few feet of him, which he could have touched. "But I know I'll never serve it." He spoke like a seer. His hearers thought he must mean either that he knew himself to be so far advanced in some deadly disease, or so resolute in the intention of suicide, that he would serve no term of imprisonment at all. But he had meant simply that he believed he had established this preposterous story of his innocence by his appeal. He did not know what was known to several persons in court: that his appeal had already been rejected. This situation made him pitiful, but left him still repulsive.

The third of these tainted witnesses, John Welch, came from Durham, a northern county of rocky seacoast and upland moors and coal mines, and therefore spoke in an accent which English hearers associate with austerity and the more rugged type of trade unionism. But he was a tiny little creature, built like a hoofer,

with bright and shifting blue eyes and a slight harelip, which gave
him a surprised and petitioning expression, and a mass of brown
hair rising from his forehead in the cast-iron undulations of an
old-fashioned marcel wave. He surveyed the world with the bogus
loving-kindness of a Riviera bartender. He would strike naïve
people, when they first met him, as ready to do anything for anyone. Stoker Rose, who had hardly looked at Martin and Galaher,
turned on Welch an eye heavy with hatred. The young man, however, was not abashed. He had given evidence against Galaher;
he had given evidence against Martin; now he was giving evidence
against Rose, and it was not his fault if the results were any less
serious.

He seemed as repulsive as Galaher. Yet in another court another aspect of him was to appear. It is the besetting sin of the
recorder to see those who make victims as fixed in that role, and
to overlook the instances, so frequent as to be the rule, when they,
in some other relationship, are also victims. On the psychoana-
lysts' couches women, mothers themselves, learn to reproach their
mothers; and doubtless in the next world their mothers resent
the injustice which forgets that they too had mothers whom they
might have reproached, but forget their resentment in pity, knowing that their daughters' daughters will in time reproach their
daughters. There was just such a Janus-headed duality among
the traitors who gave evidence against their kind in the courts
martial. (They appeared not so often in the civil cases, because
the civil authorities, more experienced and apt in legal matters
than the service authorities, used such tainted evidence as little
as possible.) While they swore away their comrades' lives they
seemed just as pitiless as they seemed pitiful when their comrades
swore away their lives; and in most trials involving prisoners of
war there were disclosed circumstances which showed the man
in the dock as subjected to such coldly and cleverly planned
temptation that the heart bled for him. In another place Welch
was found guilty, and established his claim to be a victim. At his
own court martial, some months later, he looked small and young
sitting on a kitchen chair in one of the drawing-rooms of a great
house, rolling his solemn yet trivial eyes up to the plaster doves
that floated on medallions on the ceiling, to the carved vases of
fruit and flowers on the panelled walls which were not covered by

the plywood shields, to the treetops of Hyde Park, seen as a green blur through windows varnished against blast. Here a sad, small effect was mourning beside one of the causes of the deep, broad river of misery in which it had been immersed and all but drowned. For in this house Sir Edward Carson and Lord Birkenhead had rashly made their threats of armed resistance to Home Rule which had encouraged the Germans to believe it a good moment to attack Great Britain in 1914; and in this house Ribbentrop had been so hospitably received that he reported to Hitler that the governing classes of England would never permit a war to be made on Germany. The household had meant no harm, but they were more active than they were thoughtful, and most unlucky at crystal-gazing.

So now the house was handed over to the military, and the fireplace where Birkenhead and Carson and Ribbentrop had sat and dangerously gossiped with their hosts was bricked up, and seven officers sat beside a trestle table spread with army blankets and deliberated the case of John Welch. He told a story which cannot be doubted because it so closely corresponds to stories which were told by other prisoners with whom he had no contact. He had been taken out of the camp and was working in a small saw mill in a country district. His particular job was to work quite alone in the chamber which received the sawdust. One day there came to him Martha, the young daughter of the miller, who made advances to him, putting her arms round him and drawing him close to her. He resisted but, he said, in the end "I gave in to her." Soon afterwards Gestapo men seized him and he was taken before Schaper, who told him he could be shot for having sexual relations with a German woman and would be if he did not buy his safety by working as an informer.

The army required Welch to refuse to buy his life at that price, and this demand was not past reason, for many men in like circumstances found themselves able to make that refusal. It was even not so callous a demand, for most of the men who refused were in fact not killed. But Welch was not forthright, and he wavered. He was taken to a new place, where there was a prisoner-of-war camp, and a hut outside it for informers. Among a half-dozen informers living there were Martin and Galaher, who took the new boy in charge. They got him down by wisecracking about him. He recalled with smarting irritation that after Martin had brought him into the hut Galaher asked Martin what the new arrival was like and Martin had answered, "He may look dumb but might be honest." Welch also mentioned, obviously as a powerful seduction, that at his first meal in the hut he was given three eggs. After supper Galaher talked to him seriously about the sound future which would be open to him if he became an informer, saying that he himself looked on it as a business like any other. But Welch was very reluctant to make the irrevocable decision. So presently Schaper took him and Galaher to stay in a comfortable house in the neighborhood. It is quite apparent from what happened there that this unit of the Intelligence organization had got completely out of hand, that it was no longer supervised by any sane authority, and that Schaper was using his position to indulge his peculiar fantasies. But at the same time those fantasies were so peculiar that, it must be admitted, they helped Schaper to secure the ends for which he was working in his capacity of Intelligence Officer.

Schaper and he shared a bedroom with twin beds. After they had settled down for the night Martha came in and tried to get Welch to take her into his bed. It is to be noted that the Nazis found it apparently easy to draw the women they needed for the seduction and satisfaction of the prisoners of war from the ordinary local population, even from homes which might have been presumed to be respectable. While Martha was making her assaults on Welch's virtue Schaper did not leave the room, and Welch felt nothing but disgust. Finally Schaper took Martha into his bed and she remained there for the night. In the morning Schaper and Welch were in the garden, and Martha and another girl came up and talked to them. Schaper had intercourse with the other girl on the lawn, in the presence of Welch and Martha. Not long afterwards some Gestapo men came in and told Schaper that they were arresting him and ordered him to take off his uniform and put on a civilian suit which they had brought with them. Welch was apparently almost as much shocked because Schaper changed his clothes out in the garden in front of the two girls as he was by his extraordinary sexual indecencies. Stunned, Welch went back to the informers' hut with Galaher, who ingeniously devised a new way of tormenting him. He spread among his friends the story that Schaper had told him that Welch had had sexual intercourse with Martha seven times during the night, and they teased the boy about it. He complained in his statement that this made a laughing-stock of him; and he consented to become an informer. Possibly he thought that this would mean going away to various camps, and in this he was partially right, though he was always being sent back to the company of Galaher and Martin and Schaper, who was not long out of favour.

The story of Welch's entrance into the sphere of espionage was not actually to his credit, as the story of Rose's entrance was to him. But it is a pitiful and comprehensible story. The spectacle of Schaper's vast varicosed and bandaged limbs tossing in spasm must have been horrible to a young boy who had obviously been brought up in a respectable provincial home. But he did not suggest that there was such a defence for himself when he gave his evidence against Rose, towards whom, as was alleged at his own trial, he had professed friendship, and whom he had advised to become an informer, acting on the instructions of Schaper. He told the same unconvincing stories as Galaher and Martin concerning radar and Portsmouth, and said that Rose had told him that he was giving information "to get his freedom and some money," words which were unlikely to have been uttered by that lachrymose child in view of the circumstances connected with Williams' escape, which the prosecution had admitted had brought him into Schaper's power. But he then began to tell the truth, which was clearly defined as such by its unpredictability. Some time about the middle of 1944, when Rose made a last unsuccessful attempt to be sent back to a P.O.W. camp, Schaper took Welch and Rose to Frankfurt-on-Main, where they all got into the Paris express. After they had crossed the border into France a squadron of R.A.F. planes appeared and bombed the trains and they had to climb out of the carriage and run into a wood, which they found swarming with German soldiers taking cover. At the end of the raid they came out of the wood and found there was no train. Schaper handed his two captives over to some of the soldiers to be guarded until he had found an automobile. He introduced Rose to these soldiers as "his adopted son." When Welch repeated these words he fluted his harelip and looked down his eyelashes.

Schaper came back and took Welch and Rose to Chalons-sur-Marne, a town which in peacetime was specially memorable for a hotel called the High Mother of God which served a very good still champagne as part of its market-day lunch. It was not possible to judge how far Welch and Rose carried out their instructions. It can quite safely be assumed that they contributed the barest minimum which would be accepted, and that they palmed off as much false information as they could. But they certainly went through the motions of gathering information, and certainly they must from time to time have produced a little genuine information to avert the threat of Buchenwald or shooting. In any case a certain Sergeant Norman who was among the prisoners came to the conclusion that they were informers. After some weeks, probably when Sergeant Norman's convictions became widely known among the prisoners, Welch and Rose were taken out of the camp at Chalons-sur-Marne and sent back to an informers' hut outside a camp at Luchenwald, south of Berlin, where they had been before, and where they met Galaher again. He testified that Rose brought back with him from France a quantity of powder, perfume, silk stockings, and what he prudently called "other silk articles." Apparently the Nazis worked as assiduously on informers as on members of the British Free Corps to demoralize them with liquor and prostitutes, and Schaper would have thoroughly enjoyed the carrying out of this policy. But it is remarkable that Schaper worked so hard on this boy, whose languor, lack of intellectual equipment, and reluctance must have made him a poor instrument.

Some time afterwards Welch and Rose were sent to a castle near Coblentz where a number of British and Americans were imprisoned, and were put in amongst them to do their work. But, as Welch related with a smarting sense of grievance, there was a hitch in the proceedings. Hardly had they settled in when an American colonel came "stamping into the hall and told everyone to keep their mouths shut." It was evident from Welch's tone that the American colonel seemed to him a low fellow who was not playing the game, a fault he shared with Sergeant Norman, who had so far broken the rules as to have been sent to this castle from the camp at Chalons-sur-Marne. Later Welch and Rose were summoned to a meeting with Sergeant Norman, who, Welch complained, "slied out on them" and tricked them into entering into a room where they stepped into a spotlight cast by an electric lamp lying bulb outwards on a table. In the darkness behind the lamp stood some people whom they could not see but who announced themselves as four British officers and four American officers, assembled to question them as spies. Rose danced about in the spotlight shouting that he was willing to fight anyone who called him a spy. This was a curious action for a lethargic and worried young man. At this point Welch's story became confused and he simply stated that after a great deal of talk the officers had let them go. It may be deduced that Welch and Rose left the castle by giving the guards the password by which they could always gain release from a camp when they had an urgent matter to bring before the Intelligence Officers. But what bewildered Welch, so much so that he would plainly have liked the Court's opinion on it, was that when they reported the incident to Schaper he seemed pleased at what had happened. And, indeed, examination of the incident made it very hard to believe that it could be an accident. When informers were sent from camp to camp the German authorities must have exercised the greatest care to see that they made contact with an entirely fresh set of prisoners each time. It is odd that this system broke down over a prisoner who had a personal reason for certainty that these two men were spies; and that the German Intelligence Officer responsible for the breakdown should show, instead of annoyance, something like pleasure.

But there were many mysteries in this case: the most profound a matter of a name. When the informers were put into the camps they always assumed false names. Rose worked as Johnson and Muller and Jones, but the name which he chose for himself and in which he seemed to take a special pride was Aylmer. There was never a more puzzling juxtaposition of names in a law case.

> Ah, what avails the sceptered race!
>   Ah, what the form divine!
> What every virtue, every grace!
>   Rose Aylmer, all were thine.

Rose Aylmer, whom these wakeful eyes
    May weep but never see,
A night of memories and sighs
    I consecrate to thee.

It is one of those poems which will not lie down on the paper
after it has been written, but which ramble on, living its own
life in the continuance of literature. Walter Savage Landor wrote
it and the great classical scholar Walter Headlam translated it
into elegiacs; and the greater classical scholar von Wilamovitz-
Möllendorff meditated over the Greek version with that degree
of appreciation which ranks as a creative art, and declared that
if it had been found on a papyrus it would have been counted
one of the jewels in the *Greek Anthology*. And a stoker called
Rose, choosing a false name, chooses, with marked interest and
excitement, the name of Aylmer. This might be a coincidence, or
it might be that when he drove a coal-cart round Portsmouth he
sometimes descended from the drivers' seat to converse with
someone of imagination and literary taste, whom it amused to
remember verses concerned with the name of Rose. That we
shall never know, any more than we shall know why Schaper
introduced Rose to a German soldier as his adopted son, or why,
if he did not, Welch said that he did, or why Schaper contrived
quite without profit to himself a nightmare for the boy, while
he stood naked in his shame under a bright light before his fellows, who were clad in their honour, or why Schaper laughed
when he heard of it.

For Schaper was not called to give evidence. Instead there appeared an underling of his called Richard Wigge, to whom all
persons in the Court alike, sinking the marked division between
them, alluded as Mr. Wiggy. He was one of those fleshless dust-
coloured Germans with pale but fervid eyes who are perhaps as
disagreeable as any other of their nation, and though he had been
styled an interpreter in the German army, he had been employed
in briefing the informers and arranging for their pay and their
pleasures. He was a perfect example of the unassimilatability
of the German. He was a man of forty-eight who had spent all
his youth in England, from the age of two till twenty-one, and
he had lived with us for another year in his maturity and visited

us half a dozen times; and we had not made the slightest impression on him. We had not demoralized him by our come-day-go-day slovenliness. When he was asked about a department of the German army he knew its origin and its function; when he was asked about a prisoner he knew exactly where he had been at any given moment; when he was asked about a document which had been in his charge he remembered its every detail. His particularity was repulsive, however, to our vices as to the one virtue which flowers about the thresholds of our ramshackle character: which may be described, on either side of the Atlantic, as charity. Asked what clothes Rose had been wearing when he first saw him, he answered, "A blue suit, a pink shirt, I don't remember the colour of his tie, black shoes." He had not the faintest inkling that it would be better not to observe a human being so closely unless one was prepared to like him, just a little.

Mr. Wigge was not prepared to like Stoker Rose. Quietly and efficiently he damned him. He explained that he had put him to the task of questioning prisoners about their occupations, which was ostensibly a preliminary to the formation of working parties, but it was a blind for getting information. He described how, before putting Galaher and Welch and Rose into a camp, he had shown to them a questionnaire which indicated what information they were to seek; it told them to ask the prisoners about aircraft factories, jet planes, radar, rustless steel, synthetic rubber, and the like. This questionnaire, he said, had been of little use, because most of the prisoners knew nothing; behind his drab speech there glittered for an instant a sneer at the idiot Allied armies, which had not deserved to win. Rose, he said, had certainly been shown this questionnaire, but had for long turned in no specific reports. The spectators stirred with pleasure; but were still again when he went on to say that in November 1944 Rose had given him a written statement concerning information which he had extracted from a man who before he was called up to the army was in a fort connected with the boom defence of Portsmouth. He himself had translated it into German and typed it. The little man's evidence became more and more distasteful. He said that to his certain knowledge Rose had a post-office savings-bank account with between nineteen and twenty-one hundred marks all earned by good treachery, and that Rose and

Welch and Galaher talked to him about eight thousand dollars which was waiting in a Berlin bank for their use after the war, and he described with his odious particularity a contract which Rose had signed with representatives of German G.H.Q. before he went to work in France. Nothing could have been less desirable than to hear this evidence from his lips; for he was as unrepentant a Nazi as still draws breath. When he used the initials O.H.K. and the Court asked him to explain what they meant, he held his head and rolled out the words with awe—O.H.K.— Oberste Heeres Kommandantur. If there was anything he regretted about the war, it was the losing of it. But having lost it, he was willing to please those who had won it. He was anxious to load the dice against Rose, and this could not be from any personal animus, for he was too thrifty to spend emotion on a person who could be of no material consequence to him. If he had been honest in his patriotism, and honest in his evidence, he should have felt grateful to Rose for the work he had done for Germany. So he must have aimed at pleasing the government which had flown him over to give evidence at this trial. With a careful air of impartiality he said that the Germans had never used threats to make Rose act as an informer. He carried out the work, said Mr. Wigge, and gave the impression that he was interested in it, and certainly never refused to do it. He expressed the opinion that Rose could have escaped if he had really wanted to, on quite a number of occasions, when he and Rose had gone for walks together. Asked if he had not always carried a gun on these walks he agreed that he had, but, asked if he would have shot Rose in the event of an escape, said that he would not. Nazis, apparently, never used guns to shoot people.

He was a persistent Nazi, he was a rat, and he was a humbug; but there was still another reason why his evidence gave pain. It appeared in a reply of his which revealed the flaw that is nearly always found in the performance of the virtuosic linguist. His English was perfect, but it had been crystallized at the age in which he learned it. Since those days he had shed no obsolete idiom and acquired no modern one. When he was talking of the liberty the informers had enjoyed he said that when any of them failed to return by midnight he assumed that they were "on the spree," a phrase descriptive of dissipation which has been outmoded for twenty years. It was as if a bad old gentleman were leering at one out of Mr. Wigge's words. But had he spoken in the purest classical English his evidence would have offended. Though certain Englishmen had sold their brothers for liquor and prostitutes, it would have been preferable not to hear their commerce reported with cool scorn in an English law court by the Nazi who was their pimp. By hearing this witness the trial was injecting itself with the offence which it was its intention to purge. For what is treachery? It is the betrayal of familiars to strangers, of those who are near to those who are far, of those to whom one is bound by real interests to those who, being foreign, will treat one as a foreigner and maybe, in the end, turn against one. To this dangerous error the Court inclined itself by hearing Mr. Wigge, no matter if they called him Mr. Wiggy.

The truth is that it is the business of the army and the navy to fight upon land and sea and deal with the consequences of their wars and keep themselves well disciplined; but not to deal with serious crime at leisure. They have not the technique, and they have not the cold patience which makes for long views. The army is better than the navy, because it lives side by side with the law on land. The navy cultivates an intense wisdom about the sea and the ways of men in the isolation of ships which has necessarily to be counterbalanced by intense ignorance about the land and the ways of men in relation to the community as a whole. This court martial of Stoker Rose shared certain vices with the army courts martial of the traitors. It is the custom of the law not readily to accept evidence against a person accused of a crime from witnesses convicted or suspected of complicity in that crime, unless it is corroborated by the evidence of reputable witnesses. This rule has been followed in most of the traitors' trials in the civil courts, with a few exceptions, but it has been violated in many courts martial; and never so flagrantly as at the trial of Stoker Rose. When Martin had been tried on a charge of betraying to the Germans the position of a secret radio set in a prisoner-of-war camp, one of the prisoners who had been in control of the radio set gave evidence against him. But there were no such respectable witnesses called by the prosecution in the case of Stoker Rose. If Rose had left Marlag-Milag Nord not under compulsion but voluntarily, it was odd that no British

Confidence Officer came to speak of his departure. If Rose had collected information from British and American soldiers, it was odd that none of them were brought to Portsmouth to say so. Where was Sergeant Norman? Where were the eight officers that had stood behind the lamp in the castle near Coblentz? Where was the man from whom he had extracted information about the boom defence of Portsmouth Harbour? Those men could certainly have been traced. But it would have been a trouble to trace them. Some lawyer in Whitehall had known quite well that the navy would not know enough about the law to recognize the inadvisability of using tainted witnesses and had saved himself this trouble by using Martin, Galaher, Welch and Wigge.

This malpractice was not censured by the Court, which was oddly amateurish. In some ways it was a very gracious tribunal. It was pleasant to see the Deputy Judge-Advocate thank each of the witnesses for giving their evidence. They were the worst of men, but they were paying for their crimes, and he was not there to judge them. All that concerned him was that they should answer the questions that were asked them, and that they did. So to each he gave a friendly smile and said, "Thank you very much," and for a second restored them to their original value. But in other respects the Court was unhappy. It was obvious that the naval officers trusted the Prosecuting Officer, because he spoke slowly in what seemed to them creditable contrast with the professional lawyers' suspicious fluency, but under cover of his sober delivery he was talking fantastically. He maintained that Mr. Wigge was a model of all that a witness should be: that in looking after the traitors he had simply been doing his duty as a good German, and that, having committed no crime against German law, he must be regarded not as a criminal but as a perfectly respectable person. But a man who goes about with a gun controlling the movements of a prisoner of war who has been removed from a P.O.W. camp against his will in order that he should collect information for his captors (and it was not disputed that this had happened) has violated Article 5 of Section II of the Geneva Convention relative to the treatment of prisoners of war, which deals with their molestation.

There was another point, not referring to the credibility of the witnesses but to the charge itself, in which the Prosecuting Offi-

cer seemed to move without the care that would have been imposed on him in a civilian court. It had become clear that any
information about radar given by Rose must have been false
because he knew nothing; but the Intelligence Officer maintained
that this did not make Rose any less of a traitor. For, he said, the
indictment charged him with giving "intelligence" to the enemy,
and the dictionary definition of "intelligence" was information,
with nothing added to say whether it mattered that this information was true or false. Now it is true that prisoners of war are
warned against giving false information: a lie may be very dangerous. It might draw the fire of the enemy from a spot where a
military objective of a certain importance is situated to another
spot where a military objective of still greater importance is situated. It might lead to a sudden outburst by the interrogating
officer, who, detecting a lie, might bully the prisoner into a state
of confusion in which he might give anything away. It might betray a vein of knowledge in the prisoner which would betray the
existence of certain inventions or tactics. But Stoker Rose had
never been warned of this danger, because, as his commanding
officer had told the court, he was never given any security instruction; and he was certainly unable to work out the existence
of this danger for himself. It was true, moreover, that no fixed
rule could be based on the existence of this danger, for in practice many English and Americans working with the resistance
movement in France and elsewhere used to give false information
when they were captured in order to give their friends time to
cover their tracks. These were points which the judge in a civil
court would have taken up with the prosecuting lawyer, but
which, put forward at this court martial by the Prosecuting Officer, were accepted in silence by the Court.

The embarrassments of Stoker Rose were, however, not to last
long after he returned from the singular visit to the castle of
Coblentz, so long as the giving of information was concerned.
For this was early in 1945. The informers' life had become more
and more grim. As soon as Welch and Rose had come into the
orbit of treachery Galaher and Martin had tormented them by
a gloomy cynicism that was part of their tough-guy outfit: the
sort of debunkenness that is heard in small and shabby saloons

where men sit and congratulate themselves on having been hard-
boiled enough to see through deceptions which, in fact, life never
troubled to practise on them. "If you're doing this for a woman,
it's not worth it." "Well, well, if you men will sign your own
death warrants . . ." Even such small talk was running low. Galaher had had a considerable reverse. He had joined a working-
party of prisoners of war and had been recognized as an informer.
The scars on his hands which had so perplexed the spectators at
Portsmouth were made by the wounds he then received; his face
was left a bleeding jelly and several of his ribs were broken. He
planned to escape in company with Rose, but was too drunken
and nerve-rotten to keep his tryst on the appointed evening. Rose
cut the barbed wire round their compound, but turned back
when Galaher did not join him, and when the guards found the
gap did not confess but let the whole camp take the blame. They
drank, they quarrelled, they were lecherous and sentimental;
Rose grew greatly excited about one of the whores the Germans
had purveyed for the informers. But the real inflaming interest
of their lives was the map of Europe, on which the Allies were
tracing such invincible paths. They asked each other what they
should do, and never answered. They implored the Germans to
put them into a prison camp where they would not be known;
and it was the ultimate baseness of the Germans that they refused
to show this mercy to these men whom they had corrupted and
exploited. According to Welch, Rose believed until the last moment that the German authorities were going to send him by
plane to Sweden. But the bullies fell silent and fled, then the
guards went. Welch and Rose found themselves their own masters and in mortal terror. They stole bicycles and rode towards
the advancing Allied troops through deliquescent Germany, and
at Munich they joined a working-party of genuine prisoners of
war. During this time Rose constantly asked Welch not to tell
the authorities when he was repatriated that he had known him.
On the 27th of February, 1945, American troops inflicted on them
the liberation they had dreaded. Welch and Rose were separated,
the one having been in the army and the other in the navy, and
for at least a time Rose must have believed that all was going to
turn out better than he had hoped. In May he was sent back to

England and he rejoined the navy. But in August he was visited at Portsmouth Barracks by two of the great contemporary figures at Scotland Yard, J.M.C. Davis and Percy Edwards.

These are formidable people. Both of them are clean and neat in the manner of battleships, and they conceive of themselves as bringing the earth up to battleship standards. They stand for justice and not for mercy, and mercy is the better of the two; but the pleasures of mercy can be indulged in only behind the shelter of justice erected by such as Joe Davis and Percy Edwards. When they came to see Stoker Rose they knew a great deal about him. For Welch, as soon as the reports from the Confidence Officers in the prisoner-of-war camps came in and the authorities showed signs of interest in him, had told everything he knew, and had provided a full and annotated list of all the persons with whom he had been associated during his life as an informer. To his prim and self-satisfied character it would not seem that thereby he showed himself a rogue ratting on his fellow-rogue. He would see himself as a respectable young man who, under duress, had been compelled into co-operation with a gang of criminals and naturally hastened to denounce them to the police the first moment he was free. In the list of persons he prepared for the authorities he included, obviously on the assumption that they were as criminal in coercing the prisoners of war to become informers as the prisoners of war were in becoming informers, Schaper and Mr. Wigge; and in that, common sense and international law were with him.

Armed with the knowledge derived from Welch, the two inspectors said to Rose, "Have you been to Luchenwald?" He answered, "No, I've never been there." They asked him if he had been at Lamsdorff, and he denied that he had been there too, and told them a false story of sojourns in other camps which in fact he had never visited, and of a period of hiding in France. He was asked if he had ever used the names of Johnson, Muller, Jones, and Aylmer, and he answered, "You've got me mixed up with someone else." He was asked if he knew Galaher and Martin and Welch, and he said that he had never heard of them. Then he was asked if he knew Schaper, and that appalling name was too much for him. He asked for time to think. Then he said, "What I've been telling you is lies. I did work for the Germans, but I only did it so that I could escape." He was still lying. He had worked with the Germans not so that he should escape, but so that he should go on living. In his continued agony he dictated a statement which was apparently insanely and unnecessarily incriminating and unusual in its abjection. But neither before his trial or after would he consent to obey the request of the authorities and give evidence against Galaher, Martin, or Welch.

But when Stoker Rose's statement was brought forward by the prosecution it was disallowed. There is a code of legal manners known as the Judges' Rules which forbids the police to take a statement from an accused person by means of question and answer. In practice, this is interpreted as a prohibition of leading questions: of questions, that is, which are so framed as to suggest or force certain answers. It cannot be carried out to the letter because an illiterate, temperamentally inarticulate person will often find it difficult to tell a story without being brought back to the point. Joe Davis and Percy Edwards are experienced officers and are perfectly aware of the required practice and faithful to it. But when they took this statement from Stoker Rose they were acting not as police officers but as Intelligence Officers attached to the War Office, working on a matter in the "top secret" category, and they had not been so careful as usual to observe the conventions. The King's Counsel who appeared for Stoker Rose had a permanent feud with the police, and he was glad to suspect this irregularity. He taxed them with having taken the statement by question and answer, and they at once admitted it. It is doubtful whether this departure from the letter of the Judges' Rules amounted to a violation of the Judges' Rules as they are usually interpreted. But the Court, being innocent of legal refinements, took seriously the King's Counsel's claim that the Judges' Rules had been violated absolutely, and pronounced the statement inadmissible. The effect on Joe Davis and Percy Edwards was catastrophic. They had been taking statements for something not far under twenty years, and I doubt if in all that time they had had one pronounced inadmissible. For a minute it appeared as an intoxicating possibility that they would arrest the entire court martial. There were visibly present in the court not merely two conflicting elements, the navy and civil law, there was a third—there was the police administration. The Court was abashed at this. It wondered if it was handling the matter properly, and lost confidence; thereafter the Court passed into a phase of wrangling over this and other legal formalities which needlessly extended the trial. Stoker Rose kept on breathing heavily and holding his mouth open in a little square, drawing his lips outward from the teeth as people do when they feel sick. Courts martial always drag out longer than a comparable civil trial; and for him this was the dragging end of a prolonged ordeal, for five months had elapsed between his interview with the police and his arrest, and three more months had passed since then.

This Court, being uneasy, did not take the opportunity, as a judge in a civil court would have done, to throw out at the earliest possible moment the two indictments which charged Stoker Rose with giving the Germans intelligence concerning radar equipment and the defences of Portsmouth. This was a pity, for if the case could have been purged of any of its offence the navy would have drawn its breath more easily. For it is true, many men can form a single being, and that single being can grieve. The life of the barracks was usually hidden from the visitors to the court martial, for they went in and out of the courtroom at times when the naval personnel was about its business, save for a few dark figures halting at the end of remote perspectives and looking towards the court-house to see what they could. But one day the Court rose for lunch at an hour when the men were in their quarters; and from every window a row of intent and unsmiling faces, crowded towards the side from which they could see best, like beads pushed along the wire of an abacus, were looking down at the door of the court-martial house and waiting to see Stoker Rose brought out. There must have been hundreds of them, and none was speaking. The silence was absolute.

Not only that giant body, apprehensive lest it had lost its virtue, which it required as much as strength if it were to be strong, would have been relieved if the proper legal course had been followed; the whole town of Portsmouth would have breathed more easily. One night a young woman standing behind the bar of a Portsmouth hotel expressed herself in a monologue of which, in the opinion of two who heard her, this is an accurate enough transcription: "If he gave anything away about Portsmouth, and him a Portsmouth man, I hope they shoot him. Look what the Germans did to us. We kept that pub at the next corner, you've passed it every day going up to Dockyard, and it was just before the Christmas of 1940 we got ours. I shan't ever forget it. I was in the lounge, talking to a chap and a girl who were sitting at a table, and I was resting one hand on the table, and we were saying that surely we heard gunfire far away, and suddenly all the lights went out, and the silly thing was that I blamed it on my dad. To make the place a bit festive, he'd hung a line of fairy lights round the wall in and out among the pictures, and he'd been fidgeting about with them, and three times he'd fused the lights. So when it went dark I called out to him. 'Dad, you've been and gone and done it again.' And he came out of the bar and stood in the doorway quite close to me, and he said, 'Honest, I haven't touched the things since yesterday,' and then it came down on us. The chap and the girl kept on calling to me, but my father never said another word. I put out my hand to him, and I could just touch the hem of his trousers, and I kept on trying to wriggle closer and closer to him, so that I could give him a real good nip and get some sort of a sound out of him. It never struck me he was dead, but of course he was, and so were the chap and the girl by the time they got us dug out. They took five and a half hours to get at us, and it seemed forever. I could see the fireplace tilted forward and the fire still burning, and I said to myself, 'Sooner or later that'll set the place alight, and we'll all be burned alive,' but it never did, and presently the fire went out. Then the rescue squad made a little window in the rubble and passed a cup of tea to me, but I couldn't get it up to my mouth, there was all sorts of rubbish and stuff round my face. Then they scraped away some more, and got my face clear, but I couldn't hold the cup right, the tea spilled down my dress, and I said, 'This isn't any use, give me a cigarette,' and someone said, 'Bill, give her a cigarette,' and someone else said, 'Give her a cigarette nothing, don't you know there's a gas escape round here?' So I just gave up, and the next thing I was on a stretcher rolled up in blankets, and I beat off the blankets. I said to them, 'I want to be free.' They took me off to hospital, and I went to sleep, and when I woke up the next morning I realized

I hadn't a father, I hadn't the pub, I hadn't a stick of furniture or a rag of clothes, for of course what I was wearing when the bomb fell was in ribbons. Even the nightgown I was wearing wasn't my own. Then I went up to my brother's in Scotland, but after two months I said, 'I'm going home, I'm going back to Portsmouth.' He said, 'You're mad,' and I said, 'I may be, but I won't be happy till I go back.' So I came back and I did war work in the harbour, and I stuck it to the end, but I was frightened all the time, and even now I sometimes wake up in the night feeling I want to beat away the blackness. But that's an improvement, for I used to have a light all night. So what I say is that if that little blackguard had anything to do with the bombing of Portsmouth, and him coming from the place, being like one of us, I'd like to get my hands on him."

Our schools give perfunctory instruction in patriotism; and this woman belonged to a sceptical generation which, however little was taught, distrusted it all. Her culture also did not put these words into her mouth; her favorite reading was *Picture Post,* without regional sentiment save for the Parks of Rest and Culture in the U.S.S.R. Her nature had without prompting sorrowed for her birthplace when it was wounded, and knew it the supreme misfortune of her tribe if a tribesman had procured its other misfortunes. It appeared that Stoker Rose had the same disposition to feel, under ordeal, emotions often alleged to be artificially fostered by the bourgeoisie, when it was time for him to give evidence. The tall lad, who was indeed old enough to be called a man but could not be so described without inexactitude, crossed the court with the sick air of one walking on the deck of a pitching steamer, and stood there more like than ever to a plant in need of staking. Now that he was closer his fairness appeared a negative quality which sometimes charmed by association, since in certain lights it approximated to that positive fairness which is radiant; now he was mouse-coloured, now he was golden, an interested observer would never have been sure which he was. And his nervousness, which was extreme, might have been charming to some. It must have given Schaper great pleasure to see this boy grow pale and droop at a threat of pain, and revive at a promise of mercy. A sadist could hardly hope for more delicate meat.

He muttered that he had done nothing against his country. He repeated the story of how he had switched identities with Williams, and had then been taken out of his camp. It appeared that the agent who had been sent to fetch him was the odious Galaher, who had been described to him by the guards as a Gestapo agent. Galaher had taken him to Schaper, who had put him in a cell and later had come to him and said, "You know what the penalties are for helping people to escape. Nobody knows your identity now—you would never be missed if you disappeared." He kept on, Rose said, "threatening to have me done away with." Then he was turned out into a hut to live with Galaher and Martin and Welch, who picked a quarrel with him and tried to fight him. This nightmare had subdued him. He talked of it drowsily. Again it was in Shakespeare. Emilia asks Desdemona, after Othello has been raging at her, how she does; and Desdemona says, "Why, half asleep." It was natural enough, however, that the Royal Navy should fail to appreciate a stoker who recalled Desdemona. He confirmed the stories of the traitors that he had struggled in the net. He spoke of interviews with superior officials at which he had begged and prayed to be put back in a P.O.W. camp, and he swore that, though these efforts had been fruitless, he had not been a traitor. Had he signed a dossier concerning the defences of Portsmouth? Absolutely no. Had he ever had a post-office savings-bank account in Germany? Absolutely no. Had he ever signed a contract to work for the German High Command? Absolutely no. He spoke without pride, not claiming, as Galaher and Martin and Welch had done, that he had been serving England. Simply he sighed that he had not betrayed her.

At last, when all specific charges had been denied, his examination ceased, and the Investigating Officer began to cross-examine him. The boy cringed before this man who wore the uniform of the service which he knew he had disgraced, and agreed with him whenever he could. Though he persisted that he had never been instructed not to tell the Germans anything but his name, rank, and number, he accepted the far-fetched suggestion that he should have deduced this instruction from the "Careless Talk Costs Lives" which he had seen on English walls before he sailed; and meekly he admitted that, although it was true that

Schaper had threatened him, it was also true that he had never put these threats to the test; and that he had never made a determined attempt to escape. Nor did he lose his patience when the Investigating Officer sternly taxed him with inconsistency because he had once described as "moonshine" the bottle of spirits which Schaper gave him at one of his interrogations and at another time had described it as cognac. The cross-examination was interrupted by one of these unpleasant incidents which were bound to crop up when a trial is held in unsuitable premises. The statement taken by Joe Davis and Percy Edwards had been pronounced inadmissible. That is, the Court was supposed never to know what confessions he had made in the course of that statement. But when the Investigating Officer asked Stoker Rose certain questions he consulted and read from a document which, as the courtroom was so small, could be clearly recognized by the President and the rest of the court as Stoker Rose's statement. It then became perfectly obvious what had been in the statement, and it was as much a part of the court proceedings as if it had been admitted. The King's Counsel who was defending Rose steamed with a sense of injustice, and the gentle Deputy Judge-Advocate, his left hand combing his hair with his spectacles and his right hand jerking free his sword, which kept on getting wedged against the leg of his chair, provided a picture of a good man who has got mixed up in something he does not feel happy about, which would have been recognized anywhere. But Stoker Rose drooped in the dock, unresentful of injustice, borne down by noise. He was ensphered in a certain resolution. He had been a coward in Germany. He was determined not to be a coward in England. He was not going to lie to save his skin; and in excess of abnegation bent his neck beneath the yoke of what this man told him was the truth. In his examination he had denied that he knew anything of a sum of eight thousand dollars he and Galaher and Welch were supposed to have to their credit in a Berlin bank. But now some recollection of the traitors' trade babble came back to him, and he stuttered, with desperate accuracy, that he remembered taking part in talk of some such sum. His efforts at accuracy, made in the confusion of abject fear and its counter-blast of suicidal courage, were further complicated because he had accepted the Investigating Officer's extreme theory of the equal criminality of giving the enemy false and true information, and he spoke continually, and with an air of shame, of communications he had made to the Germans which were in fact nonsense. At last, when he had covered himself with a web, the Investigating Officer said to him, "I suggest to you that right from the start you knew that what you were doing was wrong. Is that not so?" The boy did not answer for a long time. His face became greenish-white, then the discoloration cleared and left it steadfast, though still languid. "Yes, sir," he said. It was the truth, and he told it when he was being cross-examined on a capital charge.

The moment was, from his point of view, satisfactory. He had always known that he should have resisted the Germans to the point of death, and he felt cleansed by this confession of long-standing cowardice, which was of the sort that is more usually made to a priest or a parent than to a lawyer in court. Plainly he felt about this Investigating Officer as young Kenneth Edward had felt about Captain Notman. So deep did this confession mine in the young man's nature that it satisfied the demands of art; on its revelation a writer could have founded a novel. That revelation was touching but not agreeable. A delicately moulded face may at once please by its delicacy and disquiet because it exposes the faults inherent in human bone structure, such as the dangerous fragility of the temples; so his confession pleased by its desperate candour, but disquieted by its reminder that our instincts are not so nicely balanced as to commit us to sane action: that, before the instinct for self-preservation will swing level with the instinct for self-respect, pressure must be applied by the finger of the will, which is often so stiff and clumsy. But Stoker Rose knew that as well as the spectator. He had said, "I am inferior to the Investigating Officer because I did not uphold the values that he has always upheld." He had gone down into the depths of his nature, he came up again elated because he had dared to do so. A minute later his own attorney asked him, "Did you do what you did with the purpose of betraying your country?" He answered, with a new strength, "Absolutely no, sir." "Why did you do it?" asked his attorney. He answered, "I had no alternative," and added with a little laugh, "I was frightened to death." "You mean," said the attorney with a smile, "you were frightened of your life." They were both eased, because the exact truth, as the boy saw it, had been told.

That ended the third day of the trial. On the morning of the fourth day, Rose was called back into the witness-box to answer two questions put by the President of the Court. He was asked if on repatriation he had reported the activities of Galaher, Martin, and Welch. He answered that he had not, because he knew he had been mixed up with unscrupulous characters. This was not a very sensible question, for a man in Rose's position could hardly be expected to volunteer a statement which would certainly incriminate him. Then the President asked, "While a prisoner of war, did you at any time represent your particular case to anyone in authority in the Allied Forces?" and Rose answered, "No, I was too frightened." Again, this question was not so sensible as it sounded. The case of Kenneth Edward had shown that British Confidence Officers in the same camp from which Rose was abducted had been utterly unable to help an unhappy boy who had been caught in the web of treachery, and had even thought it wiser not to mention his name to the German authorities. Then Rose went back into the dock, and was succeeded by people who spoke of the innocence which coexisted in him with his guilt. The first was a petty officer named Ellenore, a sturdy young naval officer who had been in camp with Rose when he was first captured. He remembered very well how Rose had switched identities with Williams, and how this had been discovered, how the German guards had said that a Gestapo agent was coming, how Galaher had arrived and taken Rose away with him. When he had not returned, Ellenore asked what had become of him, and for that was at once thrown into a cell. "What happened to you then?" asked Rose's attorney. "I was beaten into unconsciousness," said Ellenore. He smiled as he said it, holding his round head high and straightening his short spine, unaffected by the memory. Again, as at all the treason trials, the injustice of nature was apparent. It was not fair that Ellenore should have a compact and controllable body through which his blood coursed at a good sensible speed, not rushing at every fear from his face to his heart and back again, to the total confusion of his thought, while Rose should have this lank body, difficult to mobilize by the will, a long hiding-ground for his timid life. Elle-

nore himself spoke of this difference with the direct unsentimental sympathy of a realist, and told how he had several times taken
Rose to the sick bay because he had fainted. There was a B.B.C.
monitor, to say that there had been no broadcast from London
about a raid on Portsmouth such as Galaher had spoken of in
his testimony. Two witnesses came to tell how well-behaved a
lad he had been in earlier days. Rose's father, Jack Rose, former
stoker in the Royal Navy, son of a naval rating, grandson of a
soldier in Queen Victoria's army, was as pitifully spruce, as
closely shaven, as the fathers of accused persons not previously
in trouble are apt to be. He said that he had never had any
trouble with his son at all. "He has always been a very good boy
to his mother," he said. Last came an old man with thick white
hair, a city councillor, the coal merchant who had employed both
Roses, father and son, to drive his lorries. He spoke in the deep,
slow accents of the West Country, and his voice was burdened
with the woefulness the old feel when they fear that the story
which they hoped was going to end peacefully is to be disrupted
by one of those catastrophes they hoped they had outlived. He
said that he had known young Rose ever since he was born, and
his character was "wonderful good." He had never known him
to refuse duty, and if the foreman was up a tree, all he had to
do was to ask the boy to lend a hand. This evidence was plainly
true. Stoker Rose was a most biddable lad. Every time he had
coughed in court—and he had quite a troublesome cough—he
had been mindful to raise his hand and cover his mouth, as he
had been taught when he was a child. Again, the injustice of
the world was manifest. It was iniquitous that these prim and
decent men should have been put to live in this wild world,
where there was war and fear and lust and grief. It had been
stated in court that Stoker Rose had been allowed out of prison
in February in order to get married. This neat old Jack Rose
could be imagined standing in front of a group of people, not
letting life destroy them though it had got out of hand.

The Court adjourned to give its verdict. Outside, the town
passed the time quickly enough for those who cared to take a
stroll. It seemed sometimes less like a town than the setting of a
ballet, because of the troops of nimble sailors that sped through
it. Over the main street a low bridge runs to the railway station,

and across it coursed a party of bluejackets, carrying their long
blue-grey kit-bags that look as if each might hold a swaddled girl:
a leaping, bounding frieze of figures, large and dark against the
sky, free from care now, yet still not free from the mark of discipline. The pillars of the great Guildhall stand now round nothingness; behind its hollow menace there is a cosy public park, set
thick with memorials to naval campaigns and disasters erected by
the survivors in the days when campaigns kept their distance, disaster confined itself to moderate figures. One memorial bore a
testy inscription: "This monument was removed from Town
Hall Square at the request of the survivors." There must have
been a godalmighty row, but it happened in the early nineties,
nobody will ever know the truth of it now. A Wren officer, handsome and middle-aged, confided to a stranger: "I have to leave
the Wrens in a few weeks. I am so miserable. I do not know what
to do. I have no family left, and I will have to look for a room,
and God knows where I shall find it. And when I do, I shall be
so lonely. Here, when I come in at night, there are always people
I like, but in a room of my own I shall have nobody, and I am
too old to make new friends." In a cage there was a marmoset,
very engaging with its fine black guide-hairs rising from its downy
yellow-brown pelt. Some boys were giving it little ice-cream
cones, and it licked up the first, and it licked up the second, but
the third it did not eat. Very gravely it looked from face to face
of those who were standing in front of the cage, like an old yogi
in search of an apt pupil. Suddenly it sent the ice-cream cone
flying over our clothes, shrieked in joy and turned a somersault,
in salutation of the spring that was pushing the blue scillas
through the black earth in the beds near by. A gate led out to
the ruined district by the harbour. A walk between chestnut
trees looked as if it went to a church, and indeed at the end of
it was a high house which had an air of hieratic difference from
an ordinary dwelling, which might have been a presbytery when
it had windows or floors or a roof, and beside it the long grass
grew to the edge of a pavement of coloured marbles. It kept its
past a secret as blitzed buildings do not often do. It was impossible to find where the altar had been, or the pulpit, or the font.
This was disturbing, like looking at a clock-face and finding it
was inscribed with some unknown measure of time. A woman

setting out her baby in a pram to sleep in the spring sunshine said that it had been, not a church, but a synagogue. Such differences are there between acre and acre and between minute and minute. A man who is kept to the same square yard or so of a cell and has his time artificially drained of variation must miss them sadly.

By a curious custom, all the witnesses at a court martial are set in the front rows of the court to hear the verdict. The expert on radar sat between Mr. Wigge and little Welch, who pursed his mouth as if he would like to whistle, just to show that he did not care what anybody thought of him. Percy Edwards and Joe Davis, who, since the rejection of their statement, had been looking on the proceedings with the melancholy disdain of aristocrats painted by Van Dyke, sat on each side of Martin and Galaher, who were divided by the captain of the boat on which Rose had served. At the end of the row sat the B.B.C. monitor, and then Jack Rose and the white-haired old coal merchant. These men's faces were as distinct as notes of a scale; in a row they made a phrase of wild music. They had their eyes fixed on the prisoner, who was drooping in the dock, the Master-at-Arms' naked sword a bright erect line behind his head. He did not return their gaze, his face was twitching, his too-mobile blood was there and went and came again. The President of the Court announced that the Court had found him guilty of the first charge, which related to treacherous correspondence with the enemy, but innocent of the two charges relating to the communication of intelligence concerning radar and the defences of Portsmouth. The boy's head rolled forward and he swayed. Then he was taken from the dock, and the court was cleared, for, by a raw cruelty of procedure, a court martial pronounces its verdict, then retires again and deliberates on the sentence. Where there is a jury, and one judge, the jury brings in the verdict; if it be "guilty," evidence regarding the prisoner's character is given, and the judge makes up his mind on the spot; but where there are several judges who are also the jury, as is the case in a court martial, they have necessarily to retire before they can pronounce sentence. That this delay is made inevitable by the form of the Court does not make it any easier for the prisoner to bear. Stoker Rose had been found guilty of a capital charge. He might

have been sentenced to be shot, and he had to wait for nearly
an hour before he knew that that was not the intention of the
Court; and he must have suspected, as we all did, that such a
delay meant that some of the Court had been in favour of shooting him. Then the witnesses were led again into the front row.
They sat in a different order this time, though Jack Rose and the
old coal-merchant were careful still to sit together. They did indeed need each other's company. For the President announced
that the Court had sentenced Stoker Rose to sixteen years' penal
servitude.

The announcement stunned and horrified and, at the same
time, amused, for the severity of the sentence entailed a certain
drollness; a man who puts too much of his strength into a swinging blow falls over. The seven men in gold lace and blue serge
sitting at the long table now seemed absurdly naïve. That side
of the courtroom was like a magnified scene from a Punch and
Judy show, while the other side, where the pale and awkward
boy quailed under the respite from death which was too harshly
conditional to be a relief, was like a scene from a school play
representing a martyrdom, perhaps because he was now too exhausted to feel anything more than remote and clouded emotion.
A more lively despair was made manifest on the face of Welch,
though his expression had but slightly changed. He had yet to
be tried, and now knew what he might expect, and was in any
case being at this time horribly savaged by the demon which
takes charge of the services in their relations with the law. This
demon, which means no harm, was taking enormous trouble to
protect his dignity, during his presence at Rose's trial, by back-
ing the truck which brought him to and from his jail so that nobody should see him as he crossed the pavement, and by preventing anybody from meeting him in the corridors. But it was shut-
ting him up throughout the trial (and he was obliged to attend
it every day) in a small room with Galaher and Martin, against
whom he had given evidence, who, as all parties knew, were to
give evidence against him. According to his testimony at that
trial they told him they were going to "fix him." Whether these
words were spoken or not, the act of enferming persons joined
in this horrible relationship for four days in a small room is of
a sort that might well be left to the jail authorities in Hell.

As the boy moved dreamily out of the dock and was led away by the man who held a naked sword, we were left in confusion. For an immediate discredit fell on the total protest a humane person would wish to feel against a sentence which sent a man to prison from the time he was twenty-three till he was thirty-nine for an act committed under the influence of fear. It was certainly an excessive sentence compared with the standards set by the civil courts, which had been sending people of a like degree of culpability to prison for periods varying from three to seven years. But the courtroom was full of men with stern though sometimes very young faces, who pitied Stoker Rose yet wanted no gentler justice for him than he had received. They said various things, but what they all meant was that members of the fighting forces should, owing to the extreme temptations by which they are beset, be protected by stronger deterrents than civilians, for the sake of both the individual and the services. This sentence on Stoker Rose would warn men of a real danger; for at all costs men must not consent even to enter that hut outside the prisoner-of-war camp, lest they be not so lucky as Stoker Rose in his comparative futility, and commit such a villainy as Martin perpetrated when he betrayed the position of a wireless concealed in British prisoners' quarters. Without passion these men and boys explained their special need for penalty, as scientists who work with dangerous substances might explain their special need for cumbersome protective uniforms. As for the argument that it is harsh to call a man to account for what he does under the threat of death, all of us knew the graves, in land or under water, which answer it. Certainly these men and boys had the right to the last word, for on their heads the blood would be. There was therefore no opportunity for the bland, relaxing happiness of mercy, no escape from the boundless horror of a heroic age.

Yet, after some months, the sentence was reduced. The Sea Lords brought it down to five years: perhaps because justice, like everything else, cannot be overstrained, and the severity of sixteen years retained its drollness under scrutiny; perhaps because the trial had been so rich in irregularities as the waving about of the inadmissible statement under the Court's noses. It was young Welch who, in the end, was to be given the larger sentence. None of his kin came to the great house in Park Lane where he was tried early that summer. Sitting on the kitchen chair in the fine room under the high gilt-and-plaster ceiling, he looked a tired wisp. He had been nearly a year in custody. His neatness and the careful combing of his strange upright palisade of wavy hair made a claim to self-respect. The evidence of the Intelligence Officer who had first examined him showed that, like young Kenneth Edward and Stoker Rose, he had believed absolutely in the standards he had violated. He had felt shame before this man as Kenneth Edward had felt it before Captain Notman, as Stoker Rose had felt it before the Investigating Officer. Galaher and Martin gave their odious testimony, odious as his had been, and he looked primly past them. After the Court had brought in a verdict of guilty he walked alone down the great staircase, his small, canny face, with self-exhortation to take the inevitable sensibly, floating in many places on the walls, in the drowned distances of the old mirrors. In the hall waited his guards to take him back to prison, where he was to spend several weeks, according to the barbarous custom of military trials, before he learned that he had been sentenced to ten years' imprisonment. This sentence was not reduced on appeal. It is, of course, unlikely that he will serve ten years, if he is as well behaved as one would forecast. But by comparison with Stoker Rose's five years his sentence seems as heavy as it would have seemed light if the Admiralty authorities had upheld Stoker Rose's original sentence of sixteen years. Sentences cannot, in any system of jurisprudence, be standardized, because guilt is not standardized; but such disharmonies as these show that the court martial is a very wild garden indeed.

But it was not the penalties suffered by Stoker Rose and Welch which make them so notably pathetic; it was the futility of their sufferings. The whole elaborate drama had been completely pointless. What they had done had seemed at least to have had the justification of serving the Germans' purposes; but it had no such effect. Mr. Wigge had been very naïve when he said that the traitors' activities had been useless because the silly Allied prisoners had known nothing. For it was not with the traitors as he, and they, thought. The predominant condition of their lives must have seemed to them loneliness. When they spoke of themselves they sounded solitary as one had not thought men still alive could be. Galaher told of a Christmas party they had held in their hut; the Germans had given them some extra rations, cake and wine and brandy, and had allowed them to ask their favourite prostitutes. (The ill luck which dogged Stoker Rose was faithful to him here: his girl-friend could not come.) No explorers among Arctic snows, no shipwrecked sailors on a desert island, could have been so far from human fellowship as these wretched creatures, who were not only physically but spiritually divided from all people they had ever known except a few of their enemies. So they believed; but were mistaken, for at the same time they were bathed in a strong light which they themselves could not see. Hundreds of thousands of men, of several nations, had been instructed in their names, all details of their appearances, and their designs. Their fame had run from lip to lip, as if they were great statesmen or soldiers or comedians. For complete descriptions of all the informers, at a very early stage in their operations, had been sent through the channel of communications which was, by means not yet revealed, maintained throughout the war between the P.O.W. camps and England, and were circulated among all persons likely to become prisoners of war. So the degradation of Stoker Rose and his fellows had served no purpose, not even an evil one. It was sheer waste. There was no answer to that sum but zero.

3

CHILDREN sometimes go away with strangers who offer them cakes and sweets; and the ending of that story is not usually happy. Whoever loves a child will leave it with its natural protectors unless they are false to their trust, and then the loving stranger buys the child, if he can, but does not steal it. Stealing is not the way of love. It is, however, the way of lust, and of crime seeking an accomplice; and once the child has submitted to the act of lust, once it has crept through the narrow window and opened the door from within, it becomes a tedious burden to a potential betrayer. It may even inspire fear simply by being what it is. A child, seen in twilight by a person with disordered nerves, may be mistaken for a malignant dwarf; and crime is a dusk, and criminals often overtax their serenity.

Mr. Wigge illustrated the kidnappers' situation on the terrain of war. To seduce his charges from their dignity and duty had pleased his appetite which, less gross than Schaper's, was still pricking. But their stupidity had bored and disgusted him; and the baring of his teeth during his testimony suggested that he had not always known he had no need to be frightened of them, even if the worst befell. Versions of this same situation are bound to occur wherever one nation is attempting to dominate another. Simple, defenceless people are bought by bribes of one sort or another to betray their own kind, and their buyers despise them for their venality, are fatigued by their obtuseness, and are alarmed lest these creatures, whom they conceive, since they do not understand their alien culture, as being more mindless than they really are, turn against them. The men at Dublin Castle felt loathing for the peasants who were on their payroll. The men who did like work in India felt that the vast ramifications of Intelligence throughout the native population were the ultimate proof of its unfitness for self-government. Those who were sent to Kilmainham Jail and the Andaman Islands were not all rebels. Many there knew the hopelessly inglorious martyrdom of informers who had fallen under suspicion. This reversal of ignoble fortune was seen often in the Ottoman Empire, in the first years of this century. Macedonian Albanians who had lived as pleasantly as may be, turning in reports on the Greeks and the Bulgars and the Serbs, might suddenly die, having been seen hanging about the synagogues in Monastir, or other places where the Young Turk Movement was coming to birth.

The children who go from their homes with strangers because they have been given cakes and sweets are unsustained by pride when the unkindness falls on them. They know well that they have done wrong. A person should be loyal to his father and mother, to his brothers and sisters, to his friends, to his town or village, to his province, to his country; and a person should do nothing for a bribe, even if it takes the form of a promise that he should live instead of die. This is the faith which such children hold: to which they feel they must be true, if they are to be saved, if they are to be loved, by others or by themselves. When Kenneth Edward came face to face with the jovial serenity of Captain Notman, when Stoker Rose was asked by the Investigating Officer if he had not known what he was doing was wrong; when Welch sat down with the Intelligence Officer and told him all he had done, opening his breast to him with surgical honesty: it was apparent that this was the faith in which they believed, that they felt themselves lost because they had betrayed it, and that they looked up to these men who had been true to it as, according to ancient cosmogonies, the damned look up at the happy in heaven. This attitude was clearly distinguishable from regret for having been on the losing side, and it was not feigned; the rush of blood from the cheek after the shameful admission, the greenish swaying sickness of repentance, are inimitable. It is not an attitude which has been taught them by an exploiting class. They were born into a tongue-tied age, and neither their school-teachers nor the culture within their reach had given them such positive instruction. The judgment they passed on their own disloyalty and the loyalty of others was a spontaneous reaction to experience. Those who would call them foolish to suffer for having violated a faith so local, so provincial, so national, should consider what satisfaction they derived from their international ties: with Plack, who did not answer letters; with vigilant Mr. Wigge; with the playful Herr Oberleutnant Schaper, rolling on the grass. Their parents were kinder to them: with whom they can never again be as they were, since with the natural parental love there coexists a natural consternation, a natural horror.

EPILOGUE

THE trouble about man is twofold. He cannot learn truths which are too complicated; he forgets truths which are too simple.

Today we have forgotten that we live outwards from the centre of a circle and that what is nearest to the centre is most real to us. If a man cut his hand, it hurts him more than if he cut some other man's hand; therefore he is more careful to guard his own. Even if he spend his whole life in teaching himself that we are all of one body, and that therefore his neighbour's pain is his also, he will still suffer more when his own hand is hurt, for the message then runs straight from his palm and fingers to his brain, travelling at a speed faster than light or sound, which bear the news of others' accidents. Throughout his life it remains true that what is nearest to his body is of greatest interest to his mind. When a baby is given food and held warmly by a certain woman, he grows up to feel a closer concern for her than for other women of her generation, and at her death will feel greatly disturbed. Should he be institution-bred and have no woman as his particular slave and tyrant, grievance will sour him till his last day.

If in his maturity he should live with a woman for any considerable period of time, he and she are apt, unless they are overtaken by certain obviously disagreeable circumstances, to behave as though there were a complete community of interest between them. There must have been some instinctive liking between them or they would never have been drawn together in the first place; they became involved in each other's prosperity; experience has taught each how the other will behave in most eventualities. Therefore they do better by one another than strangers would. Should he have children by this or any other woman, they will have great power over him, while other children will have little or none. He will know so much more about them. The veiled moment of their conception is his secret, and resemblances to him, to a familiar woman, or to his kin, enable him

to trace their inner lives, disguised though they be first by their
inarticulateness and then by their articulateness. He can read
them by the light of his own nature, and read his own nature by
their light, and will have a sense of fusion between himself and
those who are so inextricably tangled with that self.

If that man live in a house during the days of his childhood,
he will know it better than any house he lives in later, though it
shelter him forty years longer; and though the staircase wind as
deviously as any in the world he will find his way down it in the
darkness as surely as if it were straight. All his life long, when
he hears talk of woods, he shall see beechwoods, if he come from
a Buckinghamshire village, and a castle to him shall stand on
Castle Rock, if Edinburgh was his home; and in the one case he
shall know Southern English country folk, and in the other Low-
land Scottish townsfolk, better than other Britons. Born and
bred in England, he will find it easier to understand the English
than the rest of men, not for any mystical reason, but because
their language is his, because he is fully acquainted with their
customs, and because he is the product of their common history.
So also each continent enjoys a vague unity of self-comprehen-
sion, and is divided from the others by a sharp disunity; and
even those who profess the closest familiarity with the next world
speak with more robust certainty of this world and seem not to
want to leave it.

This is not to say that a man loves what is nearest to him. He
may hate his parents, his wife, and his children. Millions have
done so. On the tables of the Law it was written "Honour thy
father and thy mother, as the Lord God hath commanded thee;
that thy days may be prolonged, and that it may go well with
thee in the land which the Lord thy God giveth thee," and it is
advice of almost gross practicality aimed at preventing the faithful from abandoning themselves to their natural impulses and
wasting all their force on family rows. St. Paul, that great artist
who perpetually betrayed his art because he was also a great man
of action, and constantly abandoned the search for truth to seek
instead a myth to inspire vigorous action, tried to gild the bondage
of man to the familiar. "So ought men to love their own wives
as their own body," he says. "He that loveth his wife loveth himself. For no man ever yet hated his own flesh, but nourisheth it

and cherisheth it, even as the Lord the Church." But countless men have hated their own flesh. Everywhere and at all times men have carried such hatred to the point of slaying it, and still more have persecuted it by abstinence and mortification and debauchery. It has a value to them far above their loathing or their liking. It is their own flesh and they can have no direct experience of any other. Not with all the gold in the world or by incessant prayer can we obtain another instrument-case, packed with these our only instruments, the five senses, by which alone we can irradiate the universe that is a black void around us, and build a small irradiated platform in that darkness. A wife is someone who has stood on that irradiated platform long enough to be fully examined and to add the testimony of her own senses as to the nature of that encircling mystery. She may be loved or hated, or loved and hated, and still serve in that research.

A child knows that what is near is easier for him to handle than what is far. All men took it for granted till recent times, when it was challenged, together with some other traditional assumptions, not because they had proved unsound, but because a number of urbanized populations from which the intellectual classes were largely drawn had lost their sense of spiritual as well as material process. They had lost their sense of material process due to the development of the machine; goods which had formerly been produced by simple and comprehensible processes, often carried on where they could be witnessed by the consumer, were now produced by elaborate processes, not to be grasped by people without mechanical training, and carried on in the privacy of the large factories.

The reason for their ignorance of spiritual process was the urban lack of the long memory and the omniscient gossip enjoyed by the village. The townsman is surrounded by people whose circumstances he does not know and whose heredities are the secrets of other districts; and he is apt to take their dissimulating faces and their clothed bodies as the sum of them. People began to think of each other in a new way; as simple with a simplicity in fact unknown in organic life. They ignored the metabolism of human nature, by which experiences are absorbed into the mind and magically converted into personality, which rejects much of the material life brings to it and handles the rest to serve the interests of love or hate, good or evil, life or death, according to inhabiting dæmon, whose reasons are never given. Man conceived himself as living reasonably under the instruction of the five senses, which tell him to seek pleasure and avoid pain.

The first effect of this rational conception of life was cheerful vulgarity; and there are worse things than that. Man might well have felt this view of his destiny as a relief after the Christian philosophy, which abased his origin to criminality, and started him so low only to elevate him to the height, most disagreeable to most people, of company with godhead, after dragging him through all sorts of unpalatable experiences, including participation in a violent and apparently unnecessary death. Insofar as a man adopted the new and rationalist philosophy he could be compared to an actor who, after spending a lifetime playing Hamlet and Othello and King Lear, retires to keep a country pub. All was thenceforward to go at a peaceable jog-trot. Children were to grow up straight striplings of light, undeformed by repression, unscarred by conflicts, because their parents would hand them over in their earliest years to the care of pedagogic experts. Divorce was not to be reckoned as a disgrace nor as a tragedy nor even as a failure, but as a pleasurable extension of experience, like travel. Furthermore—and this was considered as the sanest adjustment of all—the ardours of patriotism were to be abandoned, and replaced by a cool resolution to place one's country on a level with all others in one's affections and to hand it over without concern to the dominion of any other power which could offer it greater material benefits. It was not out of cynicism that the benefits demanded were material: it was believed that the material automatically produced the intellectual and the spiritual. These reasonable steps having been taken, there was to follow harmony. The only peril was that it might become too sweet.

But the five senses had evidently not been rightly understood. Such children as were surrendered by their parents to expert treatment, complained against that surrender as if it had been any other kind of abandonment. They quarrelled with the pedagogues as much as they would have quarrelled with their parents; but, the bond of the flesh being absent, there was something sapless in their quarrels, and there was less energy engendered.

Sexual life was not noticeably smoother than it had been. The epic love of marriage and the lyric love-song of the encounter both lost much by the pretence that they were the same. Nor, as patriotism was discredited, did peace come nearer. Indeed, the certainty of war now arched over the earth like a second sky, inimical to the first. If harmony had been our peril, we were preserved from it, both within and without. For it was plain that, as Christian philosophy had so harshly averred, the world was a stage on which an extraordinary drama, not yet fully comprehended by the intellect, was being performed; and its action was now an agony. But, owing to the adoption of the rationalist philosophy, some of the actors filling the most important parts were now incapable of speaking their lines. It appeared that *Hamlet* and *Othello* and *King Lear* would be no longer cathartic tragedies but repellent and distressing farces if the leading characters had, in the climactic scenes, been overtaken by the delusion that they had retired and were keeping country pubs.

So the evil moment came and was clear: not surpassed in evil since the days of the barbarian invasions. The devil of nationalism had been driven out of man, but he had not become the headquarters of the dove. Instead there had entered into him the seven devils of internationalism, and he was torn by their frenzies. Then what is against all devils came to his aid. The achievement (which, as yet, is unfinished, since peace does not reign), was accomplished by a continuance of the drama in spite of the difficulties created by the rationalist philosophy. Since the actors cast to play the leading parts would not speak, the action was carried on by the peoples who used to walk to and fro at the back of the scene, softly laughing or softly weeping, or simply quietly being. Now these people streamed across the continents, inscribing their beliefs on the surface of the earth by the course of their flights, and on the sites of their martyrdoms. They defeated fascism by not being fascist. They showed the contrast between fascism and non-fascism so clearly that the world, wishing to live, defended their side because it could be seen that they were the representatives of life. As they exorcised the devils from the body of Europe they seemed to affirm certain values. It was perhaps true that the origin of man was in criminality, for once a community refused to make the effort of seeking the company of godhead it certainly became criminal. It was perhaps true that hedonism is an impotent gospel, for now it could be seen that pleasure means nothing to many men. As fast as those who ran to save their lives ran those who ran to slay them, even if their pursuit, pressed too hard, might change them into fugitives whose own lives were in danger. Now the scorned bonds of the flesh asserted their validity. It was the final and unbearable misery of these flights that husbands were separated from their wives, and parents lost sight of their children. The men who performed the cruellest surgery on these families, who threw the husband and wife into the gas chamber while the children travelled by train to an unknown destination, had themselves been brought up to contemn their own ties of blood. The anguish of the divided was obviously holy. The contentment of those who felt no reluctance to procure their division was plainly damned.

In this day of exposition those who made the other sacrifice of the near for the far, and preferred other countries to their own, proved also to be unholy. The relationship between a man and a fatherland is always disturbed by conflict if either man or fatherland is highly developed. A man's demands for liberty must at some point challenge the limitations the state imposes on the individual for the sake of the mass. If he is to carry on the national tradition he must wrestle with those who, speaking in its name, desire to crystallize it at the point reached by the previous generation. In any case national life itself must frequently exasperate him, because it is the medium in which he is expressing himself, and every craftsman or artist is repelled by the resistance of his medium to his will. All men should have a drop or two of treason in their veins, if the nations are not to go soft like so many sleepy pears. Yet to be a traitor is most miserable. All the men described in this book were sad as they stood their trials, not only because they were going to be punished. They would have been sad even if they had never been brought to justice. They had forsaken the familiar medium; they had trusted themselves to the mercies of those who had no reason to care for them; knowing their custodians' indifference, they had lived for long in fear; and they were aware that they had thrown away their claim on those who might naturally have felt affection for them. Strangers, as King Solomon put it, were filled with

their wealth, and their labours were in the house of a stranger,
and they mourned at the last when their flesh and body were
consumed. As a divorce sharply recalls what a happy marriage
should be, so the treachery of these men recalled what a nation
should be; a shelter where all talents are generously recognized,
all forgivable oddities forgiven, all viciousness quietly frustrated,
and those who lack talent honoured for equivalent contributions
of graciousness. Each of these men was as dependent on the good
opinion of others as one is oneself; they needed a nation which
was also a hearth. It was sad to see them, chilled to the bones of
their souls, because the intellectual leaders of their time had professed a philosophy which was scarcely more than a lapse of memory, and had forgotten, among much else, that a hearth gives
out warmth.